# AN INTRODUCTION TO ENVIRONMENTAL EDUCATION

# AN INTRODUCTION TO ENVIRONMENTAL EDUCATION

### Edited by

**James E. Otiende**
**William P. Ezaza**
**Brother Raymonds Boisvert**

## University of Nairobi Press

First published 1991 by
University of Nairobi Press
Jomo Kenyatta Memorial Library, University of Nairobi
P.O. Box 30197 – 00100 Nairobi

*E-mail: nup@uonbi.ac.ke*          **http://www.uonbi.ac.ke/press**

Reprinted  2010

The University of Nairobi Press supports and promotes University of
Nairobi's objectives of discovery, dissemination and preservation of
knowledge, and stimulation of intellectual and cultural life by publishing
works of highest quality in association with partners in different parts of the
world. In doing so, it adheres to the University's tradition of excellence,
innovation and scholarship.

The moral rights of the authors have been asserted.

University of Nairobi Library CIP Data
          An introduction to environmental education/ed. By J.E. Otiende,
  GF    W.P. Ezaza (and) R. Boisvert – Nairobi: University of Nairobi
 26.15   Press, 2007
          270p.
          1. Environmental education. 2. Conservation of natural resources –
          study and teaching.
          I. Otiende, James E. II. Ezaza, William P. III. Boisvert, Raymond

**ISBN 9966 8 46 13 1**

## Dedication

To the late Dr. William Paul Ezaza
who worked so hard to translate the ideas in this
text into the concrete reality it is.

# Table of Contents

## List of Abbreviations

| | | |
|---|---|---|
| APCD | - | Air Pollution Control District |
| BHC | - | Benzene Hexachloride |
| CCOL | - | Coordinating Committee on the Ozone Layer |
| CFC | - | Chlorofluorocarbons |
| CSDP | - | Child Survival and Development Programme |
| DDT | - | Dichlorodiphenyltrichloroethane |
| EE | - | Environmental Education |
| EEC | - | European Economic Community |
| EIAS | - | Environmental Impact Assessment Statement |
| EPA | - | Environmental Protection Agency |
| FAO | - | Food and Agriculture Organisation |
| GNP | - | Gross National Product |
| IAFA | - | International Atomic Energy Agency |
| ICRP | - | International Commission on Radiological Protection |
| ICSU | - | International Council of Scientific Unions |
| IEEP | - | International Environmental Education Programme |
| IMF | - | International Monetary Fund |
| ISES | - | International Solar Energy Society |
| IUCN | - | International Union for Conservation of Nature |
| IUD | - | Intra-Uterine Device |

| KEPI | - | Kenya Expanded Programmes on Immunisation |
|------|---|-------------------------------------------|
| LDC | - | Less Developed Countries |
| NEEMA | - | National Environmental Enhancement and Management Act |
| NEPA | - | National Environmental Policy Act |
| NGO | - | Non-Governmental Organisation |
| UNCTAD | - | United Nations Council on Trade and Development |
| UNEP | - | United Nations Environmental Programme |
| UNICEF | - | United National International Children Emergency Fund |
| UNHSS | - | United Nations Human Settlement Secretariat |
| WCED | - | World Commission on Environment and Development |
| WCOTP | - | World Conference of Organisations of the Teaching Professions |
| WHO | - | World Health Organisation |
| WMO | - | World Meteorological Organisation |
| WWF | - | World-Wide Fund for Nature |

## List of Contributors

**James E. Otiende**, joint editor and co-ordinator of this book, is a Senior Lecturer in Educational Foundations Department, Kenyatta University.

**The late William P. Ezaza**, joint editor was a Lecturer in Geography Department, Kenyatta University.

**Brother Raymond Boisvert**, joint editor, is a teacher of English, Mangu High School, Thika.

**Abidha N. Ombech** is a Research Fellow in the Basic Education Resource Centre, Kenyatta University.

**Jackson O. Ogeno** is a Lecturer in Educational Foundations Department, Kenyatta University.

**John O. Shiundu** is a Senior Research Fellow in the Bureau of Education Research. Currently he is the Director of the Basic Education Resource Centre, Kenyatta University.

**Eric M. Aseka** is a Lecturer in Department of History, Kenyatta University.

**Levi I. Libese** is a Lecturer in the Department of Educational Administration, Planning and Curriculum Development, Kenyatta University.

**John M.A. Orodho**, is a Research Fellow in the Bureau of Education Research, Kenyatta University.

**Nelson T. Muthiani** is a Lecturer at the Centre for Environmental Education, Kenyatta University.

**Janet W. Kabeberi-Macharia** is a Lecturer in the Faculty of Law, University of Nairobi.

# Foreword

Environmental Education is a relatively new area of study in schools, colleges and universities. It is an education innovation that dates back to the early 1970s, when three major conferences on the human environment – held in Stockholm (1972), in Belgrade (1975) and in Tbilisi (1977) – created a totally new awareness about "the environment" in the world of today. The establishment of UNEP (United National Environment Programme) at this very time reflected the seriousness with which the international community wished to tackle the environmental problems of the globe. The fact that UNEP had its headquarters in Nairobi, Kenya, was not only an event of international importance, but also of tremendous significance to the African continent, and to Kenya in particular. This is evident from the various workshops, symposia and conferences held in Africa during the late 1970s, which dealt specifically with environmental problems in Africa.

Environmental Education as an area of study is the immediate outcome of the above developments, both at international and national levels. Within the Kenyan context we must single out Kenyatta University College (as it was known then) for the special role it played in promoting Environmental Education from 1975 onwards. Initially, a number of environmental topics were included in a course titled Man and the Universe, offered to students undertaking Diploma in Education courses. In 1976, the first field course in Environmental Education was mounted by the Department of Education Communication and Technology. Thereafter a fully developed course on Environmental Education was introduced. Prof. J. Waithaka, then Deputy Principal (now Director of Education), was instrumental in bringing this plan to fruitition. In 1990 the Chancellor of Kenyatta University, His Excellency President Daniel arap Moi, announced that there were plans to create the very first Faculty of Environmental Education in Africa. Plans to establish this Faculty are now in progress. The publication of this book therefore comes at a timely moment.

An *Introduction to Environmental Education* is really a collection of various articles on environmental education that have been put together by a group of lecturers from both Kenyatta University and the University of Nairobi. The authors have closely followed the undergraduate syllabuses for environmental education in Kenya's public universities. I have no doubt in my mind that this book will greatly promote the teaching of environmental education in schools, colleges and universities.

**Prof. H.O. Ayot**
Dean, Faculty of Education
Kenyatta University
April, 1991

# Introduction

J.E. Otiende and W.P. Ezaza

## Background

Environmental education has been conceived as a process of recognising the value and various conceptions of the environment with the prime aim of determining the skills and approaches necessary for understanding the relationship between man, his culture and the biophysical environment (UNESCO, 1988).

## 1. Africans and Environmental Awareness and Education

The term 'environment' is not new to most African societies. Indeed, *environmental awareness* is as old as those societies; its roots go deep into time immemorial. For example, many African languages and dialects have related words which equate with the English word *environment* or with the German word *umwelt*. Again, the Swahili word *mazingira*, (*mazingazinga*) is often simultaneously used to describe a man's immediate surroundings and the available resources he manipulates within that environment.

Similarly, the use and misuse of the immediate surroundings and the consequent degradation of the quality of the environment created considerable concern in almost all African communities. Without environmental awareness, African societies would have perished; therefore they had to understand and adapt themselves to their environments.

For instance, it is argued that neither the domestication of animals nor the development of agriculture were imported into Africa. The widespread adaptation to changing environments and the advance onto the ecologically fragile lands led to widespread experimentation and adaptation of crops and methods of farming. African peasants have been innovative in adopting new crop cultivation approaches, cropping methods and marketing strategies throughout their history. If they had failed to do this, African societies would indeed have completely died out (Odhiambo, 1988).

Today, the concept of environmental awareness is being replaced by environmental education, which for many African societies may be new altogether. This new approach to the environment is yet to be fully integrated into the everyday thinking and activities of the African people. Nevertheless, there are several questions which could still be raised in connection with environmental education. First, what does environmental education represent with respect to managing the environment? Second, what must environmental education teachers know and do in order to disseminate the needed knowledge about the environment? Third, how does man adjust himself meaningfully to the ever-changing environment of which he is part?

This is because, in African countries, the content of environmental education essentially differs from that offered in developed industrialised countries. For example, since time immemorial, the African environment satisfied people's societal needs in terms of air, water, food, energy, clothing, shelter and even recreation. These needs not only influenced African lifestyles but also determined the levels of satisfaction different societies derived from life (Ferrari, 1989).

However, developed industrialised countries still regard Africans as having exclusively been involved in unproductive activities. In fact, it was the forces of colonialism which disrupted the natural balance which African societies steadfastly struggled to maintain (Johnson and Anderson, 1988).

In both Tanzania and Kenya, for example, European settlers disrupted the ecological balance which the Maasai had maintained for centuries. Throughout the centuries, the Maasai tolerated the severe environment and survived in spite of limited permanent water, disease and war. They also restricted the biotic potentials of people and livestock. For this reason, their pastures were stocked below the potential carrying capacity and there was constant energy flow and sustained productivity both for the well-being of their livestock and for the wild savanna ecosystem.

What the European settlers did was to upset this ecological harmony by encroaching on the most important dry-season holdings and better grazing lands. They introduced veterinary care, developed bore holes, water-points and dams, all of which resulted in the removal of biological controls and disrupted the ecological balance (Naveh, 1967).

Thus, the introduction of the money-economy dilapidated much of Africa's viable resource base. This left Africans with an environment which in reality was a mere product of history, an environment socially shaped by colonialism. The freedom struggle was, therefore, as much a search for a return to

3

environmental stability as a struggle for political independence.

Environmental awareness may not have been a new concept among the industrialised developed societies, but the fact that they realised its importance only recently is far from puzzling. Until recently, industrialised countries perceived their development and their environment as independent of each other (Tolba, 1987). Today they have realised that the two are actually interdependent and that without environmental awareness, development would be in danger and vice versa.

This new environmental awareness has emerged out of the pollution of wealth due to the high and wasteful consumption levels of the developed countries. Problems that may threaten peace and security emanate from the accumulation of nuclear arms, acid rain, global warming due to the green house effect, chemical waste disposal and oil slicks. Even the African environment is affected. These problems are a result of industrialisation; they are therefore quite different in both their causes and effects from the environmental and developmental concerns usually mentioned in the African situation.

In analysing the current environmental problems and finding solutions to them in both rich developed and poor developing countries, there is need to look back to the past and discover how the environment has been polluted in both worlds. It is now realised that in Africa, poverty is driving the majority of the peoples to engage in activities destructive to the environment.

Clearly, the approach to environmental education must differ in content when it is taught in developed and developing countries. Environmental education in Africa ought to determine the place and role played by traditional education in the overall environmental management. This calls for restructuring of the school curricula so that the place and role of cultural and socioeconomic conditions can be taken into account. It is doubtful if the two worlds of wealth and poverty can work out a unified environmental education programme which can satisfy the requirements and needs of such different worlds.

In Kenya, for example, attempts have been made to introduce two approaches to environmental education. One is based on integrated environmental education through the existing educational system and the other involves teaching environmental educational especially at the university level. These approaches are strongly supported by the government and the United Nations Environmental Programme (UNEP), the International Union for Conservation of Nature (IUCN) and the World Conference of Organisations of the Teaching Profession (WCOTP).

It is the purpose of education to foster debate about the value and validity of knowledge and understanding in connection with major issues and concerns of the times in which we live (Lacey, 1987). Today, there is an emerging debate and concern regarding African crises and predicaments; there is considerable international concern on the impact of human development processes on the environment. Africa's present predicament can also be described as a justification for implementing external policies of conservation in Africa.

But first we musk ask whether there was an environmental awareness among Africans before the European intrusion and disruption of the African continent. The answer is an emphatic 'yes'. It is evident that from childhood, the African was quite aware of the imbalances caused by his many activities such as hunting, gathering, cultivation and pastoralism; viewing his environment and its resources in terms of his culture. Although he may have handed down the environment to his immediate kith and kin without much regard to its quality, his mistakes were simultaneously and harmoniously adjusted by natural checks, political strife, cultural decisions, and natural rythms.

These natural and cultural adjustments were harsh on individuals and groups. They were not only available but also offered the only means of conservation. So the terms used to describe Africa's problems as crises require that distinctions be made between natural crises and the more common occurrences such as droughts, diseases, floods and even earthquakes. A distinction must also be made between traditional African economies such as hunter-gatherers and cultivator-pastoralists; these two economies are often practised together and do not necessarily follow the social Darwinian progression (Anderson and Johnson, 1988).

This tradition goes on with societal groups moving back and forth through time, from herding to cultivation and back to hunting and gathering as opportunities and needs dictate. All of these factors underline the role played by traditional environmental awareness. They signify a form of social and ecological strategy of security and conservation against ecological diversity.

Moreover, African traditional practices and cosmologies have often possessed notions of logic and scientific appropriateness. There is a vast amount of information which is stored in the form of words, proverbs, songs, rituals and even idioms which form expressions of utility and conservation of resources. For example, among the Nilotic peoples of Uganda and Kenya, logical and scientific information has been used in the fields of medicinal plants, in monitoring the effects of mixed farming and mixed cropping, in mulching and green manuring, in pasture management, in cultivation of crops and in monitoring the impact of domestic changes on livestock, crops, and soils.

Although this type of information can hardly be documented as 'scientific' in the modern sense, it forms a pragmatic approach to environmental management. Developed by 'rule of thumb', such techniques were very much connected with environmental parameters and formed part of African environmental education.

In analysing the social and behavioural dynamics operating in different communities within the African environment, there is need to recognise these dynamics as playing an important role in fostering environmental awareness. In other words, these dynamics help to minimise the environmental hazards that characterise the harsh and precarious African environment. Even amid resource abundance, no society in Africa could have achieved a perfect elasticity in its response to environmental changes.

In all African societies, the biophysical environment was, and still is a condition for survival. Moreover, to many, culture and ecology are inseparable. Thus, the current environmental development and population crisis, indebtedness and poverty syndrome all have to be viewed against the socioeconomic and cultural backgrounds of African societies.

Until the Stockholm Conference on Human Environment in 1972, the global understanding of the African environment was limited to a few problems such as drought, disease, population explosion, poor economic performance, illiteracy and deforestation. Indeed, there has been little understanding of the human impact connected with soil erosion and desertification or urbanisation and rural migration, energy and food requirements in Africa. Clearly, developed nations have little knowledge and understanding of the relationship between African culture and ecology. It is against this background that African scientists need to re-educate the world about their crises and predicaments.

Meanwhile, the immediate African problems hinge on increasing demands for food, fuel and water, all of which affect the environment. Increasing population pressure and particularly the growth rate, the size and the pattern of distribution, the loss and deterioration of the quality of surface and underground water, and the loss in genetic diversity of various crops, pose serious environmental concerns. These issues call for re-educating the African people, because these problems tend to intensify each other over time.

Such problems are now being exacerbated by stagnant economic growth, ill-conceived policies, diverse cultural practices, and, most important, the heterogeneous and vulnerable nature of the African ecosystem. These crises present a very gloomy picture of Africa and indeed give the impression that African countries face very serious obstacles in development which are not likely to be solved in the foreseeable future.

## 2. The Scope of the Text

The introductory remarks provide the reader with the key themes discussed in the various contributions. The book addresses itself to some important environmental problems in Africa, with particular reference to Kenya. The perspectives used in the contributions, therefore, vary in approach. Some have a regional focus while others have local foci. The variations in approach and perspective are useful since they contribute to the finding of solutions to the complex problems of maintaining, sustaining and improving the resource base on which our lives depend.

In the succeeding chapters, the contributors have attempted to introduce and highlight issues related to the environmental crisis in Africa. They attribute the current environmental and developmental crises to lack of environmental education because of the colonial experience in almost all African countries. The argument is advanced that environmental education, if introduced in educational institutions, should serve as a vehicle for the transmission of societal knowledge and values which stress a harmonious co-existence with the environment. National education programmes in Africa, particularly in Kenya, should express the environmental aspirations of the different co-existing societies.

The contributors examine and discuss the environmental situations prevailing in Africa while being mindful of where environmental education should find its place.

In Chapter Two, Environmental Education in Perspective, Otiende outlines and discusses the historical evolution of environmental education and related concepts in Kenya and elsewhere. He clearly spells out the aims, role, objectives and achievements of the International Education Programmes (IEP) and the pedagogical approaches and problems in teaching environmental education.

In conclusion, Otiende argues that the concepts and evolution of environmental education have considerable potential for the development of natural resources in the future and affirms that this potential will only be realised if the environmental education teachers are well trained. Clearly, this is a matter which requires international efforts.

The problems most African countries have encountered in the last two or three decades in incorporating environmental education into educational curricula, particularly in secondary schools and in higher institutions of learning, are many. According to UNESCO (1988), the most important setbacks to many African education systems are: lack of appreciation of the importance of environmental education; a shortage of adequately trained educators; too little scheduled time in crowded programmes; insufficient educational materials; lack of financial assistance for teacher's use; and last, inadequate opportunities for field studies. These matters are highlighted in this chapter.

In Chapter Three, Teaching Environmental Education, Omech further discusses the objectives and the different approaches to teaching environmental education at different educational levels. Considerable attention is paid to the approaches and strategies for teaching and presenting environmental education.

Chapter Four, The Earth: Its Environmental Systems and Resources, constitutes the core of all the contributions. Here, Ogeno explores and explains the laws which operate at different physical, biological and social levels and how each of these levels obeys its own laws. The chapter is unique in that it addresses itself to the interaction between different levels of various systems. Relevant application to the 8-4-4 curriculum in Kenya is highlighted.

Poverty in Africa has been exacerbated by the rapid population growth. The optimum contribution of human resources to achieve sustainable development without overloading the environment is discussed by Shiundu in Chapter Five: Human Population and the Environment. Shiundu adopts a Malthusian approach which discusses issues dealing with population carrying capacities and basic human requirements such as food, energy, shelter and clothing.

In particular, Shiundu examines the underlying causes of rapid population growth with examples from Kenya. In his analysis, he notes the direct and indirect attempts to ease population growth in Kenya and how the present growth, size and distribution affects the environment in terms of population. He concludes that the current population growth in Kenya has created new forms of pollution which he terms as pollution in disguise.

While Chapter Five adopts a Malthusian approach, Chapter Six, Human Settlement, takes a historical perspective. Aseka gives a historical evolution of settlements in Africa and discusses how such settlements, urban and rural, influence the distribution and allocation of resources. Issues connected with human settlement such as urban decay, lack of access to clean water and the poor sanitation, which continues to cause widespread disease and death, are exemplified using Kenyan and other African urban situation as examples.

Aseka concludes that both human settlement and resource exploitation are historical phenomena and one has to look at them in connection with the past to establish future trends in ecological and social change. He suggests, in his conclusion, the launching of a massive campaign to restore high quality environment in Africa. Human society, whether urban or rural, according to Aseka, needs a coherent political-ethical ideology to make the meaning of an ecologically-based environmental policy clear and acceptable to the public.

Developing countries account for about one third of the world's energy consumption but do not have proportionate access to it. Most countries depend on oil imports, biomass and animal energy. Wood, which provides the bulk of the energy, is becoming scarce, while over-fetching is leading to serious environmental hazards. These and other related issues connected with recourse use and the technology used to harness energy, are discussed by Libese in Chapter Seven, Technology and the Environment.

Technology is seen as a tool to utilize the environment in order to provide for the increasing demands generated by basic needs. Using examples drawn from other developing countries as well as from Kenya, Libese discusses different forms of energy application. He also discusses biotechnology and telecommunication, both of which promise to have a far-reaching impact on the environment. He concludes that biotechnology and telecommunication may not only change the style of human interaction with the environment but can also improve human health care, food production and the quality of life.

Chapter Eight, Development and the Environment by Orodho to some extent discusses issues already raised in Chapter Six by Aseka and in Chapter Ten by Ezaza. He argues that environmental problems in most developing countries fall broadly into two categories: problems arising out of poverty and those arising out of the very processes of development. He also discusses processes of development in traditional and modern agriculture, industry, transport and human settlement plus the role of environmental policy formulation.

Industrial development brings obvious benefits, but it frequently entails damage to the environment and to human health as well. The main negative consequences, according to UNEP (1988) are: wasteful use and depletion of scarce natural resources air, water and soil pollution; congestion, noise and squalor; accumulation of hazardous waste; and, accidents with significant environmental impact.

In Chapter Nine, Industrial Pollution and Its Effects on the Environment, Muthiani exhaustively discusses the causes and effects of atmospheric pollution on the biosphere. He sees the coordination of international legal action with regard to atmospheric pollution as a measure of safety with which the community of nations will design solutions and minimise the *greenhouse effect* and its social and economic consequences.

Chapter Ten, Perspectives on the African Environment and Development, Ezaza broadly outlines the main features and processes which describe Africa's problems exclusively, in terms of *crises*. It is argued that the current 'pollution of poverty' in the developing nations and the 'pollution of wealth' in the developed nations, present two distinct typed of environmental pollution. For this reason, it is doubtful, according to Ezaza, whether the two contrasting groups of nations, the wealthy and the poor, can work out a unified environmental conservation programme as envisaged by the Brundtland Report entitled *Our Common Future*. It would appear that the future and destiny of these two widely dispersed worlds are already clearly shaped by the poverty syndrome and wealth accumulation.

However, Ezaza notes that the future prospects in Africa are not really bleak as some African countries have begun to realize that there is a limit to the use and misuse of resources. In the last section of his chapter, Ezaza provides options for sustainable development in Africa and concludes that much of the rethinking, policy orientation, mobilization of resources and participation which are required must be generated, from within Africa.

Since we all inhabit the same earth, there is an urgent need for wealthier nations to assist Africa to overcome poverty in order to avoid the repercussions of global environmental degradation. In the meantime, the place of environmental education must be emphasized everywhere.

Environmental legislation should provide a practical framework for implementing environmental standards and for regulating human enterprises in the light of environmental objectives (UNEP, 1988). Kabeberi-Macharia's Chapter Eleven; Policies and Laws Affecting the Environment, addresses these critical legal matters with reference to both developed and developing countries, though with specific reference to the Kenyan situation.

Legal protection of the environment and public health connected with pollution of the atmosphere, biosphere and the hydrosphere in Kenya re-examined in detail. Environmental management policies and the law in Kenya have to address the question of environmental protection and socio-economic development as a measure of protecting the environment. She elaborates her argument by discussing these issues and providing examples found in the local situation.

## Bibliography

Anderson, D. and Johnson, D. *The Ecology of Survival – Case Studies from Northeast African History*, (Lesser Crook: Academy Publishers, 1988).

Ferrari M. Environmental Action in Africa: The Cairo Plan of Action in Integrated Management of Resources in Africa, (Nairobi: UNEP, 1989).

Lacey, C. and Williams R. (eds). *Education, Ecology and Development: The Case for an Education Network,* (London: The World Wildlife Fund and Kogan Page, 1987).

Navel, Z. The Determination of Agro-ecological Site Potential of Tanzania, Masailand: A Challenge for the International Biological Programme, (Haifa, Israel: Publishers 1967).

Odhiambo, T. (ed). *Hope Born Out of Despair: Managing The African Crisis*, (Nairobi: Heinemann Kenya Ltd., 1988).

Richard, P. (ed). *African Environment Special Report 1: Problems and Perspectives,* (London: International African Institute (IAI), 1975.

Tolba, M. Sustainable Development: Constraints and Opportunities, (Nairobi, Butterworths and UNEP, 1987).

____, Evolving Environmental Percepts: From Stockhold to Nairobi, (Nairobi: Butterworths and UNEP, 1988).

UNESCO, Living in the Environment. A Source Book for Environmental Education, (Paris: UNESCO, 1988).

# - 2 -

# Environmental Education in Perspective

J. E. Otiende

## Introduction

It is now widely recognised that our survival depends on a fragile ecosystem. Mismanagement of the earth's natural resources poses grave dangers to the biosphere which includes the atmosphere, oceans, soils and forests as well as the global climate. It follows that there is an urgent need for critical environmental awareness and better protection of the world around us. Clearly, if there is to be sustained development to meet ever-increasing human needs, it has to be accompanied by wise and careful management of the earth's natural resources. This is where environmental education comes in. This chapter will introduce the concept of environmental education, its historical development and key issues as well as consider a possible methodology for introducing environmental education into the classroom.

## 1. The Concept of Environmental Education

The term 'environment' means a number of things:

- the home environment with its human population and its physical surroundings.

- the local environment with its immediate surroundings and the neighbourhood where we spend our days.

- the man-made environment resulting from the hustle and bustle of human activity and enterprise.

- the natural environment which is inclusive of the atmosphere , the oceans, land, trees and wildlife.

- the social environment which includes ourselves, our actions and our interactions with other people.

- the cultural-environment which is the dynamic life shared by a group of people

The term environment is, therefore, all-inclusive; our homes, localities and man-made surroundings; natural and social ambiences make up the total or universal environment. Inevitably, there is an overlapping and constant interaction across the variety of environments. The survival of the universal environment, however, rests on keeping and maintaining a balance within the ecosystem. It is the maintenance of such a balance that guarantees the preservation of life on earth. Endangering any part of the biosphere, however distant it may be, will .ultimately affect the balance of the entire ecosystem.

If, for instance, because of man's interference with nature, a small percentage of the Arctic or the Antarctic ice cap was to melt, the effect would be felt in all the world's oceans and the climates of the whole globe would be altered. Similarly, destroying even one tenth of the Amazon Forest of South

America would affect not only that continent but also North America as well.

Human beings are the only ones capable of ensuring that the environment remains inhabitable. Whatever our activities, whatever 'progress' we achieve, we must ensure that the biosphere is neither destroyed nor adversely affected. This is no easy task as major disasters (such as Bhopal, 1984; and Chernobyl, 1986) can easily be caused by attempts to improve living conditions.

Other dangers to the environment are directly caused by modern warfare which does not hesitate to use chemical and biological weapons in the form of lethal gases, defoliants and atomic explosions. It seems that only a greater awareness of our environment can help prevent the global destruction of our fragile ecosystem. Indeed, this has always been true but the problem has assumed greater urgency now that the artificial environment of cities and industrial complexes has started affecting not only our immediate neighbourhood but also the outer atmosphere with its protective ozone layer. For many centuries the dangers of pollution were not realised, but within the last four decades a number of voices have been raised and accusing fingers pointed at man's irresponsible use of his habitat.

Man's faulty approach to development and progress has now been revealed in the light of a number of environmental disasters. The new concern for the natural environment has led to a concerted global call for environmental education. International conferences, seminars and workshops have been organised on the subject and declarations of support for the environment are both frequent and forceful. Environmental education is seen as the only way of developing an awareness of the environment and a sense of responsibility for its protection. It is the most effective vehicle for persuading the human race to adopt a rational attitude towards the natural environment and to avoid the deterioration of human life as a result of unwise exploitation and misuse of nature.

It is through education that both individual and group efforts, collective initiatives and responsibility can be set in motion. Given the extent of pollution, isolated individual efforts would be like a mere drop of water in an ocean; ineffective and frustrating. All of us must learn to care for the environment. Concern for nature must be emphasised. Prevention of environmental problems must feature prominently in any programme of environmental education. In particular, people must be persuaded that personal advantages will accrue from increased care of their surroundings. Environmental education must demonstrate that humanity depends on the earth's natural resources; and therefore, the impact of human influence on the environment and the ecosystem must be carefully assessed.

It is only through informed understanding of the environment that the global population can be convinced of its responsibility.

Creating a sense of environmental concern through education calls for more than mere knowledge and understanding; it demands positive attitudes towards the maintenance of the earth's geological integrity. All earth-linked studies, both theoretical and practical, can enable individuals to enjoy their environment fully as well as develop a responsible attitude towards it., Environmental education must therefore:

• *Teach people about the natural world around them.* Obviously, areas of study such as biology and geography are in tune with this aspect of environmental education.

Because it is through investigation, observation and discovery, individuals come to learn interesting, useful, and even vital facts about their surroundings.

- *Involve people in real situations.* Opportunities need to be created where individuals can ask questions about their environment, and find answers to them. Problems are set and solved by using the surroundings as a source of information.

- *Enhance acceptable and responsible attitudes towards the environment.* Given the interdependence between humankind and the various environments, an understanding of the ecological system must be developed together with a genuine concern for the environment. Environmental education enables students to develop positive attitudes towards their environment; these include awareness, concern and care.

Environmental education can, therefore, be said to be concerned with understanding the skills and attitudes necessary for enhancing environmental conservation. Positive action with regard to the environment goes beyond mere information; it involves sustaining healthy surroundings while keeping at bay agents of destruction. Environmentalists need to be resourceful, creative and innovative. They must also be persuasive, for many millions of individuals show nothing but lack of concern and apathy towards the problem.

Environmental education must be seen as not merely a strategy for creating awareness of the environment, but also as a means towards developing positive concern for maintaining the quality of life on earth. Environmental issues must be treated with the confidence that since human beings can reason and act morally, there is room for hope that the situation will improve.

Environmental education is integrative; it must deal with understanding, skills and attitudes. Indeed, environmental education must not only serve the needs of general education; but must also show concern for practical life outside the classroom. It must include the implementation of studies covering such areas as biology, economics, geography, chemistry, health education and ethics. Environmental education should therefore, be understood as a study oriented towards meaningful, lifelong education.

## 2. The Evolution of Environmental Education

Environmental education, in the sense of understanding the environment, has always been with us. Informal education has always attempted to prepare the young to take their place in both the natural and social environments. Before the 1970s, all African societies tried to educate their people about the interdependence between human life and the rest of the natural world. In Europe, in the nineteenth century, it was the Industrial Revolution and Darwin's *The Origin of the Species* (1859), which awoke attention to the fact that environment and nature were not unaffected by man.

At that time, the degrading living conditions of most European countries showed that environmental problems were approaching an unhealthy level. The environmental effects of the Industrial Revolution were horrifying. Individuals such as Professor Geddes ( 1854-1933), a botanist, showed concern at the poor environmental and educational situation and pressed for better living conditions. He saw a close link between the quality of education and the environment. Any improvement in education, he felt, would have a significant impact on attitudes towards nature. For this reason, Geddes can be said to be the father of modern environmental education.

Unfortunately, when he died, his ideas on the environment were generally misinterpreted. Other educators like Dewey (1856-1952) shifted the emphasis from using education as a means of bringing about environmental change to using the physical environment as a means for bringing about learning. It was not until the 1960s that interdisciplinary and multidisciplinary models of environmental education, with a child-centred curriculum, became fashionable and studies related to the environment found firmer footing in many teachers training institutions and schools. What remained to be decided was what this discipline should consist of and how the programme should be implemented. Such matters were to be discussed at regional and international meetings, conferences and seminars in the 1970s and later. Should environmental education merely be concerned with conservation or applied ecology? Such issues needed discussion and resolution on a global basis since matters pertaining to the environment were inescapably universal and urgent.

Increasingly in the 1970's, professional organisations such as the International Union for Conservation of Nature and Natural Resources (IUCN), the International Council of Scientific Unions (ICSU), and World Wide Fund for Nature (WWF), grass root organisations and even individuals throughout the world, advocated the need for a global body to deal with environmental issues. Indeed, it was the professional and non-governmental organisations which led to the 1972 Stockholm Conference and also pressed for the creation of UNEP.

The 1970s can thus be said to be the years of thinking and reflecting in concrete terms on environmental conservation and education. The 1970s also saw the birth of a number of bodies sponsored by the United Nations for the conservation and improvement of the environment - for instance Habitat. A number of international conferences deserve particular mention:

### (1) The United Nations Conference on the Human Environment Stockholm. Sweden, 1972

Environmental education, as a global movement, was effectively established at the United Nations Conference on the Human Environment held in Stockholm in 1972. The Stockholm Conference clearly recognised the close interrelationship between the environment and society. It concerned itself with environmental quality and studied the pros and cons of human settlement. Most important, the Conference discussed ways through which education can create effective environmental policies and management.

The agenda for the Stockholm Conference reflected the concerns of the day, particularly environmental pollution and the need for a global conservation strategy or programme. For the developed industrialised countries, the priority was environmental pollution arising from the impact of industrialisation on the ecosystem; conserving the earth's natural resources was recognised as vitally important The developing countries had a rather different agenda; for them the problems of human settlement, clean water, disposal of human waste and elimination of poverty were paramount.

Evidently, these different priorities were reflected in the discussions. While the developed countries would have liked to put more emphasis on conservation efforts, developing countries saw this as unrealistic. They were keen on initiating industrialisation and unhappy about possible restrictions that might be imposed on them in the course of doing so. They did not see the need for such emphasis on curbing global pollution.

In the end, the delegates to the Stockholm Conference resolved to seek inexpensive alternatives to industrialisation while endeavouring to reduce the accompanying pollution. In their Declaration on the Human Environment, the delegates concurred on the need for:

* new principles of behaviour, approaches, responsibility and concern for the environment;

* a global action plan to map out clear measures for cooperation with respect to environmental issues; and

* institutional and financial arrangements or mechanisms for realising a global action plan.

A few months later, the recommendations of the Stockholm Conference on establishing an international programme for environmental education - which was to be interdisciplinary in approach within the United Nations network-was endorsed under the General Assembly Resolution 2997 (XXVII). It resulted in the creation of the United Nations Environmental Programme (UNEP). The UNEP was to work towards educating all peoples on the simple steps to take to manage and control their environment effectively.

To this end, UNEP cooperated with United Nations Educational, Scientific and Cultural Organisation (UNESCO) in attempting to develop and establish environmental education at an international level. Both bodies carried out research and initiated programmes; by 1975 these efforts revealed that needs for environmental education were not the same in different countries across the world. In many instances, methods used for effective environmental education included devising programmes and teaching aids as well as resolving the problem of lack of trained and skilled personnel. Given the cooperation between UNESCO and UNEP, many countries have made significant advances in environmental education in terms of programmes, training, materials, research and even exchange of information.

The UNEP has endeavoured to demonstrate the close link between humankind and the ecosystem. All nations need experience based and problem-oriented education related to the environmental needs of their particular situation. Environmental education must therefore be integrated within the curriculum, and be available to all the peoples of the world if they are to develop the required knowledge , awareness, attitudes and skills for rational environmental decisions and actions. The UNEP has been faithfully trying to implement the concerns of Stockholm and the resolutions of the Assembly. There is evidence that most nations are now keenly aware of the dangers of pollution; this was particularly illustrated by the recent refusal of poor African countries to accept attractive payments for their soil to-be used as dumps for toxic or atomic waste.

### (2)　The UNESCO-UNEP International Environmental Workshop, Belgrade, Yugoslavia, 1975

Following the exploratory investigation of worldwide environmental education needs, UNESCO and UNEP organised a Workshop for exchange of views in Belgrade in 1975. The Belgrade Workshop produced the Belgrade Charter which singled out the goals, objectives, principles and target audiences for effective environmental education programmes. The workshop was able to come up with a framework for environmental education. In effect, the Belgrade Workshop amounted to the launching of the UNESCO-UNEP International Education Programme. The Programme would develop relevant knowledge, skills, attitudes and values for the improvement of the environment both for the present and future generations.

The Belgrade Workshop considered the objectives of its International Environmental Education Programme as:

- To help individuals and social groups acquire an awareness of, and sensitivity to, the universal environment and its problems.

- To enable individuals and social groups attain a basic understanding of the universal environment, its attendant problems and humanity's vital responsibility and stewardship in conserving it.

- To help individuals and social groups develop positive attitudes towards cooperation on global environmental matters in terms of environmental protection as well as improvement.

- To enable individuals and social groups attain the necessary skills for dealing with and solving environmental problems.

- To help individuals and social groups assess and evaluate environment-related measures and programmes in their entirety.

- To enable individuals and social groups inculcate, in themselves and others, a sense of responsibility and concern for environmental matters or issues.

The International Environmental Education Programme was to be aimed principally at the general public, even though the formal and non-formal education sectors were to constitute other major target groups. The Belgrade Workshop unanimously adopted guiding principles for its environmental education programme.

These guiding principles were meant to be holistic in approach, that is, they were to consider the total environment. Moreover, the process of education was to be continuous and life-long both in and out of school; interdisciplinary in its approach; emphasise participation in finding preventive measures and solutions; examine the environment globally; focus its attention on both present and future circumstances, by examining development and growth issues from an environmental point of view; and finally, promote the value and necessity of cooperation at all levels , when seeking solutions to environmental problems.

### (3) Intergovernmental Conference on Environmental Education, Tbilisi, USSR, 1977

The Belgrade Workshop was followed in 1976 and 1977 by national and regional meetings involving experts. These meetings discussed and reflected on the events of the Belgrade Workshop and laid a structure for the future directions of environmental education. Once this was done, the way was open for the Tbilisi Conference in the course of 1977. This was the first intergovernmental meeting ushering a new phase in environmental education. This conference was organised by UNESCO in conjunction with UNEP at the invitation of the USSR and was a follow-up of the Stockholm Conference of 1972 vis-a-vis its implications on education. The Tbilisi Conference was charged with implementing the International Environmental Education Programme, a product of the Belgrade Workshop of 1975. The major achievement of the Tbilisi Conference, however, was the precise description of the nature of environmental education, its aims, characteristics and strategies at all levels. Environmental education, according to the Tbilisi Conference, should be an integral part of any realistic problem-solving and life-long education; it should be particularly concerned with the well-being of human settlement across the world.

The Tbilisi Conference not only advocated for all efforts to be made for a definite inclusion of environmental education in the curriculum, but it also agreed that the subject use an interdisciplinary approach to give existing school subjects a significant role to play in addressing environmental problems and providing solutions. However, since education on its own cannot solve all the complexities of environmental problems (which involve economic, social and cultural matters), the Conference recommended that the rational use of science and technology in providing environmental education could, indeed, bring about global justice and fairness. This, it was thought, could provide for the eventual creation of a new international order with respect to development. National and regional co-operation were to be stressed. While this was a worthy ideal, it should be noted that conferences, even those recognised by most nations, have no executive powers over their own recommendations and decisions. The implementation of such resolutions must perforce be left to each sovereign nation.

Above all, however, the lasting contribution of the Tbilisi Conference remains the formulation and endorsement of environmental education goals, objectives and founding principles. It is these which have been instrumental in devising and developing almost all activities regarding environmental education worldwide. In addition, the Conference recommended that member countries establish national policies and strategies for developing environmental education; drawing up and promoting research in environmental education; exchanging experiences, information, research results and facilities; and, aiding the international community in strengthening collaborative efforts in environmental education for the cause of international peace.

In many respects, the Tbilisi Declaration, with its 41 Recommendations sought to achieve its purpose by formulating recommendations for concerted action at all levels in developing environmental education. Following the Tbilisi Conference, much of what has been achieved in the field of environmental education has been within the context of the declaration and recommendations of this important Conference. This has resulted in many national initiatives being later taken towards positive action.

Since that time, UNEP has gone on with its catalystic coordination role in environmental education with respect to national and international policies and institutions as spelt out by the General Assembly in its resolution 2997 (XXVII) of 1972: "To keep under review the world environmental situation in order to ensure that emerging environmental problems of international significance receive appropriate and adequate consideration by governments. Since 1974, UNEP has been issuing annual reports on the state of the global environment.

From 1977, these reports have become selective in their treatment and discussions. In 1985, the Governing Council of UNEP recommended that future publications should report on alternate years (a) on economic and social issues and (b) on issues involving assessment of the environment. The state-of-the-world-environment reports were to make use of the available data and assessments coming out of the Global

Environmental Monitoring System. The first of such reports was produced by UNEP in 1987.

At the heart of UNEP's concern then, is the quest for stimulating sustainable development which does not mismanage, misuse and erode the global natural resources on which such development depends. In this respect, UNEP maintains that general public environmental awareness is the key factor in this critical exercise. All levels of society have to be made aware of environmental matters and indeed, participate in maintaining the ecosystem's balance. As increasing numbers of schools and universities now encourage environmental education, UNEP, in close liaison with UNESCO, has been in the forefront of the campaign to promote the environmental components of curricula both in and out of school.

By 1987, 45 countries had included environmental studies in their school curricula, while 140 others had got involved in UNEP's International Environmental Education Programmes. The UNEP's quest for new thinking on environmental matters, using education as a vehicle, has still not been given the priority it deserves. The UNEP makes available vital information that enables individual nations to take necessary action to enhance the environment. In its approved system-wide medium-term programme for the period 1990-1995, environmental education is given a pivotal and critical role in bringing about environmental awareness and understanding.

The UNEP sets out new objectives and strategies for achieving sustainable development in relation to matters of the atmosphere, water, terrestrial ecosystems, coastal and island systems, oceans and the lithosphere. In order to keep down the cost of implementing its programme, UNEP establishes some priorities in its education and training objectives for 1990-1995: The following steps are progressively more costly:

- Integrating general environmental education in the formal educational policy and system at all levels.

- Increasing environmental awareness among all people through non-formal educational activities.

- Integrating an environmental component into the education and training of occupational and social groups such as engineers, architects, administrators and economists who are likely to influence environmental management and public behaviour.

- Continuing to provide population education to all by emphasising the effects of excessive population on the environment.

- Providing specialised training relating to the understanding, assessment and management of the whole environment; incorporating into this training the concept of sustainable development.

- Providing interdisciplinary training for managers and national decision makers in sustainable natural resources development, land-use planning and environmental protection.

Thus, to achieve sustainable development, environmental education and training, together with public information, are expected to feature strongly in the 1990s.

To realise these objectives, a variety of strategies within the framework of the Global Strategy will be implemented. Every effort will be made to integrate environmental education into the policies and programmes of the member states. In order to effectively sensitise the general public to environmental education, the 1990s will be declared a World

Decade for Environmental Education. This will be done jointly by UNEP and UNESCO. Again, constant and consolidated efforts will be made by the United Nations bodies to provide population education and show the pressure exerted on the environment by allowing the population to grow without any check.

### 3. Some Issues in Environmental Education

Considerable efforts continue to be made to integrate environmental education into national policies and processes, but little will be done without agreement on the nature of programmes, teaching methodologies, approaches and resources.

#### (a) The Nature of Environmental Education Programmes

A meaningful programme of environmental education must not only foster understanding and positive attitudes but must also include practical knowledge of immediate problems, concern for morals and aesthetics and a feeling of responsibility when the ecosystem is allowed to deteriorate.

Clearly, the task of designing an environmental education programme becomes complex if such features are to be incorporated. This poses problems if environmental education is to be treated as a study subject of its own unless this merely means consolidating the treatment of environmental issues across the curricula under one heading. It is also necessary to consider the fact that environmental education should not only be institution-based, but should also include the rest of the community through non-formal contacts.

Essentially, the problem is how to treat complex environmental issues which are not only broadly based but are also related to parallel subjects. When specific problems are resolved, others tend to arise in an endless succession.

The question is, what should constitute relevant environmental education at every stage of formal and non-formal education? This question arises because the range of possible topics for an environmental education programme is virtually inexhaustible. Decisions have to be made, therefore, to rank possible topics for consideration in terms of their relative importance in relation to other topics and availability of research based resources. Adequate consideration must be given to the interrelationship between the environment and the complex impact of human activities upon it. In order to achieve meaningful understanding of the subject, a concentric approach is recommended in order that the same topics may be approached repeatedly at deeper and deeper levels.

Attempting to realise such an objective using traditional or existing educational methods and programmes would hardly be feasible. In many cases, national education aims and programmes are not at all environmentally oriented, even though allusions may be made to the subject. Indeed, the expressed environmental aims cited in policy documents are merely expectations to be realised along the way; typically there is no clear-cut commitment to their being achieved.

The additional problem of coordination arises in attempts to include environmental education in existing education programmes. Even allowing for the inevitability of an overlap with other areas of knowledge, there is still the need for an overall education policy that will ensure that gaps are bridged and overlaps kept to a minimum. Introducing environmental education within an existing education system is not done in vacuum for subjects which are firmly established in the education system tend to resist what could be interpreted as uncalled for interference and unwarranted duplication. Success in avoiding conflicts will depend largely on cooperation with other subjects and departments.

The magnitude of the problem cannot be wished away. It is largely a question of deciding what the nature of environmental education is to be and thereafter deciding whether to integrate the subject with, or separate it from, others in the curricula. Concrete action in terms of course content, institutional structures and working relationships with the wider community must be achieved. Final decisions remain a matter for each country to make after considering specific needs, aims and priorities.

### (b) Methodology or Pedagogical Approaches in Environmental Education

Since environmental education is a practical subject, decisions must be made on what programmes should be taught and how. It is vital that environmental education should inculcate knowledge, skills and attitudes that will help improve the quality of the environment.

A comprehensive methodology must include a variety of overlapping pedagogical approaches to the subject. These include:

- The inquiry method, where the learner openly plays an active role in the educative process. In this discovery oriented method, the educator largely guides the learner to define a problem; formulate a hypothesis; collect and analyse data, and then report findings; test the original hypothesis on the basis of the findings, formulate conclusions; and finally, attempt to solve the problem. .In essence, the inquiry-discovery method offers the learners an opportunity to deal scientifically with environmental issues.

- The systems method, where consideration is given to broad environmental concepts. A case in point could involve considering broadly the concept of ecological interrelationships in the total environment. In this way, the learner would be exposed to environmental facts, and could use these facts, to propose solutions to environmental problems or even devise theories about environmental issues.

- The relevance method, where the criteria for drawing up environmental education programmes are governed by issues of social relevance and actuality. When this method is used, reference to environmental matters is incorporated into discussions on other curriculum disciplines.

- The process method where environmental education programmes are designed with greater emphasis on the scientific approach irrespective of the discipline involved. In many ways, this method is much the same as the inquiry-discovery method but differs from it in its dispassionate approach to the interrelationship between humankind and the impact of his activities on the ecosystem.

- The value clarification method, where particular consideration is given to an understanding of the cultural connotations of environmental education. This is especially pertinent in matters related to population growth and control. This topic can often give rise to heated discussions. In considering population growth and control, therefore, due care should be taken to learn and understand the traditional and, or accepted cultural values in order to treat vital topics in a manner acceptable to the target group.

## Problems Related to the Methodology of Teaching Environmental Education

The use of a diversity of pedagogical approaches may create a number of problems. One such problem is how to decide which method is suitable for which ability level; another is whether the teaching should be formal or non-formal and whether there has to be complete agreement among teachers and tutors on both the course content and its specifications across the educational system.

All matters must be decided with regard to the needs and relevance of the particular context.

Educators may not be familiar with the variety of interdisciplinary or multidisciplinary approaches available in dealing with environmental issues. Environmental education is a relatively new discipline. Moreover, the trend in teacher education is increasingly oriented towards specialisation.

In the rigid institutional structures of certain educational establishments, effective or 'action-oriented' environmental education may not be welcome. Solving such problems largely depends on how similar problems affecting other related disciplines are solved. In an ideal institutional atmosphere, educators have mutual trust and respect, and they engage co-operatively in dialogue across their disciplines. In reality, this is not always the case due to increasing compartmentalisation and specialisation.

Again, the choice of approach may depend on an already existing set of ethical, aesthetic, religious and economic values that are regularly used for assessing any situation and offering solutions. This may not facilitate effective environmental education where new situations are constantly experienced and require not only additional information but also a re-examination of attitudes and a reappraisal of traditionally accepted beliefs and taboos.

In an already crowded curriculum, what precisely will constitute environmental education and justify its inclusion? Clearly, learners need to be given an opportunity to investigate, discuss and analyse environmental concerns. Even then, due care and caution need to be taken in order to arrive at sound and effective curriculum decisions.

#### (c) Resources for Environmental Education

Whatever direction the programmes and methodology for environmental education may take, the matter of educational resources is of critical importance towards the realisation of the ultimate goal of this subject. Neither the availability and integration of environmental education programmes nor the use of a comprehensive methodology will ensure success unless both human and material resources are available to both teachers and students. Such resources should include textbooks, charts, tables, illustrations and specimens together with resource persons well informed on the local problems.

Ideally, educational resources for environmental education must not only be readily available and locally prepared but they must also clearly illustrate the purposes of the activities planned. Materials should be of good quality and produced in sufficient quantity; in addition, instructional aids must be appropriate and meet the needs of the group. Teaching aids that are frequently used must be handled carefully and the information carried upto date. Instructional aids produced for use in industrialised societies may not necessarily be suitable in less developed societies and vice versa. Environmental concerns or problems are not only different from country to country but are varied in different areas of the same country. In Kenya, material used in Nakuru may be largely irrelevant in Maralal.

Teaching materials and aids do not necessarily cost a lot and the most appropriate may also be the cheapest. Local priorities must be considered before any financial commitment is made. Yet effective environmental education can hardly be dispensed without some public expenditure on the production of instructional aids designed to make the local population not only aware of environmental factors and problems, but also be involved in decision-making and problem-solving.

Effective environmental education will certainly rely on available human resources. In fact it is the calibre of the teaching personnel that may be the decisive factor in creating a lasting impact. Such personnel must be trained and fully conversant with the aims of the subject. Ideally, they will be able to make full use of the available instructional aids and develop their own instructional aids utilising local resources. Clearly, the newness of environmental education in the curriculum means that the subject cannot yet rely on many specialists. Much, therefore, needs to be done to reappraise teacher education programmes to include environmental education in their curricula. Again, this will depend on the country's educational priorities as well as the availability of financial resources.

## Conclusion

In discussing the concept and evolution of environmental education and related issues, it is evident that the subject has considerable potential for development in the future. Much will depend on the training of educators who will need drive, initiative, imagination and special concern for the environment in order to be effective.

Much will also depend on the quality and availability of instructional resources. Local, national, regional and international efforts therefore need to be directed towards resolving these urgent matters in the interest of environmental education.

## Questions

1. Attempt to define the concept of environmental education.

2. Trace the history of environmental education from the previous century to the present.

3. Consider the lasting implications of the Belgrade Workshop for environmental education.

4. Discuss fully any specific issue in environmental education, paying particular attention to its history and its scope as well as its possible solutions.

## Bibliography

Bakishi, T.S. and Naveh, Z., (eds.). *Environmental Education: Principles, Methods and Approaches.* New York: Plenum Press, 1980.

Basic Education Resource Centre, "Basic Education and the Environment" *BERC Bulletin*, 16 Kenyatta University. Nairobi: Basic Education Resource Centre, Eastern and Southern Africa, 1987.

H.M.S.O. *Environmental Education.* Edinburgh: HMSO Press, 1974.

Lacey, C and Williams, R. (eds). *Education, Ecology and Development: The Case for an Education Network.* London: The World Wildlife Fund and Kogan Page Ltd., 1987.

Martin, G.C. and Wheeler, K. (eds.) *Insights into Environmental Education.* Edinburgh: Oliver and Boyd 1975.

Schools Council, *Ethics and Environment.* London:Longman Group Ltd., 1975.

UNEP, *The State of the World Environment.* Nairobi: United Nations Environmental Programme, 1987.

UNEP, *Profile.* Nairobi: United Nations Environmental Programme, 1987.

UNEP, The United Nations System-Wide Medium-Term Environmental Programme 1990-1995. Nairobi: United Nations Environmental Programme, 1988.

UNESCO, *Environmental Education in the Light of the Tbilisi Conference.* Paris: United NationsEducational Scientific and Cultural Organization, 1980.

# -3-

# Teaching Environmental Education

### A. N. Ombech

## Introduction

Environmental Education (EE) is an important component of education and deserves to be taught at all levels and in all types of education for the purpose of understanding and addressing environmental problems. We are concerned about the environment because we appreciate that today the human race is in the process of transforming nature drastically and may, in the near future, cause irreparable damage to our natural environment.

This environment is given various names, including habitat, ecosystem, nature, surroundings, and biosphere. Because its components interact with each other, destruction of any individual component can cause an undesirable imbalance. Our environment or our surroundings include all the factors that influence growth, behaviour and development; it also involves a complex interaction between natural and social phenomena (UNICEF, 1987).

Sound environmental behaviour is a direct result of good attitudes and a thorough understanding of certain values. These values cannot be absorbed all at once and our attitudes are developed throughout our lives. This is why environmental education is seen as process of continuous learning, a gradually acquired realisation of the importance of natural resources and the need to use them wisely. The best strategy to adopt is to make environmental education an integral part of the learning process throughout life. Environmental education is also described as the process by which one becomes gradually aware and critical of attitude towards the environment

Rugamayo (1983) states that environmental education should be conceptualised as a process and not as a single subject because it involves all human activities. The attributes of environmental education are shown in Fig. 3.1 which illustrates the relationship between learners and subject matter.

**Fig. 3.1**

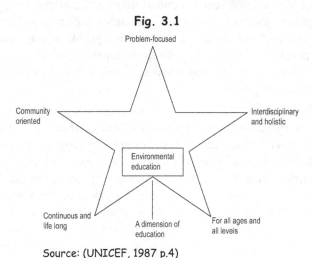

Source: (UNICEF, 1987 p.4)

## 1. Objectives of Environmental Education

As discussed in the previous chapter, the aims of environmental education are most likely to be achieved through cooperation between individual nations, non-governmental organisations and the United Nations Environmental Programme, UNEP. Teaching is an intentional activity, hence it must be founded on well defined objectives. Experts from various disciplines must join forces to enable EE to achieve specific aims. The Intergovernmental Conference on EE, (UNESCO, 1977) laid down guidelines for the provision of EE. These have proved very useful (CONNECT, 8, 1983, 2.) to organisations and institutions concerned with the development and implementation of curricula.

## 2. Incorporating Environmental Education in the School Curriculum

To achieve the objectives of environmental education, the Tbilisi Conference recommended that each country set up or strengthen the organisational structures necessary for the realisation of the objectives. A central problem was how to incorporate the teaching of environmental education into existing, traditionally structured curricula without interrupting the education process.

It is possible to let each school merely 'link' the teaching of each subject with a discussion of environmental problems as an appended reminder. For example, a geography teacher might include, under the topic of soil erosion, a discussion on the environmental degradation caused by soil erosion. The emphasis here is on soil erosion as an aspect of mass wastage and not on the degradation of the environment as such. This is one way of linking both subjects in the curriculum. The other way is a 'fused' curriculum in which the (geography) teacher discusses soil erosion and environmental degradation as one entity. In this approach the learners might begin by observing the effects of soil erosion on the environment.

The difference between 'linking' and 'fusion' in curriculum development is exemplified in Fig. 3.2 (UNICEF 1987; 9).

**Fig. 3.2**

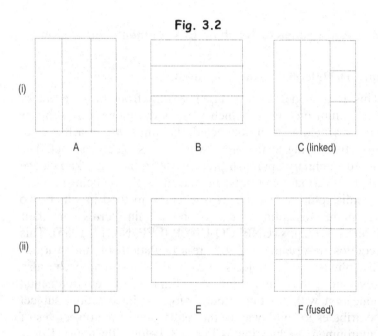

In (i), A and B, the subjects of study, are linked to form C. The linked parts of C may receive varying emphasis depending on the teacher. The linked parts are treated as separate entities. In (ii),the fused parts are fully interwoven and receive uniform emphasis during instruction. It should be noted that fusion in curriculum development results in another academic discipline closely related to the disciplines that were fused. Fusion and linkage are closely related to the traditional organisation of the formal learning environment. The result is two distinct approaches to environmental education: interdisciplinary and multi-disciplinary. There are other approaches more suitable to other learning groups, such as the community based approach and the problem-solving approach.

## 3. Approaches to Teaching Environmental Education

### (a) The Interdisciplinary Approach

This is a model of teaching resulting from the concept of curriculum linking, in which various disciplines and subjects are presented as inter-connected; the aim being to achieve the objectives lying in the areas where the subjects interact. The interdisciplinary approach presupposes a thorough knowledge of the various concepts in the disciplines being linked. Interdisciplinary teaching is a teaching method in which two or more disciplines are expressed in terms of their interrelationships (UNESCO-UNEP IEEP, No. 14, 1985). This requires re-orientation and re-articulation of the various disciplines and subjects involved. This approach also advocates the integration or linking of environmental education with existing school subjects. Each school subject contributes in some way to the realisation of the objectives of environmental education as Fig. 3.3, below, illustrates (Korir-Koech, 1987).

Recommendation No. 12 of the Tbilisi Conference urged member states to either initiate efforts or continue to strengthen the existing ones in order to incorporate environmental issues in various disciplines. In this approach, each discipline brings to the study of environmental issues its particular vocabulary, approach and its instruction process independent of others. Teachers then single out relevant points on which to concentrate. This method aims at bringing an awareness of the correlations existing in certain environmental phenomena that might be overlooked in a single disciplinary approach (UNESCO-UNEP-IEEP, No. 14, 1985).

**Fig. 3.3**

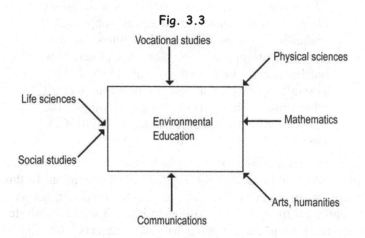

The successful use of an interdisciplinary approach, presupposes flexibility and a readiness to include appropriate aspects of environmental education within existing curricula. It might even require the formulation of new curricula that require teachers and learners to place themselves in situations that are really related to the environmental problem. Incorporating interdisciplinary into educational practice is an arduous enterprise that can be achieved only by degrees. The educators require a new kind of training and even a reorganisation of the teacher training institution. This is thoroughly discussed in the inter-disciplinary curriculum development for EE in UNESCO-UNEP, IEEP No. 14 1985. In this approach, some specialised training of the teachers is required in order to enable them to teach a wider variety of topics within each discipline.

### (b) Multidisciplinary Approach

"Time-old compartmentalisation of disciplines coupled with old-style teaching approaches makes it appear as if present disciplines, the way they are, are appropriate. New disciplines, new teachers and new pedagogical methods are possible to inspire a new initiative in overall education. This is perhaps, what the multidisciplinary approach attempts" (UNESCO-UNEP-IEEP, No. 14 : 110).

The multidisciplinary approach is then, the result of a 'fused' curriculum design for environmental education. In this approach, disciplines and subjects use the environment as a resource for their teaching. (Refer to Fig. 3.3 which illustrates the multidisciplinary approach). All subjects are linked through EE.

As an example, art as a subject "reveals itself when, as a result of communing with the environment, the learner comes to appreciate its aesthetic value and expresses it through songs, paintings and poems. The artist's product helps persuade people to admire, cherish and conserve the environment.

The appropriateness of this approach depends on the nature of the learners and the learning resources available. Teachers using this approach need to have a very wide background of general knowledge and some specialised training.

### (c) The Problem-Solving Approach

This approach is practically oriented and aims at finding solutions to specific problems of the environment, or minimally, making the participants better equipped to provide solutions. It focuses on problems more than on learners and therefore it is contrary to the traditional school certificate based approach. It requires a thorough re-thinking of the educational process and a new orientation of teaching strategies towards solving environmental problems rather than an academic knowledge of what they are and how they affect us.

UNESCO-UNEP IEEP, No. 75, is committed to the implementation of this method. Seven approaches to problem solving are discussed. These are:

- the discussion group approach;
- guided environmental interpretation;
- clarification of values;
- gaming and simulation;
- experimental demonstration workshop;
- a practical action project;
- action-oriented research.

In discussion groups participants have access, through a facilitator, to information needed for active participation. The group then aims at:

- creating-awareness of the problem;
- analysing the situation to find the most effective solutions and remedies;

- searching for improvement after discussion of the means available and expected results;
- applying the solutions and evaluating their effectiveness (UNESCO-IEEP No. 15:7).

The following is an example of a problem which a community solved by discussion :

*Problem:* Something uproots germinating maize and eats it up.

*Solution:* Discussions revealed that squirrels had eaten the germinating maize. After several suggestions were proposed, it was decided that maize with pepper be scattered in the squirrel's path; upon eating the 'bait' squirrels scratched their tongue and eyes and finally bled to death.

The solution was cheap and affordable.

Elaboration of the other seven approaches can be found in UNESCO-UNEP IEEP, No. 15. The central point throughout these approaches is that the teacher or leader must make sure that the participants are consciously aware of the environmental problem, clearly understand what constitutes a solution to it and are motivated to discover that solution. Thereafter, the participants are guided towards solving the problem. The process involves:

- identification of the problem, its causes and effects;
- collection of relevant data;
- formulation of hypotheses and testing their feasibility; and planning for effective action.

The particular strategy to be followed depends on the nature of the environmental problem, the nature of the participants, the competence of the teacher and the teaching-learning resources available. It cannot, therefore, always be predetermined. The teacher is expected to prepare his strategy carefully but he must be prepared to alter or adapt it if necessary.

### (d) Community-Based Approach

This approach can be used effectively in non-formal and adult education. 'Community' should be understood here as a relative term which includes all those affected by a given environmental problem. Even global environmental problems can be studied by a village or a nation and then, the village or nation acts as a community. The community-based approach involves action by the entire community (including the schools) towards the solution of the problem. It is a learning process for all those concerned. Community participation as a process of teaching environmental issues can either be defensive (to guard against change) or developmental (to attempt to alter a situation.) Often it is a mixture of the two. *Harambee* projects in Kenya are examples of community-based approaches if the project is aimed at solving a community problem.

The strategy for action depends on how large the community is. At the national level, it may involve:

- identification of community problems to be studied with full community participation;
- developing an appropriate curriculum
- training teachers; and
- evaluating the environmental education curriculum.

This could very easily involve a mass-media programme directed at some particular target group. Community based education can include all forms of non-formal education programmes such as nutrition, health or population education. Programmes like the Kenya Expanded Programme on

Immunisation (KEPI) or Child Survival and Development (CSDP), championed by UNICEF, are large-scale community-based approaches aimed at the improvement of the environment. There are several thousand community associations for the protection of the environment through which millions are being educated. The mass-media support these programmes and continue to play a key role in stimulating and extending awareness of the environment. Yet there are still many other groups and communities that have not been reached and efforts must continue in order to create environmental awareness. Fig. 3.4 shows areas where a whole community can be used to solve problems of environment.

Another organised non-formal sector of the community that can be useful in the provision of environmental education is the group involved in adult education classes. To effectively educate adults, Rugamayo and Johnson (1987) suggest that:

- the interests of adults must be stirred to increase their motivation to learn;
- learning must be based on experiences within the community: learning must be based on real problems;
- the inadequacy of the adult's environmental knowledge must be shown.
- the expected gain must be clear and an opportunity given to practise new knowledge, skills and behaviour;
- appropriate methods of imparting knowledge should be employed.

**Fig. 3.4 Some of the Spheres of Interest and Involvement Influenced by the Formation of Environmental Groups.**

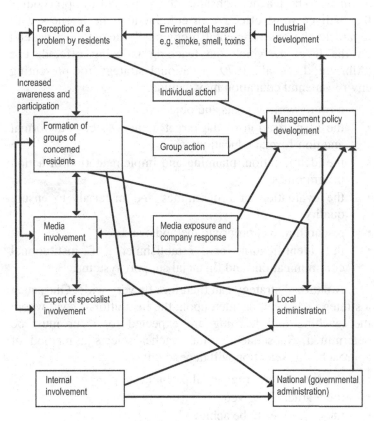

Source: (UNEP-IEEP No. 23: 18)

### 4. Strategies for Presenting Environmental Education

Strategies refer to the processes used to present environmental problems to the learners. This involves predetermining the steps that will be used vis-a-vis the teaching resources available. The teacher considers the steps and the procedures that will be most effective in enlightening the learners with regard to the environmental problem. Strategies also depend on the level at which the teaching is being offered. For (Albright, J. et. al., 1979) a national strategy for presenting environ-mental education may include:

- a framework of goals and objectives;
- the identification of the target audiences in both formal and non-formal education;
- the identification, planning and implementation of action programmes;
- the evaluation of programmes and materials to ensure quality;
- research into appropriate methods; and
- the identification and establishment of institutional communications and financial support systems.

A national strategy can therefore be very wide. Once such a strategy has been decided upon, the institutional level where the teaching and learning are expected to occur must be determined. Subsequently, the teacher selects a method of approach; this selection will depend on:

- the specific environmental problem:
- the learners involved;
- the objectives to be achieved;
- what the teacher know about the problem (i.e content arid competency); and
- the teaching and financial resources available.

These points will usually vary from context to context and means that the teaching strategy will be environmentally specific. What is important is that each teaching strategy be:

- practically feasible;
- meaningful and stimulating to the audience; and
- able to promote maximum use of the knowledge and skill acquired.

The teacher will consider the above points and select his teaching strategy. He/she must determine clearly the steps he/she intends to follow. Some of the methods available to the teacher include;

- case studies;
- demonstrations;
- field trips and environmental encounters;
- laboratory;
- conferences and seminars;
- panel discussions;
- experimental workshops;
- action research;
- role playing;
- discussion groups;
- simulation and gaming;
- application of knowledge and skills.

For some specific environmental problems, a teacher may, for instance, decide to include in his teaching a four-step strategy used over a number of lessons that is:

- a field trip or environmental encounter;
- laboratory work;
- a group discussion;

- some fieldwork where the knowledge acquired can be applied.

At the end of the unit or on completion of the four steps, it is necessary to evaluate both the method used and the results obtained.

## 5. Instructional Aids

Whenever possible, teaching aids should be used to reinforce the method used. Newspaper cuttings, for instance, can help make some views more acceptable. Advanced planning is important. It is not possible to limit oneself to any specific resources while teaching environmental issues. The resources have more appeal when they closely relate to the participants' environment and when they can easily be prepared by the learners. The list below may help teachers prepare or select resource materials (UNESCO-UNICEF, 1987: 16):

- specimens from the local environment;
- written materials of all types;
- locally produced low-cost equipment and aids;
- films, videos, slides, TV;
- library facilities;
- broadcast and pre-recorded materials, e.g. a speech by an influential personality;
- local, national and institutional publications;
- museum facilities and specimens.

Experimental work done by the students brings them closer to reality and concretises the problem. This allows learners and personal handling of equipment in that environment. The learners are also given a chance to search for and experiment with alternative solutions to the problem. The learners must be reminded of the fact that experiments are small-scale representations of much larger problems and hence their limitations.

Field trips enable the students or participants to visit appropriate localities and see what resources are available in solving actual problems or what is actually done in that direction.

Action research may be complex but it is most satisfactory when successful. The teacher organises a research study that can lead to practical applications. The participants are expected to integrate several theories, data and other teaching-learning resources to arrive at solutions or recommendations. The successful instructor is the one who is able to select the best strategy and use the most efficient combination of the above methods. This is another reason why teachers must be specifically trained for environmental education;

Displays and exhibits, such as pictures, charts and models permit learners to see details related to the environmental problem under study. This is useful when the participants cannot travel to the locations to be studied.

It will be cheaper for an individual to go and film a place with a video camera than to have a big group go and visit it. Whenever possible, however, learners should take field trips to get first-hand experience. Media resources like radio, television and newspapers can be used to reach larger audiences and may be quite effective.

## Conclusion

There are two main approaches in the teaching of environmental education. One approach is the one where the discipline – which is relatively new in education programmes -

can be integrated into a number of other disciplines such as geography, biology, botany, geology and others, to show how the knowledge of the environment and the care it requires affects our lives in many ways.

Another approach would be to teach environmental education as a separate discipline right through the existing formal education system. Informal education, particularly with adults, relies on very practical problem solving activities for effective instruction.

Environmental education teachers must be specially trained, and this may require that colleges of education to develop new curricula and equip special workshops and laboratories specifically for this purpose.

## Questions

1(a)   What are the arguments for and against an interdisciplinary approach to environmental education? How can any obstacles be overcome?

(b)   What are the arguments for and against multidisciplinary approach to environmental education? How can obstacles be overcome?

2.   "Adoption of sound environmental practices depends on the development of proper attitudes during youth. Adults attitudes are not easily changed. Discuss the validity of this statement.

3.   Discuss the difficulties your country may face in trying to follow guidelines laid by UNESCO for the provision of environmental education.

4.  What is the difference between the problem-solving approach and the community-based approach? Which of the two can incorporate the other? Explain.

5.(a)  Identify one environmental problem in the community in which you are a teacher.

(b)  State the strategy you intend to adopt and list the methods you will use in teaching the topic.

(c)  State what you will emphasise at each step.

(d)  Write the first two-hour lesson plan and mention which instructional aids you will use.

## Bibliography

Abidha, N.O. "The Need for Basic Environmental Education." *BERC Bulletin* No. 17. Nairobi, Kenyatta University (1987).

Albrigh, J. et. al. "Toward a National Strategy for EE." *Education Documentation and Information Bulletin,* No. 217, 1980.

Carson, S.M. *Environmental Studies.* Windsor, Berks: NFER, 1973.

CERI, Environmental Education at Post Secondary Level (1974).

Connect, UNESCO - UNEP Environmental Education Newsletter (All Volumes).

Korir-Koech, "Environmental Education and Population Education" *BERC Bulletin* No . 17. Kenyatta University, (1987).

Muyanda-Mutebi, "Towards CSD through Environmental and Population Education", *Digest* No. 20 (1988)

Rugamayo, E.B. "Environmental Education in the Training of Basic Education Teachers in Africa" *A Working Paper for UNEP*. Nairobi (1983).

Rugamayo, E.B. and Ibikunle V.O., *Environmental Education Through Adult Education*. AALAE ( 1987)

UNESCO, "Education for a Better Environment" *Prospects**\* No 4 (1978).

_____, Intergovernmental Conference on EE Tbilisi 1977: Final Report, 1977

_____, Environmental Education in Asia and the Pacific, Bangkok: Unesco 1981.

_____, Environmental Education, Educational Documentation and Information Bulletin of the IBE, No. 217, (1980).

Unesco-UNEP Internation Environmental Programme (IEEP) series, all numbers, Paris.

_____, 'Subregional Training Seminar on the Incorporation of EE into Industrial Education in Asia' Final Report, 20-27 April 1987, New Delhi, India.

_____, EE Module for In-service Training of Science Teachers and Supervisors for Secondary School, Paris, 1986.

_____, EE Module for Pre-service Training of Teachers and Supervisors for Primary Schools, Paris, 1986.

UNICEF, "Teaching and Learning Methodology Guide for Environmental Education including Population Education". UNESCO/ Nairobi UNICEF:, 1987.

Environmental harzads: oil spillage

Gabions: a modern way of conserving soil

Demolishing shanties – keeping the city environment clean

Soil erosion – poor land usage

Tree planting: taking part in conserving the environment

Poor drainage system in a slum area

Population explosion

A dairy farm

# -4-

# The Earth: Its Environmental Systems and Resources

J. 0. Ogeno

## Introduction

This chapter is divided into two main sections. The first section discuss the earth, its form (shape), its dimensions, composition and its major physical environmental systems; the second section identify various resources found in the earth's physical environment.

## SECTION I: THE EARTH

The earth - a solid body - is one of the nine planets of the solar system.

## The Form and Dimensions of the Earth

The spherical shape of the earth can be observed optically with the help of various recently developed technologies such as satellite photography. However, the earth is not an exact sphere. It is like a spherical body that has been compressed along the polar axis and bulges slightly around the equator. The equatorial radius of the earth is therefore slightly greater than the polar radius. Because the earth is not perfectly spherical, its form is referred to as oblate or ellipsoid. It is sometimes called an ellipsoid of revolution. This form is accounted for by the plastic nature of the materials that compose the apparently solid body of the earth; a cross section through the poles would be an ellipse rather than a circle. An equatorial section would be a circle with the largest possible circumference of the earth. But, even this description is not quite exact.

A further study of the earth's shape shows some slight variations due to different features on the earth's surface. The science of geodesy studies the form and nature of the earth in relation to the sun. The geodesists, through the use of extremely precise surveying methods and delicately refined determinations of the force of gravity, confirm that the earth has a unique shape they refer to as geoid.

**The Dimension of the Earth**

Although the earth is not a perfect sphere, it is so close to it that it is measured in the way any sphere is. The earth in equatorial diameter is approximately 12,757 kilometers and its polar diameter is 12,714 kilometers. The equatorial circumference is approximately 40.093 kilometers.

**Fig. 4.1**

Looked at from a position in space right over the pole, the earth looks like a circle whose outside limit is the equator. If you divide the circle into 360°, it is easy to see that the farther you are from the pole the greater the distance one degree will cover. Here are the mathematics which describe this point numerically.

The length of the earth's circumference at the equator

$$= 2\pi r \quad \frac{2 \times 3.1416 \times 6378 \text{ km}}{360} = 111.317 \text{km} = 1^0 \text{ of the}$$

circle at the equator.

**Fig. 4.2**

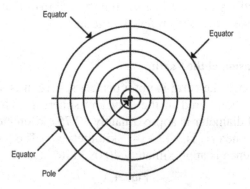

But the actual length, in kilometers of a degree of longitude depends upon where it is measured. At the equator, and at every parallel line of latitude, one degree may be computed by dividing the circumference by 360. It is important to note that if we reduce the earth to the size of an ordinary desk globe, neither the roughness on the surface nor the oblate shape of the earth would be noticed. Even variations due to some high mountains and ocean depths disappear with such a reduction in size. However, these variations are significant on the actual surface of the earth. Knowledge of the form of the earth thus becomes important not only for human navigation but also for our understanding of the earth's physical environment and its effects on man.

## The Composition of the Earth

The earth is divided into two parts: the solid globe itself and the surrounding atmosphere.

The solid globe is what we may refer to as the body of the earth from its surface to its centre. It comprises the core, the mantle and the crust. These make up the internal structure of the earth.

The core is a spherical zone of about 3475 kilometres in radius. The inner part (the core) is solid or crystalline while the outer core is somewhat liquid or at least fluid. The solid core is composed of iron-nickel.

The mantle, which separates the core of the earth from its outer crust, is a layer about 2895 kilometres thick and is composed of mainly mineral matter in a solid state (magnesium and iron silicate) which comprise an ultramatic rock called *dunite*.

The outermost and thinnest part of the earth's interior is the crust. This is a layer which varies from about 8 to 40 kilometres in thickness. It is largely made up of igneous rocks. The surface of separation between the crust and mantle (mohorovicic) is sharply defined. It is composed of an upper (granitic) and a lower (basaltic) continuous layer. The upper or granitic layer constitutes the bulk of the continents.

It is important to note that the density of rocks, their gravity, temperature and pressure increase towards the interior of the earth. This information about the earth's interior is largely obtained by means of instruments that measure earthquake waves, earth magnetism and the force of gravity. Their interpretation is the work of geophysicists and is based on established laws of physics.

The exterior of the earth, unlike the interior, is difficult to delineate precisely. What can be done is simply to identify the spheres that surround the solid earth's external environment. Layers are identified as the atmosphere, the hydrosphere, the biosphere and the lithosphere. Even among these spheres (zones), we still find it difficult to separate (by strict boundaries) the hydrosphere and biosphere from the atmosphere. Moreover, the lithosphere is not strictly external because it is part of the earth's crust which is considered to be a part of the interior of the earth.

However, for the sake of our discussion, we shall deal with the atmosphere, lithosphere, hydrosphere and biosphere as the earth's physical environmental zones that have direct effect on man. We hope the knowledge gained from this discussion will provide the basis for understanding some of the earth's environmental issues to be dealt with in later sections of this chapter.

## The Earth's Environmental Systems

We shall use the word system to refer to a collection of things confined in a particular space, but working together in a regular relation. Such physical and human environmental systems can be identified from the surrounding of the earth to its crust. We shall limit ourselves to the physical environmental systems and remember that their boundaries can be fixed arbitrarily only.

### The Atmosphere

The atmosphere is the gaseous envelope that surrounds the planet earth to a height of many kilometers. It exists largely in gaseous state though it contains varying amounts of substances in liquid and solid state. These gases are held around the earth by gravitational attraction. At sea level, the density of these gases is highest. The upper limit of the atmosphere may be drawn approximately at a height of 10,000 kilometres (see Fig. 4.3) which is divided into the lower homosphere and the upper heterosphere.

The name homosphere is applied to the lower layer of the atmosphere (80 kilometers and below). It is further subdivided into three layers according to altitude, temperatures and zones of temperature changes. These are: the troposphere, the layer with approximately uniform environmental temperature lapse rate, which extends from the surface of the earth to the height of about 15 kilometres; the stratosphere, the layer where the temperature first holds constant with increased altitude; and; the mesosphere, a transitional zone between homosphere and heterosphere. The tropopause is the boundary between the troposphere and the stratosphere while the stratopause marks the boundary between the mesosphere and stratosphere.

It is important to note that the homosphere is composed largely of nitrogen (78%), oxygen (21%), argon (0.9%) and carbon-dioxide (0.03%). The remaining gases of the homosphere include neon, helium, krypton, xenon, hydrogen, methane and nitrous oxide. The latter named gases occur in extremely minute amounts by volume. Whereas nitrogen is just a neutral 'filler' substance that does not readily enter into chemical union with other substances, oxygen in the atmosphere is chemically highly active. It readily combines with other elements in the process of oxidation leading to combustion of fuels and decay. Carbon-dioxide is also useful in the absorption of heat thus allowing the lower atmosphere to be warmed by heat radiation coming from the sun and from the earth's surface.

## Fig. 4.3 The Structure of the Atmosphere

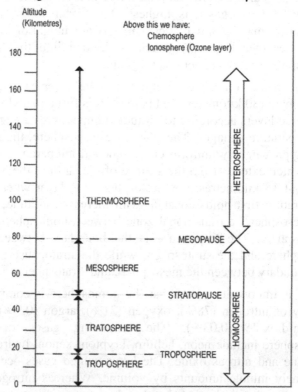

It is important that these proportions are maintained, otherwise there would be a danger of global warming or cooling. For example, if the percentage of carbon dioxide increased, there would be global warming from what is called the green house effect. This will be discussed in more detail further on.

In addition to the gaseous substances named above, the homosphere contains water vapour that may be compressed to form humidity. Humidity is important as a component of the earth's weather phenomena. The homosphere also contains myriads of tiny dust particles that have been swept into it by strong winds from dry deserts and exploding volcanoes. Smoke from bush fires and countless meteors vapourising from the heat of friction, also account for these dust particles. These particles serve as nuclei around which water vapour condenses to produce precipitation.

It is important to note that the stratosphere and the higher layers of the atmosphere are almost free of water vapour, dust particles and clouds, although winds of high speed are observable. The balance within the atmosphere from the lowest layer (troposhere) to the uppermost layer (ozone layer) must be maintained if man is to continue living on the planet earth. For this reason, the meteorologists and the climatologists provide us with continuous information about the state-of-the-earth's atmosphere. Thus, the recent discovery of the depletion of the ozone layer is causing considerable concern and even anxiety.

**The Lithosphere**

Lithosphere refers to the solid state of the crust of the earth that constitutes the continents and some parts of the ocean floor. Beneath it lies the soft, weak layer called the asthenosphere. The entire lithosphere of the earth is considered to be divided up into lithospheric plates, which include six major ones and many other smaller blocks within or between the major plates. These constitute the six major continents of the world.

The lithosphere is basically composed of mineral matter in the solid state; it supplies mineral resources to man. This mineral skin is also the source of soil and other sediments vital to life including the salts of the sea. The most abundant elements of the lithosphere in terms of percentage by weight are oxygen (46.6%), silicon (27.7 %), aluminium (8.1%), iron (5%) and magnesium (2.1%). However, because oxygen normally exists in the form of oxides, silicon and aluminium are considered to be the most abundant and hence the name SIAL is given to it from the first syllables of Silicon and Aluminium.

The lithosphere is normally studied by geologists. Geomorphologists also study it but concentrate particularly on the processes that shape the surface of the earth, (e.g denudation and deposition accounted for by the process of gradation).

**The Hydrosphere**

The hydrosphere is a generalised word for all the free water of the earth, whether in gaseous, liquid or solid form; it is the earth's global reserve of water in the form of vapour, liquid or ice. The bulk of the hydrosphere is found in the world oceans.

One of the roles played by the oceans in the overall environmental system is that of modification of climate in terms of tempering seasonal extremes. Oceans supply water vapour to the atmosphere and thereby affect climate. They also sustain a vast and complex assemblage of marine life, both vegetable and animal. The world's oceans cover about 71 per cent of the globe with an average depth of 3.8 kilometres. It is important to note, that about 75 per cent of the globe is water, this includes rivers, lakes and icebergs.

Above and within the world's oceans, there exist winds, waves, currents, sea ice, fog and other forces which may be favourable or hazardous to man. For this reason, hydrologists and oceanographers keep us informed about the levels of ice, water and humidity all over the globe.

### The Biosphere

The term biosphere is used to refer to the zone of organic matter on the earth where life exists. It occurs at the interfaces or zones of contact of the 'life layers' of the atmosphere and the lithosphere. Man interacts with his physical environment in these shallow layers, which lie at the contact surface between land and atmosphere, and between ocean and atmosphere. These zones normally experience intense activity in the form of exchanges of energy and matter from one environmental system to another; this is referred to as an 'open' system.

Through interaction with other life forms, man participates in the processes that affect the biosphere. From his physical environment, he receives the resources necessary for the life processes. He not only responds to the forces of the physical environment but also acts upon them and modifies environmental processes and forms.

Because the biosphere is a zone of contact, it is best studied by the sciences that deal simultaneously with atmosphere, hydrosphere and lithosphere. Among those, ecology, in particular, is interested in the processes within ecosystems and their global distribution as they are influenced by variations in the physical environment. Environmental science has thus an interdisciplinary role to play in analysing the environmental problems caused by man as well as by other forces.

## Discussion

After considering some information pertaining to the earth's physical environmental systems, it is necessary to make some important observations and clarify certain parts.

First, the attempt to delineate the earth's four environmental systems needs comment. The four systems relate to each other in such a way that they form one integrated system. This is observable in terms of transfer of energy and matter in various forms. Even the boundaries between them are set arbitrarily for theoretical rather than practical reasons.

Second, to understand the earth's environmental systems one must consider them as forms of one system because of the intense flow of energy and matter between them.

The whole of man's environment must thus be treated as one system. The terminology and principles gained from the science of thermodynamics are particularly useful.

### The Science of Thermodynamics

Thermodynamics is the science concerned with the relationship between heat energy (thermal) and work (dynamics); or simply, the science of the laws of energy transformation. Thermodynamics provides principles used to explain the state of the events involving energy and work that occur in the physical world. The principles are stated in what are called the First and Second Laws of thermodynamics.

The First Law of thermodynamics states that the total energy of the universe remains constant in that it is conserved though it can be converted. It also states that energy cannot be created from nothing.

The Second Law of thermodynamics deals with a property called entropy, - and states that the entropy of the universe increases. Entropy is used to refer to 'disorder' or 'randomness'. This Law also affirms that there is a limit to the conversion of heat-work.

The principle, on which the First Law is based is that heat, as a means of transferring energy, can only act when there is a difference in temperature between the system and the surrounding. Normally heat flows from a warmer to a cooler body. Here the terminology surrounding refers to the outside world or all other matters that are not within the system being discussed.

During such a transfer, heat is lost to the surrounding and the process is described as exothermic. Heat is then absorbed by the system in an endothermic process. Before either exothermic or endothermic processes can start, there has to be an 'initial state'; the condition of the total energy content of the isolated system prior to the process; and the 'final state' the condition that exists after the process.

Thus, as the system proceeds from its initial to its final state, it may either absorb energy from the surroundings or deliver it to the surroundings. In other words, a system of exchanging energy with its surroundings in the form of heat or work, either increases or decreases in its energy content. Thus, to satisfy the First Law, the equation of the state requires an equilibrium.

From the Second Law of thermodynamics, we derive the principle that any process occurring in all isolated systems must be accompanied by an increase in entropy, and that such a process will continue until the entropy reaches its maximum condition of equilibrium. This suggests that all systems tend to approach equilibrium in which temperature, pressure and all other measurable parameters of the state become uniform. Once that state is realised, there cannot be a reverse spontaneous change to a non-uniform, random state.

Entropy is defined as a randomised state of energy that is unavailable to do work. All physical and chemical processes are assumed to proceed in such a manner that the entropy of the universe attains maximum level. Entropy (or randomness in the universe) is thus assumed to be increasing in an irreversible process. Due to the tendency of all processes in a system to seek a level of maximum entropy by way of either giving up or absorbing heat, there comes a moment when the ideal of free energy is attained.

Free energy is that component of the total energy of a system which cannot do work under isothermal conditions. That is, as entropy increases during irreversible processes, free energy decreases. Free energy is normally regarded as useful energy while entropy is regarded as degraded energy.

However, we need to point out that:

•   Thermodynamics principles are best applicable to closed systems (i.e. systems that do not exchange matter with their surroundings and that can attain the true thermodynamic equilibrium).

• The earth's environmental system is more complex than the thermodynamic system.

## Thermodynamics and the Earth's Environmental System

The First Law of thermodynamics allows for a change of state. This is possible because such changes always occur in nature; for example, water can change from water liquid to water vapour (gas) or ice (solid) and vice versa. The changes require either an input of heat energy or the disposal of heat energy, depending on the direction of the change. As long as the energy of the earth is constant, the First Law is satisfied.

It is known that the flow of energy from the sun to .the earth and back to outer space constitutes a natural open system, that is, an organised configuration of matter open to the inflow and outflow of energy or matter or both.

The earth's environmental system can therefore be regarded as an open system with arbitrary boundaries, one being in the atmosphere and the other at the base of a shallow layer of soil or water. It is through the upper boundary that the open system of the life layer has its input and output of energy.

But, even within the 'life' layer, energy moves in many complicated directions that involve many subsystems and sub cycles. These movements of energy require the presence of matter to transport energy from one area to the other and for temporary storage.

Air and water normally do this task of transportation because they are highly mobile fluids. For this reason, at any given temperature, solids have relatively low entropy potential while liquids and intermediate gases have the highest entropy potential (because the gaseous state is the most disordered and chaotic). In any case, the storage of energy also requires transformation. Thus, the need for the Second Law.

From the Second Law of thermodynamics comes the principle that there is a tendency to attain an equilibrium in which the rate of input of energy and matter equals the rate of output; the quantity of stored energy and matter within the system remains constant.

This tendency also results in a striving towards maximum entropy. In the case of the total global system of the atmosphere, hydrosphere and lithosphere, energy only enters and leaves the system; matter remains within the systems boundary but within this limit, it is recycled repeatedly.

Thus, the nature of the earth's global environmental system is closed with respect to matter, while it is open with respect to energy. This openness of the system makes it difficult to apply the Second Law in a strict sense. Let us note, however, that the earth's global environmental system tends to increase 'entropy'.

In the global environmental system and subsystems, the physical environment has an added energy cycle which has an organic phase and biochemical cycle. A part of the incoming solar energy is used and given up by plants and animals; this energy is also absorbed by plants in the process of photosynthesis to manufacture carbohydrate compounds which form food for animals. All of these factors make the earth's environmental system extremely complex.

In concluding this section, the following points should be stressed:

- All natural processes are irreversible and their performance always leaves some permanent effect on the surroundings. Such processes are accompanied by an increase in total entropy (disorder) for the system and surroundings.

- For every desirable transformation that man effects, changes in the environment are inevitable. These changes are often deleterious, because they usually involve increases in temperature (note that increased temperature and entropy have a destabilising effect on environmental systems).

- Due to the above factors, it has been suggested that all the energy in the universe is undergoing constant degradation to a form that can no longer do work at isothermal conditions. The ultimate fate of the universe is the attainment of complete randomness and disorder which has been called entropic doom.

However, such comments should not sound unduly pessimistic because the earth's environmental effects are so complicated and interrelated that their complete assessment is impossible. What is being called for is proper environmental management.

Having discussed the earth's physical environment, we shall now turn our attention to the earth's natural resources.

## SECTION II: THE EARTH'S NATURAL RESOURCES

### Introduction

It is in man's ability to discover, in his physical environment the materials he needs to use in order to make his life on the surface of the earth possible. He gets those materials from the earth's atmosphere, lithosphere and hydrosphere, where they exist in the form of matter or energy. These are man's natural resources. The list of those natural resources embraces the earth's climates, terrain features, materials of composition, natural vegetation and animal life.

## Natural Resource: A Definition

A natural resource is any form of material (organic or inorganic) obtainable from the earth's physical environment to satisfy human needs.

Let us note that, before using any such material as a natural resource, technology and economic implications, cultural beliefs and the possible environmental effects of obtaining and using it must be considered. Therefore, a material thing can be considered as a resource only if the technology for obtaining and utilising it is both available and acceptable economically and culturally.

Second, if the natural resource is not exploited wisely, abundant though it might appear to be, it will soon be depleted and this will lead to serious degradation of the earth's physical environment since the loss will soon be felt. Such degradation is already producing soil erosion, the green house effect and the depletion of the ozone layer.

Let us now attempt to classify the earth's natural resources.

### Classification of Earth's Natural Resources

There are various ways of classifying the natural resources of the earth.

(1)     Natural resources may be broadly classified as inorganic and organic.

Inorganic resources are those materials, gases, liquids or solids of the earth's components that man uses directly. Some are also used as raw materials for the production of other, necessary goods. They include non-living substances such as mineral fuels, water, metalliferous ores, building stones and chemical raw materials from the earth's crust and atmosphere.

Organic resources are those derived from plants and animals (living substances) found on the earth and in the sea. They include wood, natural pasture, wild game and fish.

In this classification, soil belongs to both the inorganic and the organic classes because it is composed of materials which are both organic and inorganic in origin. Soil qualifies to be a natural resource because much of human food depends on it. Food from the sea, plants and animals are also either directly or indirectly derived from the soil.

(2)     Natural resources may also classified by considering their level of abundance: inexhaustible, non-renewable and renewable.

Inexhaustible resources are regarded as so abundant that they can never be depleted. Air and sand can be considered as virtually inexhaustible.

Renewable resources, on the other hand, are those that either come from an essentially inexhaustible source like solar energy and water or those that are renewed and replenished (relatively rapidly) by natural or artificial processes. Examples of renewable resources include; food crop, animal life, grasslands, forests, other living things and fertile soils. But, calling a resource renewable does not in any case mean that it cannot become exhausted.

Renewable resources can only be maintained if used at a rate slower than their supply can be replenished by natural or artificial processes. We call this the rate of maximum sustained yield. If the maximum sustained yield of a resource is exceeded, a potentially renewable resource may become a non-renewable resource.

Non-renewable resources are those that are not easily replaceable by natural processes because their rate of replacement is slower than the rate at which they are used. They are, therefore, vulnerable to depletion.

Non-renewable resources may be further classified into those that can be recycled (or re-used) and those that cannot be. Recycling is a process that involves collecting and re-processing a resource that has already been used while re-use involves direct use of a resource over and over again without changing its form.

Non-renewable resources that can be recycled or re-used include mainly the non-energy mineral resources which are obtained from the earth's crust in finite amounts. Examples are: ore deposits of metallic minerals (from which metals like copper, aluminium and iron are extracted), and deposits of non-metallic minerals (such as phosphate rocks from which fertiliser and nutrients are extracted).

It is important to note that; non-metallic mineral energy resources sometimes called fossil fuels (such as coal, oil and natural gas) are not easily recycled because once a fossil fuel resource is burned it is gone forever. Even uranium and other radioactive elements cannot, at least with existing technology, be recycled or re-used. Fossil fuels take a very long period in geological time to form, and their deposits, once depleted, cannot be replenished; it would take hundreds of millions of years to renew them.

We have offered broad classifications of the earth's natural resources. These classifications do not provide specific details for each group of particular resources. For this reason, it will be useful to consider some of the resources further and identify their sources of origin, modes of extraction and human uses. We will consider briefly the following resources: water, vegetation , fossil fuel and metallic and non-metallic minerals.

## Water

Water resources are not limited to the liquid substance (water) but include all the products obtained from it such as fish, mineral salts and many living organisms useful to man. This brief description will limit itself to the liquid water from the hydrosphere.

Water as a resource has a variety of uses: it is used domestically in both rural and urban settlements; it is an essential material for industrial processes; it is used for the irrigation of crops, for the production of mechanical power (called hydroelectric power); and, in the oceans, lakes and large rivers, it is used for navigation. Besides, lakes, streams, rivers-and oceans make the earth's surface very attractive.

The major sources of water include the world's oceans, wells, springs, lakes, rivers and rainfall. These sources cover over 75 per cent of the earth's surface. Some water is fresh and does not require complex processing (preparation) before use. As for the saline water found in the world's oceans and salty seas and lakes, it must be purified before use.

Today, due to many forms of pollution and the presence of some impurities even in fresh water sources, most water requires some treatment before it becomes safe for human use. It is important to note that although the supply of water is abundant, its misuse or pollution can lead to serious problems that may adversely affect living organisms.

**Vegetation resources**

Another striking feature of the earth's surface, apart from water, is its vegetation cover. Vegetation varies greatly in kind and density from region to region.

Apart from making the scenery beautiful, vegetation provides pastures for domestic and wild life as well as forest cover. The vegetative cover is an expression of the composite physical environment because it incorporates elements from both the past and the present. For this reason, vegetation is an indicator of the environment potential as a biological human habitat.

The following types of vegetation cover can be identified: grasslands, desert shrubs, tundra plants and forest plants. Here, our concern will be limited to forest vegetation. The economic activity associated with this type of vegetation is called forestry.

*Forestry*

Forestry, as a resource, provides mankind with a variety of very important products one of which is wood which is used both as domestic and industrial fuel. It may be used in the form of firewood or charcoal. Wood fuel is used as a source of power for railway locomotives and for generating electricity while charcoal is used for smelting minerals. Wood is also used in the building and construction industry and in furniture making as veneer, plywood or as fibres. Wood can be turned into pulp for the paper industry and a basis for synthetic fibres like rayon and acetate which are used in the modern textile industry.

Besides wood, forests supply a wide range of minor products including: pitch, turpentine, tannin, nuts and gums;

and medicinal products from the bark, roots, leaves and stems of the trees.

Forests are part of and depend on the earth's physical environment. The world's natural forests are products of the climatic conditions of the region where they grow. In the more humid temperate and tropical climates of the world, there are three major types of forests (differentiated by both climatic factors and the dominant types of trees), namely: tropical hardwood forests, temperate hardwood forests and coniferous forests. These are the major sources of forest products.

However, these forests are currently in great danger of degeneration. Although forests at one period of time were regarded as a renewable resource, our present experience shows that forests, if not put under wise management, face the same danger of rapid depletion as non-renewable resources. For this reason, the present forests need to be assisted through re-afforestation, improved methods of cutting, forest protection from bush fire and maximum use of the forest products with minimal wastage. If appropriate measures are not taken seriously, forest resources face the danger of exhaustion and may give way to desertification.

**Mineral Resources**

For the purpose of this discussion, a mineral resource is a naturally occurring, inorganic substance with a definite chemical composition and characteristic atomic structure. We are not particularly concerned here with atomic structure but rather with uses, methods of extraction and possible problems associated with the economic use of such resources. We identify three broad categories of them namely: fossil fuels, metallic minerals and non-metallic minerals.

*Fossil Fuel Resources*

There are various sources of energy being used by man. These include: hydroelectric power from water, geothermal energy from hot springs found beneath the earth's surface, wind power, solar energy from the sun, power alcohol from plants, wood fuel from forests, biogas from animal products, nuclear energy from radioactive elements (from both nuclear fusion and fission) and fossil fuels from petroleum, coal and natural gas.

Although all of the above energy sources are used to produce power, the major world fuels used today are coal, oil (petroleum) and natural gas. They account for over 95 per cent of the world's power supply. Coal, for example, became the basis for the industrial revolution in the eighteenth century. These three vital sources of the world's energy are referred to as fossil fuels because of their mode of formation. We shall consider each one of them in detail.

*Coal*

Coal is a black (or brown) rock substance consisting mainly of carbon. It is formed by the process of compression of vegetative remains of past geological ages. Most coal deposits belong to the Carboniferous Age (300 million years ago) but more recent deposits belong to the Tertiary age. These are lignite (brown coal) and peat which are coals in an early stage of formation.

There are various types of coal differentiated by their composition and contents: carbon, some volatile matter and moisture. These three factors, associated in varied proportions, determine the heat value of any given kind of coal and affect its market value. In ascending order of concentration by percentage of carbon content they are: peat, lignite (brown coal), bituminous, anthracite and graphite (plumbage). Graphite has the highest concentration of carbon (90%) and is not used as fuel but for such uses as, for instance, the making of pencils.

Coal is found both on the earth's surface and underground; hence it involves two broad methods of mining: surface and underground mining.

Surface mining involves either stripping (open-cast mining) or hill-slope boring. Underground mining may involve drifting (adit-mining), slope mining and shaft mining. The shaft mining method involves boring deep holes towards the coal seams that lie deep in the ground.

In both surface and underground mining methods, the earth's covering material is usually removed. This renders the surface derelict and it remains infertile once mining is over.

*Petroleum*

Petroleum is an inflammable mixture of oily hydrocarbons with very complex chemical properties. The origin of petroleum (oil) is still unclear although it is generally believed that it is derived from organic materials. The analysis of oil samples shows that it is derived from innumerable decomposed marine plants and animal organisms that were trapped in sediments deposited on the sea bed.

Some scientists believe that when an accumulation of sedimentary rocks in the ocean depths is compacted, pressure is created which then generates the heat needed to transform the decaying matter into tiny droplets of oil. Others think that oil was formed relatively rapidly after the organisms were trapped in the sediments and that no such pressure and heat were needed.

Normally, oil is trapped within porous rocks. It is capable of flowing in any direction until it is trapped by the presence of a non-porous dome of cap-rock such as shale or mudstone. When a cap-rock prevents the oil or gas from moving further (either upwards or sideways), oil is said to be trapped. This can occur in anticlinal traps, fault traps, salt plugs and stratigraphic traps. Wherever it occurs, oil is usually found in a water-oil-gas sequence. In some cases gas is found alone. How the oil is extracted from these non-porous reservoirs is the next point of consideration.

*Extraction and Refining of Oil*

There are two methods of oil extraction: the percussion (cable-tool) and the rotary method. From the drilled hole (pipe), crude oil is drawn. The extracted oil is usually crude because it is made up of various hydrocarbons which form its basic components. These hydrocarbons have to be separated to fit specific industrial and domestic uses. The process of separating these hydrocarbons is called refining.

Refining involves the breaking down of the various hydrocarbons into their respective 'groups' or fractions through a complex process of distillation. In the oil refinery, the crude oil is not only split into its various fractions but impurities such as sulphur, are removed. The chief methods of oil distillation in refineries are known as: fractional distillation, thermal cracking, catalytic cracking and polymerization.

When distillation is thoroughly done, a refinery may produce as many as eighty different oil, gas and chemical products. The modern petroleum industry recognises three principal grades of crude oil, namely: paraffin-based, asphalt-based and mixture-based. From these grades, most important fuels and products are obtained. From the lighter fractions we get petrol (gasoline), paraffin (kerosene) and benzene, and, from the heavier fraction we obtain diesel, lubricants and fuel oils. In addition, a number of residues such as coke, asphalt and bitumen (tar), wax (vaseline) and gases, like butane and propane, are produced.

Although petroleum has become a universally accepted source of fuel, it is not absolutely without danger to the environment. The smoke emitted by refineries and other associated industries has, to some extent, contributed to the pollution of the atmosphere.

*Natural Gas*

As already noted, natural gas may occur in association with petroleum; it usually occupies the uppermost part of an oil trap, but it may also be found alone.

Natural gas is a mixture of gaseous hydrocarbons of which the principal constituent is methane which makes up over 80 per cent of its volume. Its other component gases are propane and butane. Natural gas is not totally free from non-hydrocarbons. It may contain helium, nitrogen, carbon-dioxide and hydrogen sulphide.

In the past, natural gas, particularly when found in oil wells, was released into the atmosphere when the oil was extracted. Recently, due to greater knowledge and an increasing need for more fuel, it has become an important source of fuel, useful both domestically and industrially.

However, whenever this fuel is used, care needs to be taken because it catches fire very easily and can lead to serious destruction of property.

**Metallic and Non-metallic Minerals**

Unlike agricultural and forest resources, mineral mining is a 'robber' industry. This is because whenever it is carried out, irrespective of the size of the deposits, these become exhausted. Moreover, the deposits are virtually irreplaceable because they take a very long geological period to form.

*The Occurrence of Minerals*

Obtaining minerals from the lithosphere is a complex process. It involves not only a great deal of technological knowledge, but also an understanding of the nature and the mode of occurrence of various types of minerals.

Minerals may occur in veins, lodes or as a mixture with other materials. When a mineral occurs in almost pure form, we call it a native mineral. Few minerals, however, occur in this form. When found mixed with other materials they are called ores. Ores may be found in cracks, crevices, faults or joints in rocks. These may take the form of either veins or lodes. Veins are the thinner varieties of such occurrences while lodes are relatively larger.

In most cases, veins and lodes are formed when minerals in molten form, intrude into cracks and crevices of rocks and subsequently solidify. In other cases, minerals are deposited as pediments in joints and cracks of rocks by percolating ground water.

Through sedimentation, many minerals occur in beds (layers). These have been formed as a direct result of deposition, accumulation and concentration in horizontal strata of the earth's crust. Some grades of iron ore are formed in this manner. Other major metals such as tin, copper, silver, lead and zinc occur either in veins or lodes.

Another mode of mineral occurrence involves the evaporation process. This is the case for the formation of potash and salts (common salts) in dried-up lakes. It is also the case when, under certain climate conditions, deep weathering affects a variety of rocks to produce, for instance, bauxite (ore of aluminium). A mineral may also become detached from the veins by erosion of the parent rock. Gold, tin and platinum occur in this way because of their high resistance to weathering and corrosion in water.

*Identification of Minerals*

We have already mentioned that most minerals do not occur in nature in their native (pure) form. In most cases they are mixed up with non-mineralised rocks, oxides, sulphides and other substances. For this reason, the properties of mineral ores differ from those of pure metals or mineral elements.

Mineral ores refer to compound deposits with a high degree of metal concentration; these can usually be extracted and refined economically. Among those, we may identify: aluminium ore (bauxite), iron ores (magnetite, hermanatite, pyrite and limonite), zinc ore (sphalerite), copper ores (native copper, chalcopyrite and chalcocite), lead (galena) and limestone.

Most of these mineral ores occur either as oxides or sulphides. A sulphide mineral ore consists of one or more metallic elements in combination with sulphur. The most important sulphides are ores of nickel, zinc, copper, cobalt, lead, mercury and silver. Ores are generally identified by their colour, lustre, cleavage, hardness, density and chemical properties. Identification, however, is not always easy.

*Mining Methods*

The major methods of mining minerals are: open cast mining, underground mining (shaft) and alluvial mining. Once the ores are mined from the crust of the earth, the unwanted materials in which the veins or lodes occur (the gangue) must be removed. The rocks are crushed, the metal washed put and then concentrated. Normally, the final (pure) metal is obtained by further refining which might involve smelting or electrolysis.

We can now classify minerals and list their possible uses.

## Classification and Uses of Minerals

Minerals may be classified into the following groups:

Rock minerals

These are mainly materials from the crust of the earth. They are used as building materials.

Non-metallic minerals.

These are substances which are not metals: salt, potash, nitrates, sulphur, asbestos, diamond and graphite. They have varied and often very specialised uses.

Metallic minerals.

These are mineral substances such as iron, copper, tin, aluminium, lead and zinc which can conduct both heat and electricity. Iron is the most abundant and it is used in the metallurgical industry. The other metallic minerals that do not contain iron such as copper, tin, aluminium, lead and zinc are called base metals or non-ferrous metals. Among metallic minerals we have: ferro-alloys, minerals which can be alloyed with iron to produce steel and include: manganese, chromium, nickel, cobalt, tungsten and molybdenum; and precious metals such as gold, silver and platinum.

All these classes of minerals are either used in industrial manufacturing or direct consumption. In some cases, a mineral can be both directly consumed and used as an input in the industry to produce other products.

## Conclusion

The chapter described the shape of the earth as a geoid. This description is a refinement of the earlier one that states that the earth's shape is an oblate ellipsoid. This shape implies that the earth's equatorial diameter is slightly greater than the polar one. Variations due to different relief surface features on land and water do not significantly alter the general shape of the earth.

We also identified four major parts of the earth's physical environment; the atmosphere, lithosphere, biosphere and hydrosphere. These are the major physical environmental systems that have a direct effect on man's life on the surface of the earth.

From these environmental systems, man is able (through technology) to obtain the material substances he needs for his survival: the earth's natural resources. This led to defining a natural resource as any form of material (organic or inorganic) that satisfies human needs. Resources were classified broadly as either organic or inorganic; identified according to their level of availability; and recognised some as renewable and others as non-renewable. Some examples of resources like water, vegetation, fossil fuel, metallic and non-metallic mineral resources were studied in greater details. This description did not exhausted the earth's natural resources.

Finally, it should be noted that there is always a danger, not only of depleting the resources, but also of polluting the earth's physical environment while extracting and using them. As a case in point, the extraction of sulphide ores may cause considerable environmental dangers of air pollution during the smelting processes where toxic and evil-smelling and sulphur gases are usually omitted. Beside this danger of pollution, dereliction and water contamination are often the result of thoughtless and uncontrolled mineral extraction and processing.

## Questions

1. Discuss how our knowledge of the earth's shape can be applied to understand the nature of the earth's physical environment.

2. Discuss the importance of the troposphere to man.

3. Discuss the causes of forest depletion and the nature of problems associated with such depletion.

4. Explain this statement: "Good forestry implies a balance between the exploitation and conservation of timber resources".

5. Explain why different types of coal are suitable for different uses.

6. Discuss the statement: "Coal is the fuel of the past, petroleum of the present and electricity of the future".

7. In mining, what measures are to be taken for conserving natural resources?

8. Discuss some of the uses of water as a natural resource.

9. Acid rain is now considered as a very common and destructive agent of pollution.

10. Discuss the statement, Explain: "All spontaneous and artificial processes are irreversible and always leave some permanent effect on the surrounding".

## Bibliography

Alexander, W. and Street, A. *Metals in the Service of Man.* New York; Pelican (1962).

Bateman, A.M. *Economic Mineral Deposits.* New York: John Wiley and Sons (1950).

Dansercau, P. *Biogeography: An Ecological Perspective.* New York: The Ronald Press (1957).

Eyre, S.R. *Vegetation and Soils.* Chicago: Aldine Publishing Company (1968).

Fairbridge, R.W.; (ed). *The Encyclopedia of Atmospheric Science and Astrogeology.* New York: Reinhold Publishing Company (1967).

Goh Cheng Leong, *Human and Economic Geography.* Nairobi: Oxford University Press (1982).

Lehninger, A.L. *Bioenergetics.* New York: W.A. Benjamin Inc. (1965).

Leinwald, G. *Air and Water Pollution* New York: Washington Square Press (1969).

Petrucci, R. *General Chemistry* New York: Macmillan Ltd. (1972).

Riehl, H. *Introduction to the Atmosphere.* (New York: McGraw-Hill Book Company (1972).

Simpson, B. *Rocks and Minerals.* (Oxford: Pergamon Press, (1966). Strahler, A.N. *Physical Geography.* New York: John Wiley and Sons (1975).

Vernor, C. Finch et. al. *Element of Geography: Physical and Cultural.* New York: McGraw-Hill Book Company 1957).

Zimmerman, E.W. *World Resources and Industry.* New York: Harper, (1964).

# -5-

# Human Population and the Environment

J. 0. Shiundu

## Introduction

This chapter studies the relationship between human population and the environment The emphasis is, however, on the effects of overcrowding and human activities on the environment.

Ecologically, people are part and parcel of the environment; they actively interact with its components. Whether by divine design or by chance, or as a result of the process of evolution, human beings belong to a higher category of organisms or animals and have a more developed brain, a more sensitive nervous system and a greater ability to think and manipulate the environment. It is in this way that they are able to survive and realise their role as humans. They depend on the environment of which they are a part to obtain their basic needs: food, shelter and clothing. In this process, there is considerable interaction between people and the environment.

Over time, human beings have developed more effective ways of using and controlling the environment. They now realise that, if humanity is to survive, great care must be taken of all natural resources. In the past centuries and with a smaller world population, the problem was not given much importance.

Due to various reasons, including thoughtlessness, neglect of their divine duty and selfishness, men have overused their habitat. This situation has been exacerbated by the high rate of population growth in many parts of the world

Although Thomas Malthus foresaw the possibility of a shortage of food supplies about two centuries ago, his warnings were not taken seriously until the middle of our century. Malthus was quite right, for since his time, famines have claimed and are still claiming countless lives in many areas of Africa, Asia and Latin America. Hundreds of millions more are suffering from malnutrition.

Food shortage aside, there are reports of severe environmental pollution and depletion of natural resources. Most of those are related to the increase in population and the irresponsible use of the environment. Some environmentalists see this denudation and pollution as a threat to the existence of the very human race that is causing it.

Everywhere on earth people now feel the threat of environmental problems, see the need for identifying their causes and realise the urgency of finding solutions. Both the Governments, and NGO's are getting involved in studies and projects to save the environment.

This chapter briefly describes the two concepts in the relationship: *human population* and the *environment*. It then goes on to discuss the misuse and destruction of the environment by people and the threat that their activities now pose to human, animal and plant life.

## 1. Human Population

Ecologists, economists, researchers and geographers (or demographers for that matter) understand the term *population* differently. That is one reason why we have decided in this chapter to use the term *human population* which is closer to the geographers' or demographers' concept. Human population here refers to people, their numbers, their distribution and their activities within a defined environment. *Numbers* here refers to population size, growth rate and density (which is an element of distribution).

Human population is dynamic; it increases or decreases and at present, it is growing. In some regions of the world, there is a violent population explosion. The upsurge in population numbers started about 200 years ago, and was first identified in Europe by Thomas Malthus. As early as 1798, Malthus warned that the amount of food being produced in Europe would soon be insufficient for the fast growing population.

Before that time population had been growing very slowly and this was due to two generally accepted reasons: first, there was a high death rate, particularly among young children; and, second, dreadful epidemics occurred that wiped out huge sections of the population.

The Industrial Revolution in Europe is said to have been an important cause of the rapid population growth towards the end of the eighteenth century. Scholars attribute this to four main factors which have their roots in the Revolution:

- improvement in medicine;

- improvement in farming and transport;
- better health facilities; and
- better food and sanitation.

These factors greatly improved chances of human survival. In fact, while both remained high, death rates were drastically cut.

Malthus' analysis was the first attempt to systematically understand the relationship between population change and socioeconomic welfare. He asserted that man's capacity to increase his means of subsistence is much slower than his capacity to reproduce and multiply. Whereas production can only increase in arithmetical progression, population grows in geometrical progression or what Hardin (1975) terms, *exponentially*. He based this on the *Law of Diminishing Returns* when he argued that the labour supply increases with population growth, but there is little or no increase in capital supply. Output increases slowly while the supply of labour increases rapidly; the net result is a fall in per capita income.

The neo-Malthusian school believes that the process of development is impeded when the rate of population growth is high. This school of thought attributes a high rate of (population) growth to the rapid reduction in mortality; this in turn is the result of the increased effectiveness and efficiency of health services quite independent of levels of production and consumption. An economic imbalance is thus created. One alternative to this scenario would be to allow for some reduction in mortality and a concurrent and commensurate reduction in fertility so that population growth is kept to a minimum; then all efforts should be made to raise the formation of capital to a maximum.

This argument suggests that the problem is riot simply that of a high rate of population growth but a combination of growth and other prevailing economic factors. The Malthusian theory is not universally accepted: for instance various arguments have been advanced to affirm that there is no population explosion, especially in Africa.

One common argument in favour of this view is that the world is infinite. As high level technology continues to advance, more resources are being discovered and there are therefore possibilities of renewing the so called 'limited' resources. The technological advancement and discovery of new resources would offset the imbalance that would be created by the rising population. Evidence of this possibility includes the manufacture of synthetic foods, and the re-cycling of old metals to manufacture new products. Agricultural land can even be reclaimed from under the sea as has clearly been proved in the Netherlands.

In countries like Kenya, some people have dismissed as baseless the claim that there is a need to curb the rate of population increase. Their argument is that there is a lot of land lying fallow that could be occupied by additional people. Furthermore, they criticise the land tenure system which allows individuals to own a disproportionate amount of land which could be used to settle thousands of people. Some even advocate that national parks and game reserves be turned into habitable land to be occupied by the additional population.

Similarly, some people argue against population control from a religious standpoint. Any efforts to control birth are thought to be against the wishes of the Creator, who, at creation, ordered men to multiply and fill the earth. They affirm that we need not worry as everything that occurs on earth is according to the Creator's plan.

A secular variation of this view would be that nature should be allowed to take its course; in the event of overpopulation there are natural phenomena which counteract the situation and restore the balance. Natural catastrophies such as epidemics, famine and earthquakes and human events such as war and famine, are the ways nature uses to reduce men's numbers and create a balance between population and available resources.

Two other views have been advanced from the economic point of view. Some argue that more births are a blessing since the labour force increases. While this argument might be relevant in countries like China (where production is labour intensive), it could not be defended in countries where the main forces of production are capital intensive. Besides, the Law of Diminishing Returns shows that an over increase in the labour force is counterproductive.

Another school of thought (which reflects the Marxist view), has recently advanced the theory that the so-called 'problem' of the population explosion is a creation of the multinationals and their equally rich agents in the developing countries who fear for their property in case of additional numbers of poor people. According to this school of thought, most people who worry over population increase are trying to find a way to avoid relinquishing any of the privileges they now enjoy. This comes back to the old argument that the wealth of nations is in the hands of a few individuals and, if it were equitably distributed, then the issue of population increase would not arise.

It would be wise to listen to those views which should not be dismissed as of little importance given the current economic conditions. Among the world's economists and demographers, the strongly held view is that the world is finite and resources are limited. Therefore, to encourage excessive additional numbers of people is tantamount to willingly courting an imminent disaster.

## 2. Population and Land

It would be a mistake to think of land merely as space to be occupied without taking into consideration the carrying capacity of the said land; that is without considering the number of people that land is capable of supporting without any danger of depreciation. While there is considerable acreage of land in Kenya, much of it is so marginal that it can support only a minimal number of people.

Even if people were given a piece of land in such an area, they would be reluctant to settle there; areas with greater resources are more attractive and tend to be overcrowded.

Some thirty years ago, families in Kakamega and Kisii Districts of Kenya had an average of ten acres of land. Today, most families have an average of half an acre. Recently, some of the families have sought to settle in less desirable areas but even these places are becoming overcrowded. The result is landlessness, migration to towns and development of slum areas.

### (a) Growth Rate and Consequences

The Population Council notes that due to the high population growth rate, Kenya's per capita GNP rose only by 18.6 per cent between 1968 and 1972 compared to 35.7 per cent between 1964 and 1968.

In fact, the GNP has continued to fall and there is a clear indication of increased unemployment and poverty, particularly in urban slums and squatter areas. Beggars and destitute are on the increase. Moreover, continuous inflation further erodes the purchasing power of the currency in many developing countries.

The effects of population explosion are more evident in urban and peri-urban areas where it is becoming extremely difficult to provide people with even their most basic needs. Food shortages could be attributed to underproduction; but a more obvious reason is that, the demand (due to the large number of consumers) is beyond the capacity of production. Besides, formerly productive land is now leached of nutrients and exhausted.

Land produces less when there is a lack of rainfall. Weather seems to have become quite unpredictable while the rate of population growth is constant or ever increasing. Incidences of famine are on the increase and, when they occur, developing countries have to depend on rich developed countries for food. Millions of urban inhabitants cannot find decent shelter; street pavements, bazaars and disused motor vehicles have become their homes.

More population means more movement. Motorists, cyclists and pedestrians scramble for the inadequate space available on urban streets and highways.

Unemployment is the most critical issue in developing countries. Besides, the great numbers of those who depend on the few earners, keep the majority of the people on the very brink of misery and starvation.

In desperation, many people turn to such unacceptable activities as theft, prostitution and thuggery. Whenever the problem of basic human needs becomes less urgent, new needs for recreational and social facilities arise. Schools are overcrowded and yet not all school age children can be accommodated.

The critical issue is what impact the population growth will have on the limited resources available. How many people can the country provide for decently? Tremendous growth in the world population is anticipated before the year 2000. Even in developing countries, this will have severe consequences on the environment. According to Soutwick (1985), human population will increase by about 55 per cent, from 4.1 billion in 1975 to 6.4 billion in the year 2000; faster growth is expected in the less developed countries. Out of the estimated 6.4 billion people, 5 billion will be found in these countries.

### (b) Determining the Population Growth Rate

How do we determine the population growth rate? For example, when we say that the rate of population growth in Kenya is 3.8 and that it is one of the highest in the world, how do we arrive at that figure? The simplest method used by the demographers is to compare the Birth Rate and the Mortality (Death ) Rate of a given country or community.

*What is Birth Rate?* Birth Rate (BR) is the number of child births occurring per 1,000 people per year. For instant, District X in 1988 had 500,000 people and 7000 children were born during that year. The Crude Birth Rate (CBR) would be calculated as follows:

$$CBR = \frac{Births \ x \ 1,000}{Population}$$

$$CBR = \frac{7,000 \ x \ 1,000}{500,000} = 14$$

This is the Crude Birth Rate (CBR)

*Specific Birth Rate* (SBR) describes the number of births among people of a given age per 1,000 in a certain age-sex category.

*What is Death Rate?* Death (or Mortality) Rate is a measure of the number of deaths occurring per 1,000 population per year. For example, if the same district in 1988 had 500,000 people and 7000 people died during that year, the Crude Death Rate (CDR) of the district would be:

$$CDR = \frac{Deaths \times 1,000}{Population}$$

$$CDR = \frac{7,000 \times 1,000}{500,000} = 14$$

The BR represents the addition to the existing population and the DR represents the decrease in it. To determine the growth rate, we subtract DR from BR in a given year. In our example, if BR was 14 and DR was 14 , then the Growth Rate would be 14 minus 14 which is zero.

This is the *natural increase rate* which does not consider migration. Supposing BR in District B was estimated at 20 in 1989 and DR was estimated at 10 per 1000 in that same year, the difference would be 10 or 1 per cent *growth rate* calculated as follows:

$$Growth\ rate = \frac{Birth\ rate - Death\ rate\ (per\ 1,000)}{10}$$

If the value is positive, then it means that there has been a population increase. If the value is negative, it means the population is reduced.

Figures show that the world population is increasing at a high rate, especially in the developing nations. The growth rate for Africa is estimated to be between 3.0 per cent and 4.0 per cent. This is mainly due to the high fertility and birth rate.

The latter was estimated at 46 per 1000 in Africa in the mid seventies, compared to 24 in North America, 19 in Europe, 40 in Latin America and 33 in South Asia (Bernard and Walter, 1971: 150).

This is related to people's different attitudes and lifestyles. Cultural values that include a persistent desire for big families are still dominant. There is also tolerance for illegitimacy and many children are born outside marriage.

Whereas birth rates are increasing, death rates are tailing rapidly due to:

- modern health measures;
- modern eating habits and lifestyles;
- rising life expectancy; and
- declining wars and local conflicts (in the more peaceful areas of Africa).

The Death Rate in Africa is estimated at 22, (which is much lower than the Birth Rate of 46) and still the highest in the world.

In considering the population situation of a particular country or area, we must look beyond the growth rate to the age structure and distribution of the population as well as other population characteristics like sex, attitudes and traditions.

*Effects of Age on Population*

The age structure of a population affects the rate of population growth. In the developing countries particularly in Africa, more than 40 per cent of the population is under 15 years of age as compared to about 25 per cent in the industrialized countries. This has implications for both population growth and development. There are many more potential parents and, therefore, more children are being born. Young families make a heavy demand on services such as education, health, housing and social amenities.

*Population Distribution*

Population distribution is another very important factor in understanding problems related to the environment. The world population may be estimated at 6 billion, but these billions are disproportionately spread among countries; that is population density varies. Take, for example, the African continent. Here, population is unevenly distributed with over three quarters of the population being found in only one third of the continent. A country like Nigeria, which is smaller than Sudan, holds over 50 million people while Sudan has less than 10 million. Similarly, in Kenya, over three-quarters of the population occupies one third of the country. Most people in Kenya live in the south-western half of the country. A small province like Western Province has over 1 million people while North Eastern Province which is larger, has a very small and scattered population.

The density of population in an area is described as the number of persons per square mile or kilometre. A country with an area of 6,000 sq. km and a population of 60 million people would have a density of:

$$\text{Density} = \frac{\text{Births} \times 1000}{\text{Population}}$$

Basically, the density of an area's population depends on the nature and the availability of resources. In addition, there are several other physical, socioeconomic and cultural factors that influence the distribution of people and hence the density of the local population.

*Migrations*

Migrations, which are seldom anticipated or planned for, alter the population of both the country of origin and the country of destination. This is one factor that has caused considerable population change and uncertainty in the world and, especially, in many developing countries. There are numerous physical and socio-economic reasons for cross-boundary migrations including civil wars. Within countries, there are general migratory trends from rural to urban areas and from areas with relatively fewer resources to those with more resources.

## 3. Human Population as Part of the Environment

Man is part of the environment and he must use it to survive. He uses it for the following purposes:

- as a source of food;
- as a source of air to breathe;
- as a source of water to drink;
- as a source of resources like oil and minerals;
- as a means of travel and communication;
- to provide space for shelter and other socioeconomic and physical activities;
- as a source of artistic satisfaction;
- as a setting for relaxation and leisure activities; and
- as a fit ambience to stimulate human thought, research and discovery.

Through ignorance, sheer carelessness, curiosity or desire for economic and social growth, man has often misused or overused the environment in wasteful ways:

- Some methods of land cultivation or farming have led to reduction in the soil's fertility and productive capability. Over cultivation and overgrazing have led to soil erosion by wind or water.

- The overexploitation of environmental resources without providing a means of regeneration to replace them. Deforestation, excessive mining, hunting, fishing and draining of water resources, are some of the typical activities through which man has caused a serious imbalance in the environment. Excessive reduction in genetic diversity has disrupted the ecosystem.

- The use of some chemicals and/or techniques to suppress or control human diseases and enemies such as insects, animals and reptiles. These have resulted in destruction of certain species, polluting water, air and soil with effects more detrimental to man than the presence of the initial enemies. Certain drugs for protection against, or cure of, diseases have also had nefarious effects on nature.

- The use of secondary means of production in the process of industrialisation and mechanised farming puts much pressure on natural resources and leads to various forms of environmental pollution: gas leaks, radiation and chemical sprays which harm and poison people, animals and plants.

- Certain patterns of human settlement can adversely affect the environment; the congestion of people in particular areas can lead not only to pollution but also to the disruption of the natural ecosystems of these areas. Cities today are experiencing severe environmental problems.

Settlement on river banks and seashores not only interferes with the natural course of such features, but also leads to pollution as these waters become the dumping grounds for human waste.

As population grows, so does, the misuse and overuse of the environment. Dangerous chemicals and wasteful techniques are used to sustain the increasing population. More industrialisation and mechanised farming is required to provide employment and enough food for the additional people. Research centres must be established to study the new problems created by the increased population and its activities; the spread and concentration of settlements, more cultivation, deforestation, mining, hunting and fishing.

**The aesthetic argument for the conservation of the environment**

Land has been described as 'the most precious property'; all the more reason for decrying its unaesthetic use by man. The earth's beauty must be conserved for future generations.

As Samuel Ordway Jr. (1956) once observed that if destruction of the environment continues long enough, basic resources will come into short supply and rising costs will make additional production unprofitable, industrial expansion will cease and man will reach the limit of growth. This observation echoes the very early nineteenth century assertion that if *per capital* use of minerals or energy triples and population doubles, the total demand upon the earth's natural resources will be multiplied by six.

As already mentioned, there are two contrasting views of problems related to conservation: the optimistic and the pessimistic views. The optimists, among whom are technologists, affirm that man's potentiality and ingenuity are very nearly inexhaustible. The pessimists, on the other hand, behind whom rally conservationists, see the population explosion as a threat of imminent disaster. The question is, is man's technology developing fast enough to ensure wise exploitation of renewable resources? Can this technology help discover and develop presently unknown resources? In other words, can technology not only sustain but also ignore the environment?

Since World War II, the view of the conservationists seems to have gained ground over that of the technologists. Although the conviction of plenty (or the philosophy of abundance) has persisted, especially in the industrialised nations, foreseeing scholars have frequently warned of the urgent need to control the growth of population. They call for attention to the deplorable conditions in which crowded populations live and the chronic and worsening food shortages, especially in the less developed nations.

In the developed areas, the environmental movement acquired importance and has become more active since the 1960s with a sharp emphasis on reducing environmental pollution in highly developed and populated areas. In the 1970s came the energy crisis. Finally, mankind seems to have woken to the realisation that the earth does not have unlimited resources. Many of those world resources are non-renewable. Prospects of adequate reclamation of used materials are unlikely; supplies of resources so far widely used as forms of energy and strategic metals and minerals are now seen to be strictly limited. Yet, there are still some who disregard warnings on population explosion and of the long range effects of population growth. While most Western nations have come to the conclusion that world rates of population growth must be reduced, many developing countries believe that the developed countries are selfishly advocating limits to population growth in order to protect their own affluence.

**Pollution**

Heat and contamination can befoul air and water even in distant areas; this will be deleterious to the environment. Overloads of solid waste befoul not only the vicinity of the source but also the places to which it is transferred. The burden of solid waste disposal is increasing. Increased population growth is particularly conducive to increased pollution of both the atmosphere and water. The latter utility was once free when people were fewer but in many industrialised countries, drinkable water can be found only in groceries. The best arable and grazing lands available have been brought into full use; even marginal areas are now being exploited.

## 4. Visible Effects of Population Growth on the Environment

The ever increasing number of people has led to a great scramble for the limited resources available; land, food, energy, air and water. In the scramble, some people get little or nothing while others profit by their positions of power to acquire tracts of land. The land tenure policy of individual ownership leads to excessive parcelling of land, making farming and agriculture either impossible or uneconomical. This leads to frustration and social conflicts when families are unable to acquire sufficient land on which to survive.

Indigenous forest and savanna vegetation, as a home for countless wild animals, is now rare. The destruction of some animal and plant species or some organisms have affected the functional relationships between human beings and their physical environment. The food chains through which energy flows in the ecosystem and the biochemical cycles (carbon nitrogen and phosphorus cycles), essential to life, have been disrupted.

The conservationists lament the high rate at which such animals as the rhino and the elephant are diminishing in Kenya. It is not that these animals are essential to the tourist industry but that if they become extinct, the ecosystems in those areas will be disturbed and man will be the one to suffer most.

Natural forest and good agricultural land have been indiscriminately used for human settlement. In fact, there is no longer any extra land in high potential areas; there is little space to allocate to schools and other essential amenities. Schools and hospitals are overcrowded and this results in poor services and creates situations conducive to infectious and contageous diseases.

As population density grows, a larger proportion of people tend to live in hazardous locations and on marginal lands. These are prone to famine, lightning, drought, floods and strong winds. The productivity of such places is generally low. Areas recently settled in Kenya, such as Mai-Mahiu, are really more suitable for wildlife than agriculture.

For a long time, employment opportunities and greater comforts have been thought to be available in urban areas; this explains why many people continue to flock to the urban areas. The great number of urban immigrants as well as the natural population increase is putting an excessive burden on urban resources. As a result, cities, especially those in the less developed countries are experiencing great environmental problems.

The Nairobi City Council, for instance, can no longer cope competently with urban demands. It cannot provide adequate transport, water, schools, clinics, social amenities, energy or housing. Slums are mushrooming in Mathare, Kibera, Kawangware and Ngomongo.

Slum dwellers, who are mainly unemployed or underemployed, are forced to engage in informal activities both legal and illegal. Congestion and limited resources have led to increased urban crime rate, accidents, conflicts and pollution in general. Other large cities in the world are experiencing very much the same problems.

**Air Pollution**

Chemicals such as carbon monoxide from motor vehicles and other gases from industries and factories including sulphur oxide, nitrogen oxide and hydrocarbonates are continuously discharged into the atmosphere. Pulp and paper mills, iron and steel mills, petroleum refineries, smelters, and chemical plants also add toxic substances to the air. The situation is made even worse by fuel and trash burning.

In our own country, the gases emitted by the Webuye Paper Mills in western Kenya, have high corrosive effect on iron roofs in the vicinity. There is no doubt, that these emissions have similar effects on plants, animals and man himself. Los Angeles (California, USA), is an extreme case of air pollution caused by industrialisation. Smog first appeared there during World War II and even now, all the efforts made by the Air Pollution Control District (APCD), have been unable to improve the air quality. This failure may be due to the rapid population growth. Each worker is faced with the virtual necessity of using a vehicle to move around in an immense city which lacks an adequate public transportation system. More people and more vehicles, systematic resistance to smog control regulations from industries and a quasi irresistible move towards industrialisation, have combined to work against successful pollution abatement.

Cities in the developing countries may soon fall into a similar predicament. Nairobi, which was sometime in the past very cold, is said to have become much warmer. This may be due to the large expanse of metalled roads and the growing number of concrete buildings. More people means more manpower in businesses and industries; more employment tends to attract more people.

Air pollution is a threat to health. Concentration of various gases in the air leads to suffocation, heart and lung diseases, poisoning, respiratory diseases, coughing, blood clotting, asthma, bronchitis and cancer.

**Water Pollution**

The growth of industries in cities leads to an increased demand for clean water. The very same industries dissipate waste water and individual waste into the drainage system which is soon polluted by lead, detergents, acids, ammonia, oil, and mercury. As a result, sewage treatment and refuse disposal facilities are quickly outgrown. Over the centuries, the water masses in the world have been considered suitable dumping grounds for all sorts of human waste.

Population growth has also led to the need for increased agricultural production and this results in heavier application of pesticides, herbicides and nitrate fertilisers. As a result, more pollutants find their way into streams, rivers, lakes, seas and even underground water and this becomes a real health hazard to users. Attempts to introduce exotic species of fish into a body of water in order to provide more human food may also result in ecological disasters.

### Solid Waste

One of the major problems facing most cities of the world today, including Nairobi, is lack of space for the hygienic disposal of solid waste. Solid waste has became an aesthetic disaster in Nairobi, whether waste is piled up to disintegrate or burnt to dispose of it, the air becomes unpleasantly polluted. Water, percolating through burnt solid waste, soon becomes polluted and provides breeding grounds for disease-bearing organisms such as flies, rats and cockroaches.

### Geo-ecological Hazards

Whenever there is human concentration, the surface of the earth is disfigured by wasteful methods of cultivation, overgrazing, sheer movement and deforestation. Dangerous gullies and canyons appear; the natural ecosystem is soon disrupted. The remains of mining activities and the mines themselves greatly affect the biosphere as they destroy the earth's beauty.

### Pollution of Heavy Metals

Through the industrial process, metals like mercury find their way into lakes and rivers thereby polluting the drinking water. Aquatic foods consumed by human beings , such as fish, may cause both blindness and deafness. Smelting of metals and the burning of petroleum produce lead-smoke toxic to the body's organs. Lead poisoning causes miscarriages among other disastrous effects.

Heavy metals also reduce photosynthesis and endanger aquatic life. In fact the long-term ecological effects of heavy metals on the seas have not yet been ascertained thoroughly but can apparently be disastrous.

**Radiation**

Certain machines and substances used by man in relation to health, transport and nutritional requirements have proved detrimental to health. X-Ray machines, certain chemicals and foods can have serious radioactive effects on men such as genetic defects, cancer and stillbirths.

**Noise pollution**

Some modern technology is excessively noisy. Amplified music, sonic booms and supersonic aircraft produce noise that is detrimental to man's hearing. Excessive noise can cause both temporary and permanent loss of hearing.

**Pesticides and Nitrogens**

Synthetic insecticides, chlorinated hydrocarbons (like DDT), benzenehexachloride (BHC), aldrin, lindrane, endrine, toxaphene,and even the organophriphates like azodrin, phodrin, and diazonetin are all designed to kill insects, but they also affect plants, animals and man himself in many ways. Their toxicity affects living organisms either directly or through food, water and air.

In a number of instances, agriculture today can also be considered ecologically hazardous. Pesticides often kill a higher proportion of the non-target population than that of pests. Because some synthetic pesticides have a toxic effect on so many other non-target organisms, they are sometimes labelled 'biocides'.

Pesticides with persistent effects - DDT for instance - have been proved to kill or reduce the reproductive capacity in sea animals such as fish and other organisms in the soil and air. Poisonous fumes are very mobile and can be blown about the atmosphere as dust particles; they can also travel in air and water currents. They dissolve in water and also become concentrated in the fats of organisms.

A concentration of DDT in the food chain poses a definite danger to the life and the reproductive capacity of certain fishes and birds. For example, DDT caused a sharp drop in the egg shell thickness of peregrine falcons, sparrows, hawks and golden eagles between 1945 - 1947. These are vivid examples of the disastrous effects of DDT and other pesticides.

In bodies of water, DDT also reduces photosynthesis by marine phytoplankton which are the primary producers of most of the food we obtain from the sea. A significant reduction in marine phytoplankton soon results in a proportional reduction of marine food supplies.

The effects of pollutants on soils are difficult to evaluate, The soils themselves are extraordinary complex ecosystems. There are numerous and varied micro-organisms yet, only several million in each acre of soil (e.g mites, arthropods, bacteria and the microflora) are essential for soil fertility as they play various roles in the ecology of the soil. Micro-organisms are responsible for the conversion of nitrogen, phosphorus and sulfur into useful nutrients for the plants. Most of the complex physical and chemical processes responsible for soil fertility are dependent upon these soil organisms. Soil treated with deadly and persistent poisons are causing great concern among environmental biologists and ecologists. Constant use of such pesticides is certainly reducing soil fertility.

Whereas we are not sure of the effect of plant fertilisers on the soil ecology, the use of herbicides as a substitute for farm machinery and labour in cultivating crops has greatly affected the environment.

Though their direct toxicity on animals is low, herbicides have a great impact on animal populations as they modify and reduce the plant population on which animals depend. Most herbivorous animals prefer to feed on one or a few kinds of plants. Research carried out since the 1970's, seems to indicate that herbicides destroy bacteria that are symbiotic with legumes (Ehrlich and Ehrlich, 1972).

The excessive use of artificial fertilisers in the form of nitrogen and phosphates is also being questioned. Fears are expressed in regard to the effects they have on the soil ecosystem and subsequent fertility and productivity. For example, in natural soil, nitrogen is present in humus, the organic matter of the soil. Inorganic nitrogen in tropical soils, for example, accounts for less than 2 per cent of the nitrogen present. In such soils, the nitrogen cycle is tight and not much of it is removed from the soil by leaching or surface runoff.

It has been shown experimentally that by maintaining the supply of humus, the fertility of the soil can be perpetuated. But this is not possible when fertilisers containing inorganic nitrogen are added to the soil unless organic carbon, in sawdust for instance, is supplied to the solid microorganisms. The undesirable decline of humus, which often occurs under inorganic fertilisation, is due to failure of the farmers to return crop residues that contain carbon and nitrogen to the shamba.

If attempts are made to maintain soil fertility by continued application of inorganic nitrogen fertilisers alone, the capacity of the soil to retain nitrogen is reduced as its humus content drops. Depletion of humus loosens the soil particles and permits large amounts of nitrates to be flushed into rivers and lakes.

Use of inorganic fertilisers in some countries has been going on over a long period of time. One result of the dramatic increase in their use has been a concomitant rise in the content of nitrates in surface water and in the atmosphere from which it falls as rain. Another effect has been a high reduction of the original organic nitrogen content in the soil. For example, where fertilisers have been used in Kenya for a long time such as in the Kitale area, the original composition of the soil has been altered. It does not yield abundant crops unless farmers continue to use fertilizers.

Adding nitrogen to water bodies leads to a contamination that cannot be removed by either boiling or chlorination. Although the organisms in it will die, the dangerous chemicals that the water contains will not be removed or broken down. The documented fate of Lake Erie in Canada is a case in point; the nitrate content in lake Erie has been greatly increased due to the runoff from the surrounding farmlands (30,000 sq. miles). These waters are now too rich in nitrogen. Similar problems exist in other lakes in the heavily industrialised countries.

There are, therefore, several environmental problems that can be attributed to the population explosion. Whereas overpopulation cannot be blamed exclusively for this state of affairs, it is certainly responsible for intensified environmental pollution and other problems. Various approaches must be used to control the population itself so that the number of people matches the available resources.

## 5. Population Control

Policies on population control have generally taken two major forms: Indirect control and direct control.

*Indirect control* can be made effective in two different ways. First, policies may be adopted in relation to population locations or settlements. In many countries, the government controls human settlement by restricting it to certain places. For example, in Kenya, certain areas are set aside for wildlife and forest conservation while others are state-owned and reserved for future development. There are laws prohibiting settlement in some areas which are hazardous to human life. Recently, the government has designed laws restricting the sale of land, a process which could easily lead to two extremes: population concentration and landlessness.

There are also policies encouraging settlement in the marginal lands in order to avoid excessive concentration of people in some of the best agricultural areas in the country. There are several new settlements in areas of so-called low potential such as in the dry parts of the Rift Valley, the North Eastern Province and areas formerly infested by tsetse flies. These new settlements have eased the population density in certain areas like Kakamega and Kisii.

Another method of indirect population control consists of restricting and monitoring population movement. The main type of population movement in developing countries like Kenya is migration from rural to urban areas in search of employment. This is mainly due to the socioeconomic disparity which has long existed between urban and rural areas. Urban areas are often thought to offer greater opportunities for improving one's life. Most governments in the developing countries have recently adopted policies to restrict migration to towns; they strongly advocate a return to the land.

An attempt is being made to transform the rural areas and provide them with facilities similar to those in urban areas. The policy is to decentralise industries and spread major institutions for instance, throughout the country. One of the main objectives of the District Focus for Rural Development in Kenya is to ensure equal development for all districts and make them more attractive. Previous policies had emphasised development in urban areas and ignored the rural areas.

*Direct attempts* to control population occur in two ways. First, setting a higher minimum age for one to get married and start families; and second, family planning. The former approach has not received as much emphasis as the latter. Everywhere, governments of developing nations are advocating family planning; which in fact, dominates population control policies in most countries.

Several methods have been developed or identified for family planning, but those which are commonly in use today include:

*Sterilisation:* Sterilisation in males is called vasectomy while in females it is called tubectomy. In a rather simple and inexpensive operation, key tubes in the reproduction system are closed to prevent the release of either sperm or ova. It is usually a permanent method of contraception, although the process can sometimes be reversed.

*Injectable contraceptives:* This method involves injecting synthetic progestin hormones into muscles from which they are slowly released. They prevent pregnancies and suppress ovulation by causing the production of thick cervical mucus which is impenetrable to sperm.

*Intrauterine Devices (IUD):* The IUD are small plastic or metallic devices that are placed in the uterus through the cervical canal. The gadgets seem to render the uterus inhospitable to both eggs and sperms thus preventing or stopping pregnancy.

*Oral Contraceptives (the pill):* This involves regular intake of pills as prescribed by a physician. Pills are a combination of synthetic forms of the hormones progesterone and estrogen. Oral contraceptives stop ovulation by interfering with the cyclical hormonal changes required for ovulation and make the cervical mucus thick and impenetrable to sperm. Pills are taken every day in a 21 or 28-day cycle depending on the pill type. A whole cycle must be taken on schedule to work effectively.

*Condom:* The condom is a sheath or thin rubber (latex) envelope which is put on a man's erect penis before intercourse to collect the semen, hereby keeping the sperm from entering the woman's vagina.

*Diaphragm:* This is a soft rubber cup with a stiff but flexible rim around the edge which is inserted into the woman's vagina before intercourse. The diaphragm covers the entrance of the uterus; as a further measure contraceptive cream or jelly is spread on the surface which lies against the cervix in order to block sperm movement.

*Vaginal contraceptives:* These are foams, creams, jellies, tablets, sponge (today) and suppositories, all chemical substances containing spermicides. Before intercourse, the contraceptive is inserted into the vagina, where it spreads over the vagina and cervix. This contraceptives render the sperm inactive.

*Periodic abstinence* (rhythm, natural family planning, fertility awareness): This requires the couple to refrain from sexual intercourse during the estimated time of fertility. Ways to determine a woman's approximate time of ovulation and her fertile time include; keeping records of the menstrual cycle, the body temperature and the consistence of the cervical mucus (Billings ovulation method).

Despite persistent emphasis on family planning, population control methods have not proved as successful as expected in reducing the population growth rate. This is attributed to the following factors.

Contraceptive methods are not 100 per cent effective. There are chances varying between 0.2 and 30 per cent that women using various contraceptive methods can still get pregnant.

Certain methods are unpopular because of the side effects, various complications, and sicknesses ranging from simple headaches to loss of fertility.

Sickness and body deformation prevent some people from using some of the relatively effective devices.

Some people are still rooted in their traditional values and they strongly believe in having as many children as possible . In traditional African societies the more children one has, the better for one's social status. Besides, values and attitudes (rooted in traditional customs) which hamper the use of family planning methods are prevalent in developing countries.

Many married couples are not able to agree on the need and method to plan their families. There is a very strong belief among men in certain traditional societies that the main work and duties of a woman is to give birth to as many children as possible.

Some religions forbid the use of artificial family planning devices. The Catholic Church, for example, strongly condemns any use of artificial contraceptives as this is considered to be against the Divine will.

The use of contraceptives is sometimes associated with prostitution and loose morals. For that reasons, some people shy away from them. Certain family planning devices are thought by some to deny the full enjoyment of sex and prevent satisfaction. Others may be considered cumbersome and messy.

Many people lack proper and adequate education on family planning and the use of the various methods.

For a family planning programme to be effective, an attitudinal change is required so that people can accept new methods more easily. Most fears related to family planning come as a result of ignorance and prejudice. Occasionally, those who are supposed to promote family planning are known for their many wives and large families; this makes their arguments less convincing.

## Conclusion

This chapter begins with a short description of the relationship between the human population and the environment. It defines human population and some related concepts such as *birth rate* and *death rate* and discusses how these help to determine the growth rate of the population. It alludes to some factors that explain the recent high growth rate in some parts of the world.

Subsequently, a brief definition of environment is presented followed by a discussion on the use of the environment by man. The recent high increase in population has multiplied overuse and misuse of the environment resulting in pollution and degradation of resources. The visible effects of population growth on the environment are then outlined. There is need to make provisions to adequately support the large and growing population; instead there is increased pollution and degradation. Population growth even creates new forms of pollution. This is what could be called *pollution in disguise.*

The last part of the chapter explains the attempts by man to control the population by indirect and direct methods. This is not always popular. Nevertheless the need to control the population is obvious, since it continues to increase while environmental resources are decreasing very rapidly.

## Questions

1. Explain the following human population concepts:

   (i) Birth Rate;

   (ii) Death Rate;

   (iii) Population growth rat.

2. Discuss the concept of 'pollution in disguise'. How does it occur?

3. Using specific examples, explain what is meant by 'population control'. To what extent are family planning methods effective in population control?

4. Analyse the conservationist and technologist views on the relationship between population and resources in the context of the contemporary situation in Kenya.

5. "Man belongs to the biosphere but he depends on all the other spheres for survival". Discuss this statement with reference to man's relationship with the environment.

6. Explain the ways in which man has overused and misused the environment in your own city, town or settlement.

# Bibliography

Ackerman, E.A. "Population and Natural Resources." in P. M. Hauser and O. D. Duncan (eds.) *The Study of Population.* Chicago: University of Chicago Press, 1959.

Asimov. I. *Earth: Our Crowded Spaceship.* New York: UNICEF, 1974.

Bernard, F.E. and Walter, B.J., *Africa: A Thematic Geography* Vol.1. Athens: United States Department of Health, Education and Welfare, Institute of International Studies, 1974.

Boulding, K.E., "Limits of the Earth: Materials and Ideas." in Thimas, W.L. *Man's Role in Changing the Face of the Earth.* Chicago: University of Chicago Press, 1959.

Brown, L.R. McGrath P.C. and Stokes, B. *Twenty Two Dimensions of Population Problems.* Washington D.C.: World watch Institute, 1976.

Ehrlich, P.R. and Ehrlich, A.H., *Population Resources Environment Issues in Ecology.* (San Francisco: W.H. Freeman, 1972).

Farooq, M., *Economic Consequences of Population Change: The African Case.* Ife: Institute of Population and Manpower Studies, 1976.

A. Hullet, A.R., "Optimum World Population". *Bioscience* Vol. 20, (March, 1970) No. 3.

Malthus, T.R., *An Essay on Principle of Population.* (London: Reeves and Turner, 1872.

Ominde, S.H. (ed.), Kenyas Population Growth and Development to the Year 2000 A.D. Nairobi: Heinemann 1988.

_____ Land and Population Movement in Kenya,. London: Heinemann 1968.

_____ Studies in East African Geography and Development. London: Heinemann, 1971.

Ordway S.H. (Jr.) "People Limits of Raw Material Consumption." in Thomson W.L. *Mans Problem Changing the Earth*. Chicago: University of Chicago Press, 1956.

Population Council, *Country Profiles*. New York: The Population Council, 1973.

Population Crisis Committee *A Guide to Modern Contraceptive Methods (Chart)*. Washington D.C.: Population Crisis Committee, 1985.

_____ *World Population Growth and Global Security*. Washington D.C.: Population Crisis Committee, 1983.

Reining, P. and Tinker I., *Population Dynamics, Ethics and Policy*, (Massachusetts: American Association for the Advancement of Science, 1975).

Soutwick, C.H. (ed.), *Global Ecology*. Sunderland: Sinaner Association Publishers, 1985.

Spengler, J. *Population Change: Modernization and Welfare*. Englewood Cliffs: Prentice-Hall, 1974.

Thomlinson, R. Population Dynamics: Causes and Consequences of World Demographic Change. New York: Random House 1965.

Tolba, M.K., *One Earth One Home*. Nairobi: UNEP, 1987.

Tuve, G.L., *Energy, Environment, Population and Food*. New York: John Wiley and Sons, 1976.

Udo, R.K. (ed.), Population Education Source Book for Sub-Saharan Africa. Nairobi: ASSP, 1979.

United Nations, Population Perspectives: Statements by World Leaders. New York: UNO, 1985.

United Nations. Report of the International Conference on Population, Mexico City 6 - 16 August, 1984.

UNESCO, Population Education: A Contemporary Concern. Paris: UNESCO 1978.

World Bank, *Population Planning Sector Working Paper*. New York- World Bank, 1973.

A World Population, "Growth and Global Security." *Population,* No 73 September 1983.

# -6-

# Human Settlement

### E. M. Aseka

## Introduction

The concern for the nature and quality of the environment is becoming an increasingly important focus of interest both in the developed and in the developing countries. Attention has often been drawn to the problems presented by the current trends in the growth of population, the difficulties of ensuring adequate food supplies for the human race and the continued strain upon stocks of renewable and non-renewable resources. The recent intense interest in environmental questions could also be attributed partly to increasing urbanisation and lack of satisfaction with the physical and social environments that cities provide.

It is true that the rapid growth of cities has raised numerous problems such as atmospheric pollution, traffic congestion, urban overcrowding, shelter shortage, inadequate planning and the like. Nevertheless, environmental problems are not confined to cities alone; they also exist in the rural areas. It is therefore pertinent to note that problems related to both urban and rural deterioration have been with us for centuries. Man, as a herbivore and carnivore, with a very wide dietary range, is remarkably well equipped to exploit the variable habitats of the world. As a hunter, fisherman and forager, he feeds on a substantial number of different plant and animal species.

When natural systems and ecosystems are used unwisely by man, they may rapidly become unstable with associated severe and sometimes essentially irreversible changes. Historically speaking, the first small population of human beings probably appeared on earth between 1 and 2 million years ago, probably on he continent of Africa. Since then, the human population has spread out to occupy virtually the entire land surface of the planet and by the last decade of this century it will number over 5 billion individuals. In their quest to provide subsistence, shelter and recreation for specific demographic units, humans have learned to modify and exploit the environment to their advantage in a great variety of ways.

**Early Settlement in Africa**

In Africa, in the early days of the Holocene Period when the Sahara was particularly wet, the abundant fauna and flora in the area favoured man's pre-occupation with hunting and gathering. But when the drying process of the present day Sahara region became more pronounced by 5,000 B.C., adverse environmental changes in the area had already driven the early African inhabitants to more complex adaptation and development of efficient ways of exploiting the habitat. By this period, the inhabitants of the Nile Valley had already learned to till the land in seasons, sow and irrigate it in order to get a more regular and abundant food supply.

While agriculture and settlement had become possible in the area by this period, a similar process was taking place elsewhere although it may not have been at the same pace. As the Stone Age microlithic culture of hunting and gathering became enriched by neolithic traits, the adoption of agricultural practices led to man's specialisation and division of labour. Whereas the adoption of agriculture marked the genesis of a more intensified exploitation of the habitat, the resultant multiplication and localisation of food supply entailed by this phenomenon boosted population growth; it was because of this that the need for permanent human settlement arose. An era of competitive resource and exploitation with potentially catastrophic short and long-range effects unimagined previously was ushered in.

What do we mean by human settlement? The use of the term *human settlement* seems redundant; for, are not all settlements human? If *settlement* is defined as the permanent place of residence of people, then not only towns and cities but also farms are settlements. It is generally agreed that a group of farms in a hamlet forms a settlement. But we also talk of a pattern of farms dotted about the countryside as dispersed settlement. Notwithstanding the rigidity of these different images of settlement as portrayed either in rural villages or urban centres, features such as population size, function, physical character and economic activity may help in defining types of settlements. The number of residents is a simple way of classifying settlements into broad categories such as village, town, city, metropolis and megalopolis.

## 1. The History of Human Settlement

Settlements may be grouped into two major types, urban and rural. On the basis of size, settlements smaller than towns are rural and those the size of, or larger than towns, are urban. Rural settlements are associated with the land and related activities such as farming, fishing and forestry. On the other hand, urban centres are inhabited by people engaged in manufacturing and service activities such as administration and commerce. Still, whereas the notion of human settlement includes phenomena such as emigration or migration to humanise either the rural or urban setting, it also includes an increase in the percentage of the population living in urban settlements. This phenomenon is otherwise referred to as *urbanisation*.

In historic times, progressive change among Africans and other peoples of the earth was incidental; an outcome of the altering patterns of natural phenomena and their effects on the environment. There is a theory that human beings have all along been the feeble playthings of material forces before which they were powerless. It is true that natural forces have altered the conditions under which communities lived and on which they based their assumptions of life. But to what extent, and in what ways, did man purposely seek to guarantee his survival?

Africa's neolithic villages of the Nile Valley (which date from as early as 4,000 B.C.) already showed signs of changes from the neolithic agrarian pattern of the region. This urban culture became more evident with the onset of the Iron Age (around 2,000 B.C).This period slowly opened the way towards Africa's developing her ability to harness the resources of her environment by adopting new social and economic behaviours and techniques. It intensified agricultural and exchange activities which depended upon communal efforts through some form of social organisation of a large number of people.

Understandingly, ethnic groups clustered around agricultural centres, with these centres joined together to form larger political groupings. In North Africa, such groupings were already in existence between 5,000 B.C. and 3,000 B.C. It would then appear that the concept of statehood developed concomitantly with urbanisation. The rural input in the form of labour and environmental resources in these early settlements became the basis of economic and urban growth.

It is also true that the inter-play of environment and social relationships worked to establish belief and behaviour patterns. The concept of divine kingship emerged in urban and rural settlements as the basis of social control and inter-territorial exchange relations. In other words, different communities found it expedient to develop social systems and divine leadership to mediate in their social relations. Given the abundance or scarcity of environmental resources, they needed well-coordinated social systems within which they could collect, store and distribute resources appropriated from the environment and the agricultural surplus created through improved methods of food production.

In sum, when discussing the subject of human settlement, it is important to note that one of the oldest of all demographic trends is the one towards urbanisation. Pre-agricultural men, by necessity, had to be dispersed over the landscape as hunting and gathering required a vast area of territory to produce enough food for a home. Under such conditions, it was impossible to exist in large concentrations. But the agrarian revolution began to change all that. Because more food could be produced in a smaller area, people began to form primitive communities. Hence, the ability of farmers to feed more than their own families was an obvious prerequisite of urbanisation. A fraction of the rural population had first to be freed from cultivation of the land in order to form cities.

## 2. Urban Settlement

The trend towards urbanisation continues today; it has been especially accelerated since the last century. The urban population of the world increased from 1,350 million in 1970 (about 37.3% of the world total population) to 1,800 million in 1980 (41.3%). But the annual growth of urban settlements remained 2.9 per cent in the developed world, while in Africa it stood at 22.9 per cent and 28.9 per cent in 1970 and 1980 respectively. The rural population however increased at a much slower pace from 2,310 million in 1970 to 2,600 million in 1980.

The African case demonstrates the fact that rapid urbanisation has not been confined to industrialised countries. By 1968, Nairobi, the capital of Kenya, was growing at a rate of 7 per cent per year. That is more than the growth rate of Los Angeles between 1950 and 1960. Accra, the capital of Ghana, is growing at almost 8 per cent per year, Abidjan the former capital of Ivory Coast, at almost 10 per cent; Lusaka, capital of Zambia, and Lagos, former capital of Nigeria, both at 14 per cent.

Indeed, pessimism may be generated by projecting the present rate of human population growth worldwide into the future. In the not so distant future, the world population will exceed 5 billion people. However alarming the future may appear, it is clear that the 1970's marked a climax and a turning point in a gigantic transformation of human settlement patterns. In developed countries where previously the majority of the world's largest cities were to be found, the growth of urban centres began to slow down and a process of spread into surrounding areas got underway. Contrastingly in developing countries, growth continued to climb rapidly. For the first time, developing countries produced a greater proportion of big cities compared to developed nations.

Among Third World cities, only Buenos Aires had over 4 million people by 1950. By 1980, 22 cities counted more than 4 million people. By the year 2,000 the number of city dwellers may have doubled; 61 cities with over 4 million inhabitants and a few may exceed a staggering 10 million.

### 3. Technology, Human Settlement and Environmental Degradation

But how many people can the earth support? There is no simple answer to this question as 'capacity' may be defined in different ways, and it may change with time. Whether capacity is perceived as the earth's potential to barely support a teeming, crowded and squalid world or defined in terms of the number that might support with some measure of comfort and dignity, one fact remains evident: the earth has its limits.

It is not yet clear whether or not or even when we will run short of environmental resources such as land, energy, fossil fuels, water, food and renewable resources. In a previous chapter of this book, it has been pointed out that the distinction between renewable and non-renewable resources is not always a clear one. [Tie crucial question to be asked about a renewable resource is "Does the rate of production or replenishment equal the fate of consumption or loss?" For non-renewable resources, in contrast, the question that may be asked is simply "How much exists and low long will it last at the present rates of consumption?"

If the rate of consumption of a given resource exceeds the maximum sustainable yield, sooner or later the stocks will be exhausted and the human population dependent on that resource will be impoverished and possibly perish. Again, it is not absolutely certain that technology could save the earth if it had to support staggering human numbers. Their settlement patterns and demands would certainly tax the environment, understood in this context, as the set of natural conditions that define human living space.

The environment has four functions.

1.  As a source of available goods, it provides air, water, a useful and pleasant landscape and natural recreational facilities both in urban and a rural settings.

2.  As a supplier of renewable and non-renewable resources, it provides resources that are used as inputs in the communities' production activities.

3.  As a receptacle of waste, it is burdened with what is discarded in production and consumption activities: solid waste, emitted, pollutants accumulated, partly or fully decomposed, transported to other areas or transformed.

4.  The environment provides space for the location of economic systems such as land for industries and residences, agriculture and infrastructure.

As a result of these often overlapping functions, major environmental problems occur because of the unchecked use of often environmentally imprudent or inappropriate technologies. From the Stone Age onwards, man has influenced the landscape by changing forests into meadows, digging ditches and canals, building dykes and converting salt marshes into cropland. Already in Africa, vast swathes of once productive land have been desertified. Questions related to environmental problems emerge " from the study of several pivotal issues":

*   the extent of human dependence on the natural environment and the fundamental character of its disruption;

- the exponential properties of growth of the human population and its impact on the environment;
- the inter-locking nature of present problems of environmental deterioration, resource consumption, and social organisation; and
- the limitations of technology.

Patterns of human settlement and the exploitation of natural resources have contributed largely to the conditions that have bred certain chronic environmental problems. It should be reiterated that the conditions that make the earth hospitable to its human settlers result from complex and perhaps fragile balances among the great chemical cycles - water, nitrogen, carbon, phosphorus and sulphur, all powered by the energy of the sun. Organisms regulate the environmental concentrations of nitrites, ammonia and hydrogen sulphide all of which are poisonous.

The damage caused by man to the natural cycles of environmental systems in his quest for settlement, food and comfort amply demonstrates the central truth of the man-environment relation: man is still part of nature, not master of it. By exploiting 40 per cent of the Earth's land area, he has reduced the mass of land vegetation by one third.

It is a fact that the causes of environmental degradation cannot be completely disentangled and tackled separately. Neither can environmental problems and their causes be considered in isolation from the other grave difficulties that plague mankind such as widespread poverty and the over concentration of wealth, rapid consumption of the world's readily available supplies of mineral resources by the affluent nations and domestic arid international tensions of social, religious and ideological origin.

It should be clear that neither environmental nor social problems can be ignored. New technologies merely aggravate these problems in so far as they expedite the adoption of schemes that are specifically meant to maximise exploitation of the habitat. Moreover, the intensification of production caused by new technologies quite often engenders ecological liabilities that may directly affect the quality of life in the neighbouring human settlements.

Many people may approach the study of environmental problems with the notion that such matters are questions to be resolved by practitioners of science or technology and hence essentially outside the scope of sociology, anthropology, economics or history. While scientific and technological inputs are indispensable in the determination of the physical effects of human settlements on the environmental amenities, such information is not in itself sufficient for making decisions about the allocation of resources. The political implications of economies of scale in resource exploitation and allocation are profound.

Hitherto, lack of stringent policy safeguarded by African countries have sometimes led to covert continuities in the exploitation of African resources by the Western nations using modern technology. There is need for African countries to conceptualise apt economic theories and enact prudent environmental policies of their own to address issues of environmental quality as a public resource, environmental degradation and underdevelopment in Africa, resource exploitation and unequal exchange, resource utilisation and the place of African countries in the global political economy. Africa has yet to take its rightful place as a pressure group on global environmental issues.

Indeed, technology is crucial in terms of the impact, both positive and negative, which its use has on the environment. The environmental soundness of any particular technology in the local conditions for which it is intended should be a fundamental element in deciding upon its appropriateness. Environmental degradation in various regions such as the Sahel, the Himalayan foothills, the Carribean and the Indus Basin has had a demonstrable impact on the economies of the countries concerned.

Such macro-environmental problems have caused macroeconomic problems in the affected regions as they diminish the purchasing power of the local communities in world trade and raise issues of food self-sufficiency, diversion of resources to deal with environmental catastrophes, the inflationary effect of lowered economic productivity, lowered rates of investment, population growth in fragile ecosystems and environmental refugees.

## 4. Rural Settlement and the Environment
Irrigation and drainage in settled lands has brought about abrupt and sweeping transformations in natural systems. The controlled distribution of water over cultivated lands and the withdrawal of excessive water through drainage has immediate effects on the crop-producing capacity of the land. It also affects both the quantity and quality of downstream flows.

The sudden appearance of extensive areas of irrigated crops in sub-humid and arid ecosystems triggers the potential for dramatic changes. These systems become inherently unstable. Because of intensive management of irrigation, arid ecosystems which have a limited capacity to assimilate, withstand and respond to inputs of water, chemicals and energy, find it difficult to adapt to alterations in species

**145**

diversity, numbers of organisms and the stability of their interrelationships.

The modification of aquatic ecosystems through irrigation practices results in:

* shifts in humidity and sedimentation;
* nutrient concentration;
* transport and resultant entrophication of fresh waters;
* wide distribution of pesticides and herbicides;
* dissemination of aquatic weeds and phreatophytic plants;
* bacterial and viral contamination; and
* it also leads to the spread of parasite vectors.

Although irrigation may bring many benefits upon human health (improving nutrition, water supply and community facilities), it also has deleterious effects through chemical pollution and distribution of diseases such as malaria and schistosomiasis.

Control of the spread of these diseases requires an interrelation of studies of disease transmission, ways in which snail or mosquito distribution may be affected by canal maintenance, alternative patterns of human settlement and field cultivation practices.

It may also call for a fresh assessment of the practicability of changing canal design and water distribution schedules, of circumstances in which farmers may be expected to revise crop cultivation, and of domestic water use, including bathing and other practices. Clearly, as human settlement and intervention in arid ecosystems become more widespread and complex, there is an increased need and urgency to understand the physical, biological and social processes which they trigger off or interrupt.

Given that about two thirds of Kenya is semi-arid, there is need to understand the physical, biological and social processes which relate to the natural balance of ecosystems. Semi-arid land is dry and apparently unfavourable to dense and abundant life. Redemptive policy measures are required to either slow down or halt the complete destruction of much tracts of land by both natural and human agencies. Safeguarding policies must be instituted to regulate the occupation and use of such land in order to avoid environmental crises.

It should not be forgotten that the advance of the nomads towards the edges of the Sahara has contributed to the degradation of the natural environment: the Hilalian Arabs are accused of having systematically cut down the fruit trees of North Africa. Their goats and other animals appear to have hastened the destruction of some of the region's woodlands. In dry areas, therefore, while irrigation is a necessary evil that destabilises the ecosystems, nomadic pastoralism may contribute much more directly to the degradation of vegetation cover.

Much depends on the relationship between the pasture resources and the grazing load they bear. The pasture resources may vary according to rainfall while the grazing load varies according to settlement patterns and economic conditions. During the dry periods, the pastoralists cut down trees to provide leaves for fodder. They increase their flock excessively whenever they find it profitable to do so.

However, the birth rate of nomads is usually lower than that of settled people. This explains why in the West African Sahel, the supremacy of the pastoral nomads between the 15th and the 19th century contributed to the low human density in the area. However, here and in the rest of the Maghreb Africa, the onset of colonial occupation saw the expansion of agricultural settlement first on the rich soils and then into the semi-arid regions. It also witnessed the sedentarisation of nomads and semi-nomads. The rapid increase in population that followed, resulted in the destruction of forest, the deterioration of vegetation and the dangerous acceleration of soil erosion.

One may ask why soil erosion is considered such a big threat in Africa. It is obvious that the developing economies of Africa demand the full exploitation of their resources in order to provide a sound economic base for balanced growth in other sectors. Since water plays such a significant role in the life of a nation, demand for the resource has increased tremendously with increasing population and urbanisation and it is fast becoming an item of short supply.

Yet the same resource wreaks havoc when there are sudden torrential rains. The magnitude of its threat may best be exemplified by Kenya's campaign to erect gabions in vulnerable areas, a campaign that was further spearheaded by President Moi in the late 1970's. Here, as elsewhere on the continent, there is an added need to fully utilise environmental resources because of population increase. Pastures have been overgrazed; this fact led to destocking campaigns in British Africa during the colonial times.

Fig. 1   Kenya-Arid and Semi-Arid Lands

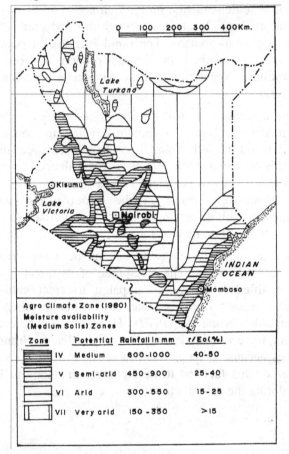

In the north and south of the Sahara, settlement has had generally unforeseen consequences. In these areas, natural resources have been heedlessly overexploited and therefore the uncertainties and the threat of disequilibrium in marginal

149

areas have been aggravated. Moreover, people's productive and extractive activities have been circumscribed by the environment. Their history of settlement, similar to that of other continental areas, has governed the conditions of their occupation of land. Thus, soil resource exhaustion is an area of exploitation with historical roots and deserts are the extreme condition arising from soil exhaustion.

In Africa, soil erosion causes a colossal loss of arable land which amounts to about 40,000 hectares per year. This specific gradation amounts to nearly 2,000 tonnes per square kilometer in Central Algeria. A comparable situation can be observed in the Arab countries of the Middle East. Indeed, a third of the semi-arid areas have recently been created by man.

It seems that although soil erosion is a universal phenomenon, there is no ultimate solution. Restoration of land quality must be a long term project. In tropical zones, human settlement has taken place in rain forests and flood plains; only disaster, pestilence and war have arrested further settlement. But in semi-arid tropics and the tropical uplands, the fragility of the soils has never allowed the human population to expand beyond low densities. It is human economic activities in the Sahel of North and West Africa that have exhausted the soil and created a semi-arid zone.

Elsewhere, the highlands of East Africa, the Cameroons and New Guinea are among the tropical uplands threatened by soil erosion. These areas are among the most complex and delicate environmental systems on earth. Given that the human population passed the 4.4 billion mark in 1980, (an increase of more than 700 million over the world population in 1970), it will be difficult satisfy the needs of an expanding human population without correspondingly modifying the environment. The basic applications of that modification can be foreseen as threefold:

(a) some renewable resources are depleted at a greater rate than they are replenished;

(b) most renewable resources are dispersed too widely to be re-collected and re-used; and

(c) residuals are discharged into some parts of the atmospheric and oceanic "sinks" beyond the rate at which they can be absorbed.

Tropical forests are still found in many countries of the world but nearly half of their total area is to be found in three countries alone, namely, Brazil, Indonesia and Zaire. Although tropical forests are the world's richest biological zones and provide a wide range of useful products (such as fuel, building materials, pulp wood, pharmaceuticals, resins, gums and dyes), they are also the home of millions of people. Currently, they are being exploited at a rate that is ecologically destructive and economically unsustainable. What is more, much of the world's oxygen production takes place in these forests and their degradation is an environmental tragedy. Inevitably, much of the forests cover will be lost by the year 2000 through complete conversion to other uses and by severe degradation. By that year, there will be an estimated minimum loss of tropical forests of 12.5 per cent.

In Kenya, natural forests are protected by government policy through the Ministry of Environment and Natural Resources. As a result, there is still natural vegetation called *highland forest* which covers certain isolated parts of the Kenya highlands where it is found at altitudes ranging from 1,976 metres to 2,736 metres. Mount Kenya , Mount Elgon and the Aberdares have this forest belt. At the Coast are found Witu forest, Mida-Gedi forest, the forested Kayas, Gongoni forest, remnants of the Shimba Hills forest, Sokoke forest and Ramisi River Valley forest. Clearly, a government protection policy had to be enacted because many of these existing forests have been reduced considerably by lumbering. In fact, charcoal burning is the greatest threat to Kenya's vegetation cover and the demand for charcoal is accentuated by increasing human settlement in Kenya's urban centres where oil and gas prices are becoming increasingly prohibitive.

From the foregoing information, it is clear that, although desertification is exacerbated by severe drought, its principle cause is human overexploitation of dry lands through 'over-cultivation, overgrazing, poor irrigation practices and deforestation. This proves the fact that even though the study of ecological change is still rudimentary, there is evidence to show that human settlement and community lifestyle have often been a dynamic element in the disfigurement of the environment.

## 5.  Settlement and the Pollution of the Environment

Nowadays, protection of the global environment is closely connected with a set of issues such as the depletion of the stratospheric ozone, the long range transport of pollutants, climatic change resulting from carbon dioxide accumulation, marine pollution and disposal of toxic waste. Pollution in this context refers to harmful substances that are released into the environment as the result of human activities. There are many kinds of pollutants which may be divided into 4 categories that cause:

(i)  direct assaults on human health (e.g. lead poisoning or aggravation of lung disease such as air pollution);

(ii) damage to goods and services that society provides (e.g. the corrosive effects of air pollution on buildings and crops);

(iii) other direct effects on what people perceive as their 'quality of life' (e.g. congestion and litter); and

(iv) indirect effects on society through interference with services that are provided for society by natural ecosystems such as ocean fish production and control of erosion by vegetation (e.g. destruction of vegetation by overgrazing and logging and poisoning of coastal waters with oil and heavy metals).

*Air pollutants* are numerous and varied. Many of them are difficult to detect. Their concentrations vary geographically and in many areas, techniques for monitoring pollutants are inadequate; moreover, long-term records are unavailable. Consequently, long periods of study are usually needed to reveal their delayed and chronic effects. Air pollution is a world-wide problem and some of the worst affected towns are found in all continents: Tokyo, Los Angeles, New Delhi, Atlanta and Sydney. On the whole, city dwellers are exposed to 20 parts of carbon monoxide in 1 million parts of air. Because of this, some of their haemoglobin is blocked. The affinity of carbon monoxide for haemoglobin is nearly 300 times that of oxygen and so a mere trace of carbon monoxide in the air we breathe can effectively destroy the oxygen-transporting ability of the blood.

Many city dwellers have detectable quantities of asbestos fibres in their lungs. Brake linings are an important source of these fibres. Also present in the inventory of automotive pollutants are oxides of nitrogen and particles of vulcanised rubber. These compounds are irritating when breathed and can cause damage to the lung tissues. Lead compounds too have insidious effects on man and many people have been poisoned when they unwillingly swallowed flakes of lead paint and window putty. It is a fact that the amount of lead that accumulates in persons depends on their place of residence and occupational exposure to exhaust fumes and other such pollutants.

Alongside air pollution, there occurs water pollution. Whereas heavily industrialised societies witness the discharge of visible or invisible pollutants into the air, some pollutants that are too heavy to be swept away by air currents find their way into surface water. Water pollution from sewerage provides one of the classic examples of environmental deterioration accompanying settlement and population growth. With increased population in most urban centres, the waste-dissolution ability of rivers and seas becomes overstrained. In some areas they have become so overburdened as to pose a threat to the existence of fish and other riverine or marine creatures.

A serious problem facing most of the developed world-and a few developing countries as well-is the accumulation of solid wastes in open dumps or inadequate fills. These dumps are not just eyesores; when burnt, they contribute to air pollution. Refuse includes cans, bottles, jars, metal and plastic bottle caps, packaging materials, junked cars and all manner of trash and garbage. On the whole, it is becoming a universally recognised problem that current methods of dealing with the solid waste material are utterly inadequate. This problem of waste disposal is increasingly encountered in the growing cities of Africa such as Cairo, Johannesburg, Harare, Nairobi and Lagos.

It would be impossible to mention all the elements of the entire inventory of pollutants; suffice it to say that the deterioration of the environment both physically and aesthetically, is most apparent in our cities. Pollution is one offshoot of man's mounting numbers and increased industrial technology. Its nature and extent depends on the type of settlement, the type of technology used and the level of scientific knowledge achieved.

Man has been polluting his environment since he began to live in large settlements, burn fossil fuels and use technology for his needs. The process of air pollution accelerated during the industrial revolution with the introduction of steam power for factories and with greater concentrations of population in manufacturing centres. The number and variety of pollutants increased still more markedly with the development of modern chemical technology in the 19th century.

### 6. Population Explosion and Settlement Problems

The growing size of urban areas is changing the whole pattern of land use. Fast metropolitan growth leads to degeneration of shelter and quality of life in suburban areas: slum sectors inevitably mushroom and soon become today's biggest challenge to mankind. Nairobi's and Kampala's slum and squatter .settlements continue to grow and along with them, the social sequences of poverty. They provide sanctuaries for deviant patterns of social behaviour including crime and prostitution.

Slums are unquestionably deplorable. They not only breed physical sickness but also overcrowding; lack of privacy and deprivation of the basic amenities of life can be demoralising. Besides, it is a sad fact that any growing town soon has a fringe such undesirable quarters.

The populations of the urban settlements are being augmented by three sources:

(a) the population explosion in the poorer and more backward parts of the cities;

(b) the rising unemployed rural population seeking employment opportunities in the city; and

(c) the attraction of the city which the rural population sees as a provider of a better quality of life and amenities such as hospitals and schools.

As rural populations are being siphoned off into urban settlements, these three reasons combine to give population growth the form of an urban explosion. But the juxtaposition of people with different levels of income, different manners and customs and of different races, produces in the city (unlike in the countryside) a social environment with unanticipated psychological effects. Though efforts are being made to cope with the development of the cities, problems often arise faster than they can be solved. The city is becoming more complex and the environmental degradation is practically unstoppable. Will mankind win or lose the struggle?

The question of human settlement has exposed the crises that exist in urban centres. But environmental problems are not confined to urban settlements alone. They also exist in rural areas. The truth is that man has produced imbalances not only in nature but more fundamentally in his human relations. In rural areas, environmental problems have arisen out of poverty, inadequate development and the process of underdevelopment itself (i.e. mass poverty, malnutrition, low quality housing, poor water supply, inadequate sanitation, prevalence of diseases, illiteracy: and natural disasters).

Eighty five per cent of Africa's population lives in the rural areas. But even there, the rapid population growth in recent times has tended to aggravate problems and impose further constraints on resources. Problems are further compounded by the increasing wave of rural to urban migration and the fact that both outsiders' and rural folks themselves look at rural life as inferior in quality and comfort. The crisis exists not only in land ecology but above all, in social ecology. While man in the urban area is literally; undoing the work of organic evolution by creating vast urban conglomerations of concrete, metal and glass, in the rural areas the characteristics of low quality environments persistently include:

*   unrewarding subsistence agricultural or pastoral economy;
*   inadequate supplies of safe drinking water, and
*   poor housing conditions.

All of these conditions result in the replacement of a highly complex organic environment with a simplified, inorganic one.

Furthermore, the situation is aggravated by the building of gigantic economic projects in the rural areas which may interfere with the regions' ecological balance. In Africa, such development projects include the Volta River Scheme in Ghana; the Aswan High Dam in Egypt, the Orange River Project in South Africa and Kindaruma Project in Kenya. These projects, which were intended to provide water for irrigation and the generation of hydro-electricity, have brought about their own unique ecological hazards and created conditions conducive to the spread of water-borne diseases in irrigated areas (e.g. bilharzia, typhoid, cholera, trachoma and malaria).

## Conclusion

In treating of human settlement, we have touched upon almost all aspects of human social and economic activity and related them to environmental questions. Where we found it useful, we have provided historical perspective because both man settlement and resource exploitation are a historical phenomena. But as noted out earlier, the *understanding* of ecological change is still in a rudimentary stage although human communities are known to have been an ever-present dynamic element in their own environment. Particularly in the last two centuries, man has been disassembling the biotic pyramid that has been supporting humanity for countless millenia.

Because history is part of the environment, examining the rural and urban settlement patterns in one's country and era involves seeing them in the context of the past so as to perceive and formulate trends in ecological and social change. Such trends are important in helping to make future projections; they underscore the need to formulate viable policies to guide societies in their resource utilisation.

However, it is equally important to note that urban and rural squalor is a most degrading human environmental condition. Yet, while there is evidence to establish that the abuse of land-based resources (first soils and then fossil fuels), has had a direct relationship to the rise in power of First World nation states, the Third World countries, who own some of these resources, have failed to exert their dominance.

As a conglomerate of historical forces, climatic variety, ethnic alliances and resources, African countries have been caught up in a web most frequently described as underdevelopment. Flows of matter and energy are re-directed to increase the human comfort, convenience and pleasure of the western societies, the repositories of advanced technology for whom African environmental resources are perpetually extracted, exploited and carted away. While African resources are precious and should be used sparingly and wisely for the benefit of the African countries themselves, the human conscience of the overdeveloped West is largely directed towards domination and exploitation. This situation will continue to be harmful to the Southern nations.

But while the overdevelopment of the West is cushioned by the relentless exploitation of Third World ecological resources; and while the Southern nations languish in liquidity problems, unfair pricing of their resources and deteriorating climatic conditions, they have yet to contend with the twin problem of technological advancement in the West. To underscore the binary relationship between the Western nations with their massive, political, economic and technological resources, on one hand and the Third World nations with their almost stagnant lifestyles and fledgling political, economic and technological resources, the West has on occasions attempted indirectly to destroy the African environment by turning it into a dump yard for its toxic and radioactive nuclear wastes. Many African settlements are threatened by these.

Whereas its resources are continually depleted and taken away using Western advanced extractive technology, the African continent continues to languish in poverty and indebtedness. This is because Africa was incorporated in the economy of production and exchange on very unequal terms with the Western nations. Disadvantaged by the less influential position which Africa occupies in this global economy, the deepening socioeconomic crisis of this economy has been pushed towards Africa and the rest of the Third

World by the increasing subordination of these territories to Western interests. The watchdogs of these interests are the Western dominated monetary institutions, the International Monetary Fund (IMF) and the World Bank which force African and other Third World countries to operate within a sort of orthodoxy favourable to the developed West.

Thus, the large-scale and systematic exploitation of Africa's natural and human resources is affected by various forms of unequal exchange. Falling prices of most raw materials extracted from its environment have been coupled with the shrinking share of Africa in world trade. This has caused a growing deficit and bred a soaring debt burden currently standing at US$1,354 million. When the debt crisis in Africa and the rest of the Third World is analysed properly, it provides a clear picture of how the global economy operates in its most thoroughly irrational mode.

It is clearly time for a massive campaign to be launched to restore high-quality environment to Africa and the rest of the world. There is increasing need to rethink and raise our economic system to a level more in line with the realities of the ecology and he global resource situation. Consequently, resources and energy must be diverted from selfish and wasteful uses in overdeveloped nations to meet the genuine needs of underdeveloped countries. Whereas this effort must be largely political, the campaign should se strongly supplemented by legal and boycott action against all environmental transgressions.

This is necessary since the Northern states have failed generally to perceive the moral and *realpolitic* implications of an ever-widening gap between the Northern 'have' states and the Southern 'have-nots'. Although the foundations of civilisations have rested heavily on their particular supplies of energy, the world community is now at an energy crossroads as environmental resources increasingly become politicised and selfishly misused. In summary, human society, whether urban or rural, needs a coherent politico-ethical ideology to make the meaning of an ecologically based environmental policy clear and believable.

## Questions

1.  How does the population explosion influence settlement patterns? Does this have an effect on resource utilisation?

2.  Discuss the role played by human settlement patterns on environmental degradation.

3.  Suggest ways in which the developing countries may use the wealth gained from their natural resources to contribute to worldwide environmental conservation.

4.  How do human settlement and productive activities cause soil erosion in Africa?

5.  Why are human settlement patterns and activities a threat to the world's forest ecologies?

## Bibliography

Ake, C. *A Political Economy of Africa*. London: Longman, 1981.

American Chemical Society. *Learning Our Environment: The Chemical Basis for Action*. Washington D.C.: American Chemical Society, 1969.

Aseka, E.M. "Precolonial urbanization in Africa: A Critical Re-Assessment". Staff Seminar Paper 5, Moi University, 1988.

Bookchin, M."Ecology and Revolutionary Thought" in R.T. Roelefs *et. al* (eds) *Environment and Society*. Englewood Cliffs, New Jersey: Prentice-Hall, Inc., 1974.

Daniel, P. and Hopkinson, M. *The Geography of Settlement*. Edinburgh: Longman, 1982.

Darkoh, M.B.K. Towards Sustainable Development of Kenya's Arid and Semi-Arid Lands (ASAL). Nairobi: Kenyatta University, 1990.

Ehrlich, P.R. *et. al., Human Ecology: Problems and Solutions*. San Francisco: W.H. Freeman and Company, 1973.

Gordon, G. and Dick, W. *Settlement Geography: Concepts and Problems*. Edinburgh: Holmes and McDougall, 1982.

Gunn, A.M. Habitat: *Human Settlement in an Urban Age*. New York: Pergamon Press, 1978.

Holdgate, M.W. and White, G.F. *Environmental Issues: Scope Report, No 10*. London: John Wilcy and Sons, 1977.

Jacobson, H.K. and Sidjariski, D. (eds.) The Emerging International Economic, Order: Dynamic Processes,

Cosntraints and Opportunities. Beverly Hills: Sage Publications, 1987.

Mabogunje, A.L. and Filani, M.O. "Human Settlements and the Environment." in Sidney B. (ed). *Development and the Environment in Africa.* Proceedings of a Seminar, Institute of Development Studies, University of Nairobi, 1975.

B. MacEwan, A. "The International Debt Crisis and the U.S. Left". *Monthly Review* , Vol. 38 (May, 1986) 1: 31 - 36.

M.I.Y., Man's Impact of the Global Environment: Report of the Study of Critical Environmental Problems. Massachusetts: M.I.T. Press, 1970.

Ndegwa, P. Africa's Development Crisis and Related International Issues. Nairobi: Heinemann, 1985.

Ojany, F.F. and Ogendo, R.B. *Kenya: A Study in Physical and Human Geography.* Nairobi: Longman,1986.

Siebert, H. *Economics of the Environment.* Toronto: D.C Heath and Company, 1981.

Sprout, H. "The Politics of Environments' Reform". in Roelefs R.T. et. Al. *Environment and Society.* Englewood Cliffs, New Jersey: Prentice-Hall, 1974.

Tordoff, W. *Government and Politics in Africa.* London: Macmillan, 1984.

Toynbee, A. *Cities on The Move.* London: Oxford University Press, 1970.

UNEP, The State of the Environment in 1972-1982. Nairobi: UNEP, 1982.

_____ The Environment in the Dialogue Between and Among Developed and veloping Countries. Nairobi: UNEP, 1984.

Wallace, B. *People, Their Needs, Environment, Ecology.* Englewood Cliffs, New Jersey: Prentice-Hall Inc. 1972.

White, L., "The Historical Roots of Our Ecological Crisis" in Reolefs, R.T. et. al. (eds.) *Environment and Society.* Englewood Cliffs, New Jersey: Prentice-Hall, Inc., 1974.

Weston, B., "Education for Human Survival: An Immediate World Priority". American Division of the World Academy of Arts and Sciences and the New York Academic of Sciences, *Environment and Society in Transition,* 2nd International Joint Conference, New York, 1974.

Willrich, M. "World Energy Policy: A Global Framework". in American Dision of the World Academy of Arts and Sciences and The New York Academy of Sciences, *Environment and Society in Transition,* 2nd International Joint Conference, New York, 1974.

# -7-

# Technology and the Environment

L. I. Libese

## Introduction

The pressures on the environment are many and varied. In developing countries, these pressures come from many diverse sources such as low levels of technology, lack of adequate education and trained personnel, poverty, underdevelopment and pollution. There are many types of environmental problems. These problems can be grouped into three broad areas: global, regional and local.

The *global problems* are international in nature; they pose perhaps the greatest dangers to humanity and the environment. In this category, technological products such as insecticides and pesticide residues have a tendency to persist for long periods of time in such agents like wind and water; chemicals in the environment frequently may travel far beyond their original sites of application.

Similarly, oceans and rivers become depositories of chemicals washed away from fertilisers, herbicides and pesticides used on farms; acid rainfalls over land and water bodies pollute such areas with air borne gases and solid particles.

*Regional problems* include increasing desertification, development of rivers that flow across national boundaries, and air pollution carried to neighbouring countries.

*Local problems* are those often confined within national boundaries. These may include: exploitation of natural resources, collection and disposal of garbage, a safe sewer system, etc. In recent years, nations all over the world have become conscious of man's relationship with the environment. Many countries , Kenya included, now realise the need to stress the value of an environmental component in their educational systems.

Man has always used his environment to provide his basic needs: food, clothing, shelter and communication. The increase in population means more pressure on these essentials. To be able to provide them there is need for more effective technology to expand and increase food production, health care, transport and communication.

The present environment - physical, social, economic and political-has , to a large extent, been shaped by technology. In order to fully utilise the potential of every citizen for development, a high level of familiarity with the tools of technology has become necessary. This is becoming more and more evident and experts predict that the effects of technology on the environment and society will be even more far-reaching and widespread in the very near future.

The chapter survey the experts view of the technologies of the future. It also discuss the shape of development in the areas of energy technology, communication technology and biotechnology as examples of technologies in the making.

## 1. Energy Technology and the Environment

Energy is an essential factor in the socioeconomic development of any nation. Wilson (1974) noted that a country's level of social and economic-development can be measured in terms of how much energy that nation or society uses. He pointed out that economically advanced societies of North America, Western Europe and Japan, consume considerably more energy than the less developed countries of Africa and Asia.

The United States of America consumed almost 32 per cent of the oil in the world, Western Europe 27 per cent and Asia 14 per cent while Africa consume only 1.6 per cent. Most of the energy used to develop present day civilisations originated from burning fossil fuels (coal and petroleum products) and wood.

The use of fossil fuels, however, has a number of environmental problems associated with it:

- The Earth's supplies of coal and petroleum are finite. It is predicted that most of the Earth's supplies of coal and petroleum will run out by the end of this millennium. There will be very little or none left for the coming generations especially as the need for energy will increase in future when the developing countries of Asia and Africa industrialise and demand a share of the Earth's energy resources.

- Fossil fuels are not evenly distributed in the world international trade; the producing nations control the fuel supplies and maintain prices at a high level. These high prices put fuel beyond the reach of most Third World societies. In Africa, for example, the increase in foreign debts is largely due to the importation of oil and coal.

• Most important for the environment is pollution which is caused by the processing and utilisation of fossil fuel. As mentioned in a previous chapter, the refinement and the burning of fossil fuels releases toxic waste such as sulphur oxides, carbon monoxide and nitrogen oxides into the environment. Each one of these waste products has harmful effects on living things.

*Sulphur dioxide,* which originates from oil refining and the use of chemical fertilisers, when released into the atmosphere, reacts with the water vapour in the air to form sulphuric acid and other sulphates. The result is acid rain which has become one of the major environmental problems in Europe and North America. The corroding effect of acid rain destroys buildings, monuments and forests. Sulfur dioxide in the air also causes respiratory diseases in human beings and animals.

Excess *carbon monoxide* in the environment comes mainly from the incomplete burning of petrol and diesel by motor vehicles. When breathed into the lungs, carbon monoxide prevents the absorption of oxygen by blood haemoglobin; the result is loss of energy which all living tissues require. Hexter (1971) showed that the mortality rate in Los Angeles, U.S.A. increased in proportion with the increased level of carbon monoxide in the air. This particularly affects the children and the old.

Most of the *nitrogen oxides* in the environment come from the manufacture and use of chemical fertilisers. Nitrogen oxides in the air have been associated with such health problems as acute respiratory diseases, increased bronchitis among school children and leaf abscision in plants which results in decreased agricultural yields.

Other waste effluents from the manufacture and the use of fossil fuels (carbon dioxide, lead and mercury etc also add to air pollution in the environment. Hare (1982) showed that there has been a steady increase of carbon dioxide concentration in the atmosphere. It is theorised that this will eventually cause a rise in surface temperature which may affect many low areas on the edge of continents. Carbon dioxide is able to absorb increasing solar radiation but resists its return flow.

This results in the general warming effect on the Earth's surface temperature. It is commonly referred to as the *'green house effect'*.

Lead and mercury in petroleum and coal are called heavy metals. They are poisonous to human beings and animals as they interfere with the proper functioning of key molecules (such as enzymes) in the body. They may also cause such health problems as brain damage, hearing impairment and psychological difficulties.

Whenever oils are spilled into the environment, especially in oceans (e.g. during transportation or drilling), marine life is badly affected by the oil: aquatic birds and fish are either killed or effected so much that they cannot be used as food.

Because of the many problems associated with the use of fossil fuels, environmental education advocates a drastic cut down on the use of this important resource; even more important is the development of the necessary technology to make use of other forms of energy, especially renewable energy resource. One such alternative resource is energy from either nuclear fission or fusion.

**Nuclear Energy**

The generation of electricity from nuclear reaction has been suggested because it is, in theory, an extremely abundant source of energy. When the necessary technology is refined, nuclear reactors can provide a practically inexhaustible source of energy for human development. The search for this technology became a matter of great urgency as a result of the oil crisis in 1973 when oil producers decided to double and even triple the price of oil.

As a result, there was a rapid increase in the use of nuclear reactors to generate electricity. The International Atomic Energy Agency noted that, by 1986, almost 15 per cent of the world's electricity supply originated from nuclear power plants. There were 335 nuclear research reactors in the world and 17 additional units planned mainly in the developing countries. It is expected that more nuclear energy will be used as soon as the necessary technology is developed and reactors are made safe.

For now, the major fear for using nuclear energy comes from the danger of accidents occurring in the nuclear power plants and the polluting effects which are associated with such leakages. Whenever such accidents occur, ionising radiation is released into the environment causing severe disruption to all forms of life in that environment.

The latest nuclear accident-occurred at Chemobyl, U.S.S.R,. in May 1986. As a result of that accident, many people died immediately while others were maimed for life. The accident which occurred in Russia spread dangerous ionising radiation to other countries such as Sweden, Norway and Denmark, to the West of the U.S.S.R and as far as Spain and Italy in the South of Europe. Radiation was also detected in North America.

Other nuclear accidents have occurred at Chalk River, Canada in 1952; Windscale, Liverpool, England in 1957; Idaho Falls, U.S.A. in 1961; Brown's Ferry, Alabama, U.S.A. in 1975; Three Mile Island, U.S.A. in 1979; and Tsurage, Japan in 1981. Nearly each time a nuclear accident occurs, human lives are lost. People concerned with the well-being of the environment support the efforts of the International Atomic Energy Agency (I.A.E.A) to promote safe technology for the generation of nuclear energy.

The I.A.E.A, the International Commission on Radiological Protection, and the United Nations Scientific Committee on the Effects of Atomic Radiation as well as other bodies concerned with the safety of nuclear power plants, recommend that the technology associated with nuclear fission should be made safe through proper designing of the power plants; the design of the power plant unit should prevent core melting and give sufficient training for the control-room personnel.

Openshaw (1988) suggests that nuclear power plants should be located in environments where there are relatively few people and computers should be used to automatically shut down a reactor whenever unacceptable levels of radiation are detected.

**Other sources of energy**

Other energy sources waiting for the necessary technology to be perfected and made affordable are solar energy, biomass, wind and tides. In Kenya, the Government has taken a keen interest in promoting technology to use such renewable energy resources.

**Solar Energy**

The development of solar energy technology, which would effectively harness the energy of the sun, could help solve our long term energy supply problem. Solar energy could be used in many ways: to heat water for bathing and washing, to warm homes during the colder season in the highland environments, to light homes and run household appliances.

A solar electrical system is made of a number of parts which include: a solar cell component which converts sunlight directly into electricity; an electric energy storage component; and wiring, bulbs, and various connectors, switches and adaptors.

*Photovotaic system:* The total amount of electricity converted by a solar call is roughly proportional to the intensity of the light in the environment as well as the active area of the cell. The conversion efficiency is calculated by expressing the maximum power output as a percentage of the incidence of light on the solar cell area.

There are a number of types of solar cells. The U.K. International Solar Energy Society - (ISES 1976) has described one type of cell called *borondoped* or p-type silicon cell. This type of cell is quite small since it measure 50 mm square and 0.3 mm thick. In most cells the active material is silicon. Silicon has many advantages as it is widely available, and there is a well-developed technology to produce it. The only disadvantage is that pure silicon is still very expensive.

Other solar cells are made from materials such as caprous sulphide and cadmium sulphide.

*Electrical energy storage:* Much more electrical energy is constantly being produced than can be used. There is therefore a need to store the excess so that it can be used when it is needed. Solar energy, for instance, is generated during the hours of daylight while lighting is needed mostly at night. Electricity is stored in batteries. For the storage of solar energy those batteries must be easily rechargeable, keep their energy when not in use, require minimal maintenance and provide efficient service. Batteries are of two types: lead-acid and nickel-cadmium.

In Kenya, solar energy is used both for heating water and generating electricity. Hankins (1989) lists a number of areas where solar energy is used on a regular basis. Places like Buru Buru in Nairobi, Egerton University, Golf Hotel Kakamega and Garissa Rural Industry use solar energy to heat water; while solar energy is also used as electricity for lighting in places such as Hola Secondary School, Kahawa Water Supply, and Karumogi Secondary School.

**Biogas**

Another renewable energy source is biogas. Biogas can be generated from agricultural residues which are readily available in the rural areas. Agricultural residues such as coffee pulp, sisal slurry, waste from wheat, maize and beans, and animal dung can be used to generate gas for cooking and heating.

In other parts of the world, biogas technology has been used since the 1940's. Hankins (1989) observed that biogas technology has made a large contribution to the industrial development of countries such as China and India. Biogas digesters have been used in those two countries to produce fertilisers and treat waste.

In Kenya, the initial efforts to produce biogas were attempted by Hutchinson, a European farmer, as early as 1957. But in more recent times, the Kenya Government has encouraged the construction of biogas plants throughout the rural areas.

The type of biogas plant encouraged in Kenya is known as the Meru Biogas Plant Model. It utilises both Indian and Chinese technologies by using a biogas digester, a gas holder, water and gas pipes which distribute gas throughout the house. Biogas plants can be found in place at Mtwapa Coast, Jamhuri in Nairobi, Bukura in Kakamega, Kisii Agricultural Centre and Koru in Nyanza.

The biomas from sugar cane was first used in Brazil for the production of ethanol which can be used instead of fossil fuel. Kenya now produces quantities of ethanol which is mixed with imported petrol and sold as gasohol.

The Kenya Government also promotes technology to use other renewable energy sources such as wind, water (hydro) and wood. There are also efforts to encourage energy conserving appliances.

## 2. Communication Technology and the Environment

Brown et al (1974) proposes that the ability to use language as well as manipulate symbols is a unique human characteristic. Because of this ability, man is usually able to obtain what he needs from his environment. Man has developed a culture which has enabled him to achieve other forms of social, economic and political development. The ability of man to communicate enables him to pass on knowledge to succeeding generations. With the help of communication technology, human societies are expected to change more in the future.

Firnberg (1981) predicts that information technology will radically change our present ways of life. Telecommunication will improve the management and administration of organisations, educational facilities, industrial arrangements and even such things as transfer of funds; money can very easily be transferred through telex. Martin (1978) predicted that as the cost of oil continues to rise, the major mode of communication will be to hold conferences by telecommunication; instead of people traveling to attend conferences, they will be linked through a telecommunication network and hold teleconferences.

Communication in the future will make increasing use of the experience and knowledge that have been gained from air space research and technology. Communication satellites and space shuttles will be the major technology involved in communication, a communication satellite functions in the same way as a radio relay in the sky. When messages from antennas on Earth are sent in the form of signals to the satellite, they are amplified and sent back to earth as stronger signals. Satellites are capable of handling large banks of information at once. They can then transmit the message to various parts of the Earth. A communication satellite can relay messages to a distance of 45,000 kilometres while a microwave relay covers only 40 kilometres. Three satellites properly sited can cover almost all of the biosphere.

Satellites can also enhance the process of broadcasting. Regular broadcasting equipment consists of one transmitter and many receivers. However, when a communication satellite is used, it serves as a two-way signal in which there are many transmitters. Each earth station becomes in effect a broadcasting transmitter since the signal it sends out reaches all other earth stations.

Satellites are capable of communicating data between computers and computer users. Technically, it is now possible to carry telephone message and television programmes in digital form through satellites.

Together with space shuttles, communication satellites will enable man to transport materials to and from space thus making space more productive. Some of the natural resources man needs for industry can be found in space in sufficient quantities.

It appears that satellites, both nationally and internationally, promise to be one of the most powerful and cost-effective media of communication; according to Martin (1978), the next century will see widespread developments in culture and unlimited development in human knowledge. The new information channels will give man access to world-wide data banks, film libraries, computer assisted instruction and digitalised encyclopaedias.

## 3.    Biotechnology and the Environment

Biotechnology is perhaps the area that promises to have the farthest reaching impact on the environment. This is because biotechnology deals directly with the specific objectives of environmental education - the protection of life. In the 21st century, biotechnology is expected to affect food production, human care, energy generation and pollution treatment positively.

Much of biotechnology has developed as a result of research into the chemical composition of life and especially the nature of the genetic system (DNA) of living things. Biotechnology is proving efficient because its methods are based on nature itself.

In the early 1960s Watson and Crick discovered that the central chemical constituent of the gene is a molecule called deoxyribonucleic acid (DNA) and also described its composition and structure. The two scientists showed that DNA is made up of I two chains of a 5-carbon sugar (ribose) and 5-nitrogenous bases (adenine thymine, cytocine, guamine and uracil) and a phosphate, molecule.

DNA has two functions: first, reproducing itself during a process called replication; and second, directing the process of protein synthesis. Synthesised proteins can either be structural (e.g. those that form tissues and make up the large part of living (organisms) or in the form of key molecules (e.g. enzymes, hormones and antibodies). It is in this process (synthesizing proteins) that DNA acts as the determinant of species, the genome.

The type of protein synthesised at any one time is dictated by DNA and determined by the linear arrangement of the bases in DNA. During protein synthesis, uracil replaces thymine. DNA is therefore the genome which determines the species of living things. Generally it is the aim of nature to conserve the uniqueness of each species. However, changes in the environment can bring about a change in the genome causing new species to be formed. In other words, DNA determines both which protein is to be synthesised at any given time and the linear arrangement of its own bases.

The discovery of the nature of DNA and how it functions led to research activities aimed at manipulating DNA. When recombinant DNA (rec DNA) techniques are used, genetic engineers extract DNA from one species and transfer it into another, learning more about the reaction between the donor and the host.

Some of the techniques developed during recombinant DNA research have practical application in industry, human health care and even in the production of food and drink. Fairlough (1986) predicts that as the 21st century approaches, biotechnology will have profound and widespread impact on the world's industries and that the relative economic strengths of different nations and enterprises will be significantly affected.

In human medical care, the biotechnology of recombinant DNA has the potential to redesign micro-organisms to produce medically important substances such as hormones. Insulin, an important hormone used to treat diabetic patients, is already produced by a particular bacterium, *E. Coli.*

Anderson (1982) observes that recombinant DNA technology has enabled scientists to synthesise hormones, vaccines to treat various human diseases and antibodies used in diagnostic techniques.

In industry, biotechnology is used to manufacture enzymes, which can be used in the synthesis of protein, the manufacture of cosmetics, disease diagnosis and the treatment of some diseases. Potentially, enzymes can be used to digest some organic waste. Towalsk et al (1986) observe that using micro-organisms to produce enzymes could ensure adequate supplies and free man from seasonal shortages.

In food production, biotechnology has enabled man to use bacteria to produce protein. Fairlough (1986) states that nuclear genetics have enabled man to specify a potentially limitless range of proteins for cells to synthesise. That capability to produce protein could be used to improve the quality of food and alleviate malnutrition in the world.

## 4.  Technology and the Ozone Layer

The stratosphere is the layer above the troposhere which extends up to 50 kilometers above the earth. The stratosphere contains a rich layer of ozone $O_3$, the natural filter that absorbs the sun's ultra-violet radiation (UV) which can be damaging to life on earth.

Carbon dioxide, in combination with water vapour, ozone $O_3$, and several other gases, plays a significant role in determining the thermal structure of the atmosphere. These greenhouse gases are transparent to the incoming solar radiation but opaque to longer wave thermal radiation from the earth's surface. As the concentration of *green house gases* increases or accumulates in the air, the solar radiation received at the ground level will not be significantly lowered, but the thermal radiation from land and water surfaces will drop markedly . When this occurs, there will be a surplus of energy available at ground level and hence the surface air temperature will rise.

The ozone layer can be destroyed by many complex chemical reactions. Over two hundred chemicals including oxygen, hydrogen, chlorine and nitrogen compounds are capable of destroying the ozone layer. Other gases that contribute to the depletion of the ozone layer include: nitrous oxide, methane, chlorofluorocarbons-CFCs (particularly CFC-11, and CFC-12) and water vapour.

Chlorofluorocarbons are man-made chemicals that are primarily used in aerosol propellants, refrigeration (as solvents) and in the production of plastic foams. Clearly, human activities and the use of various chemicals are upsetting the balance between the production and destruction processes of ozone. This has led to changes in the total amounts of ozone above the earth's surface.

Ozone depletion is believed to be responsible for: climatic changes, increased incidence of skin cancers, acceleration of ageing of the skin, increased eye disease and reduction of growth in plants and marine life. The depletion of ozone, and a consequent warning of the polar seas would pose a global environmental threat: melting ice would cause a rising of the seas and disastrous flooding of low ocean shores.

Evidently the use of technology is not morally neutral. Indeed, since nuclear energy has intrinsic dangers and is extremely expensive, it is at the moment hardly a viable option for developing countries. Communication technology is also expensive and has its own dangers and problems. While communication technology could lead to widespread changes in cultural practices as well as welcome developments in human knowledge, it is also likely to increase dependency and differentials in economic power between the First and Third Worlds. In sum, biotechnology has profound moral and political implications given its potential to new species.

## Conclusion

This chapter looked at the impact technology can have on the environment. Technology enables man to use his environment effectively and increase man's ability to communicate freely over great Distances.

It also looked at technologies of the future tele-communication, biotechnology and energy - which promise to have a profound and widespread impact on the environment. Such technologies may change the style of human interaction in most places.

Biotechnology is expected to improve human health care, food production and generally, the quality of life on earth.

Technology is also expected to find and develop new sources of energy as substitutes for the widely used wasteful and pollution-producing fossil fuels.

## Questions

1. From the knowledge of recombinant DNA research, it is theoretically possible to manufacture human body parts by 'cloning'. Discuss the ethical implications of such a possibility.

2. Discuss the role of information technology in the management of a university.

3. Discuss the implications of using solar energy as alternative to energy from fossil fuels.

4. It has been said that the purpose of modern technology is to retard the development of Third World countries and increase their dependence on industralised countries. Either support or oppose the claim.

## Bibliography

Anderson, J.K. *Genetic Engineering,* (Grand Rapids, Michigan: Zonderva Publishing, 1982).

Bloomer, A.G. "Linking Schools and Industry: A Survey of Current Practice" *Education Research,* 27 (1985) 2, pp. 79-94.

Brown, J. and Glazier, E.V.D. *Telecommunication,* (London: Chapman and Hall, 1974).

Buchanan, B.S. "Technology as a System of Exploitation". *Technology and Culture,* 19 (1962) 3, pp. 341 - 356.

Fairlough, G.H. "Genetic Engineering - Problems and Opportunities", in Jacobsson, S. et. al. (eds). *The Biotechnological Challenge,* (London: Cambridge University Press, 1986).

Firnberg, D. *Information Technology for the Eighties,* (London: Wiley Heyden Limited, 1981).

Goonantilake, S. *Science and Culture in the Third World and Europe.* Third World Seminar Publications, 31, University of Oslo (1982).

_____, Aborted Discovery: Science and Creativity in the Third World, (London: Zed Books Ltd., 1984).

Guhn, C.I.V. "Towards Scientific and Technological Innovations?" *Journal of Modern Africa Studies,* 22 (1984) 1, pp. 1 - 8.

Hankins, M. *Renewable Energy in Kenya,* (Nairobi: Motif Creative Arts Ltd., 1989).

_____, *Dissemination of Biogas Plants in Rural Areas of Kenya,* (Nairobi: Special Energy Programme, Kenya Government, 1987).

_____, *Solar Energy A U.K. Assessment,* (London: U.K. International Solar Energy Society (U.K. I.S.E.S), 1976).

Jacobsson, S. et. al. (eds.) *The Biotechnological Challenge,* (London: Cambridge University Press, 1986).

Khamala, D.C.P.M. "Science and Technology for African Development: An Assessment for their Achievements and Prospects", *Post,* (1981) 2, pp. 37-430.

Martin, J. *Communication Satellites System,* (Englewood, California: Prentice-Hall, 1978).

Mazrui, A.A. *The Africans: A Triple Heritage*, (London: BBC Publicatons,1986).

Odhiambo, T.R. "Understanding of Science: The Impact of the African View of Nature" in Gilbert, P.G.S. and Lovegrove, M.N. (ed.), *Science Education in Africa* (1972).

_____, " Introductory Address: The First Sympossium on the Utilisation of Agricultural and Agro-Industrial By-products in the Context of Rural Development in Kenya. Some Implications for Research and Development", Nairobi, Kenya, 1984.

_____, "The Management of Science-Enterprises", *The Weekly Review*, Nairobi, 29th November, 1985 .

Parslaw, R.D. *Information Technology for the Eighties.* (London: Wailey Heyden, 1981).

Serconvich, F.C. "The Political Economy of Biomass in Brazil: The Case of Ethanol " in Jacobssons et al (eds). *The Biotechnological Challenge,* (London: Cambridge University Press, 1986).

UNESCO, Environmental Education in the Light of the Tblisi Conference, 1980, (Paris: UNESCO, 1980).

UNEP, State of the World Environment, (Nairobi: UNEP, 1987).

Wilson, R. *et al Energy, Ecology and the Environment* , (New York: Academic Press, 1974)

World Bank *Environment & Development,* (Washington D.C. World Bank 1979)

_____, Accelerated Development in Sub-Saharan Africa, (Washington D.C.: World Bank, 1981).

# -8-

# Development and the Environment

## J.M.A. Orodho

## Introduction

The story of man's relationship with the natural environment dates back to the dawn of man's emergence as the dominant species on our planet. The story is indeed inseparable from that of man's own development. Although the concept of development was introduced relatively recently into the literature of economic and social affairs, the aspirations that it embraces are as old as mankind itself. Underlying the present idea of development as well as the earlier notion of progress, is the betterment of man's life on earth through an increase in the goods and services available to him. For the vast majority of mankind, the quality of life has depended and continued to depend on this factor.

Increased production of goods and services has been sought through different combinations of labour, raw materials, accumulated capital and available technology. The manner and conditions in which these factors were combined was determined within the context of different economic and social systems. In each of these systems, examples can be found of success in operating their economies to make goods available to the various social groups. The idea that social change is inherent in the very concept of development is now accepted without challenge in all economic systems. But both the concept of development and that of social change should be extended if the accumulation of goods is to have any useful effect on human life.

It is only recently that the environment has become a public issue on a global scale. Its concern first arose in the highly industrialised societies where the adverse consequences of many of the varied practices and technologies (which have produced the unprecedented affluence of those societies) first became evident. In this context, it is not surprising that many people in the developing countries questioned how this new concern for the environment was relevant to their own compellingly urgent development strategies. Most developing countries asked whether pollution was not in fact merely a disease of wealthy societies and why they should be concerned with it at all - especially at this preliminary stage of their own development.

Indeed, some of these developing countries went as far as to suggest that if more industry meant more pollution, then they would welcome more pollution. But at the same time, they asked how the action taken by the more industrialised countries would affect their own interests and wondered how accessible technical assistance would be. They were also concerned about the markets they required for their own development. Also queried was the attention which was to be given to the kind of environmental problems which directly affected them.

## Development and the Environment

This chapter attempts to sort out some of the possible answers to the above questions. A full understanding of these issues is an indispensable prerequisite to the kind of international co-operation which will be required if mankind is to deal effectively with the newly perceived environmental challenge.

It should be re-emphasised that the environmental issue is indeed of great importance to the developing countries and should therefore be considered as an integral aspect of their own development process. In effect, the reader should be clearly aware of the important differences in perspective and priority between the environmental problems of the industrialised countries and those of the developing countries.

The current concern with the human environment has arisen at a time when the energies and efforts of the developing countries are being increasingly devoted to the global goal of development. Indeed, the compelling urgency of the development agenda has been widely recognised in the last two decades by the international community and has more recently been endorsed in the proposals set out by the United Nations for the second Development Decade.

The problems experienced by the industrially advanced countries have, to a large extent, brought about the current concern with environmental issues. These problems are themselves very largely the outcome of a high level of economic development. The creation of large productive capacities in industry and agriculture, the growth of complex systems of transportation and communication and the evolution of massive urban conglomerations have all been accompanied in one way or the other by damage and disruption to the human environment. These disruptions have attained such major proportions, that in many communities, they already constitute serious hazards to human health and well-being. In some ways, in fact, the dangers extend beyond national boundaries and threaten the world as a whole.

This does not in any way suggest that the developing countries are unconcerned with these problems. They have an obvious and vital stake in them in so far as these problems have an impact on the global environment and on the socio-economic relations between developing and developed countries. The Third World has also an interest in them to the extent that they are problems that tend to accompany the process of development These problems are in fact already emerging with increasing severity in most developing societies. Wisely, these societies clearly wish to avoid, as far as is feasible, the mistakes and distortions that have characterised the patterns of development of the more industrialised societies.

As mentioned earlier, the major environmental problems of developing countries are essentially of a different kind. They are predominantly problems that reflect the poverty and the very lack of development of their societies. In other words, they are problems, of both rural and urban poverty. In both the towns and the countryside, it is not merely the quality of life but life itself that is endangered by the poor quality of water, housing, sanitation and nutrition, by sickness and disease and by natural disasters. These are problems, no less greater than those of industrial pollution, that clamour for attention in the context of the concern for human environment. They are, verily, the type of problems which affect the greater mass of mankind.

It is evident that, in large measure, the kind of environmental problems that are of importance in developing countries are those that should be overcome in the process of development itself. In the more industrialised countries, it is appropriate to view development as the major cause of the environmental problems. Badly planned and unregulated development can have a similar result in the developing countries.

However, developing countries must view the relationship between development and environment from a different perspective. In their context, development becomes essentially a cure for major environmental problems. For these reasons, concern for the environment must not and need not detract from the commitment of the world's more industrialised nations to the task of assisting the development of the less developed regions of the world. Although it may be argued that the concern with human environment in developing countries can only reinforce the commitment to development, it should also serve, to provide new dimensions to the concept of development itself. In the past, there has been a tendency to equate the development goal with the more narrowly conceived objective of economic growth as measured by the rise in gross national product. It is usually recognised today that high rates of economic growth, necessary and essential as they are, do not by themselves guarantee that urgent social and human problems will be solved or even lessened.

Indeed, in many countries, high growth rates have been accompanied by increasing unemployment, rising disparities in incomes between groups and regions and the deterioration of social and cultural conditions. As a consequence, new emphasis is being placed on the attainment of social and cultural goals as part of the development process. The recognition of environmental issues in developing countries is an aspect of this broadening of the development concept. It is part of a more integrated or unified approach to the development objective.

Whilst the environmental problems of developing countries are in large measure those that have arisen from the lack of development, it is true that problems arising out of the process of development are equally in evidence in these countries to the extent that the safety of the environment depends on their relative levels of development. As the process of development gets underway, the latter type of problems is likely to assume increasing importance. The process of agricultural growth and transformation, for example, will involve the construction of reservoirs and irrigation systems, the clearing of forests, the use of fertilisers and pesticides and the establishment of new roads and communities. These processes will certainly have environmental implications.

Similarly, industrialisation will result in the release of pollutants that will react on the environment in a number of ways. Urbanisation is already a pressing problem for many developing countries and some cities are experiencing problems similar to those of industrialised countries. In addition, with the urgent need for the rural areas to sustain a growing population, the problem of the rural environment assumes a new significance. The problems are already severe in developing countries. But with the lack of relevant educative information and resolute action, they will tend to attain formidable dimensions in the decades ahead.

The very growth of population, when not accompanied by adequate economic development, emphasises the seriousness of rising unemployment: by further impoverishing the countryside and swelling rural-urban migration, human problems of the deepest intensity are created. These can only aggravate the serious social and political tensions that even now prevail in these societies. There can indeed be little doubt about the urgent need for corrective action.

Some of the advanced environmental consequences of the development process could be avoided by better planning and regulation as we will see in the last sections of this chapter. However, it suffices to point out at this juncture that in some fields, environmental issues open up new possibilities for developing countries. The structural changes in production and trade as well as the geographical relocation of productive enterprises which might be necessitated by environmental considerations, should provide new opportunities for meeting some of the developmental needs of the developing nations.

Among such structural changes, we can mention first of all the switch in balance between natural and synthetic products and the re-opening of certain markets to the export of natural products. In some cases, developing countries may be able to increase the inflow of foreign capital and create new industries. If such opportunities are to be fully realised, they will require new and concerted measures on the part of developed and developing countries in the field of international trade and investment. The desire to redress some of the past damage to the environment and to minimise the environmental cost of future development will, in most cases, represent a new claim on productive resources and an additional element in the cost of production. Some of this burden may be reduced in the future as science and technology respond to the needs of environmental management.

Still, one of the major questions which arises from the increased concern with the preservation of the environment, is how the higher cost of future development should be shared between developed and developing countries. There are

191

misgivings in the developing countries that, given their peripheral role in the international economy, they may not be able to take full advantage of opportunities arising from environmental control, while at the same time they may have to bear a disproportional part of the extra burden which such control would entail.

The increased cost burden to developing nations should be accompanied by a greater willingness, on the part of developed nations, to provide additional assistance. On the other hand, nations should endeavour to rectify the inefficient allocation of productive resources arising from indiscriminate protection of agriculture and industry. Whatever is done should in any case provide fresh arguments for more efficient protection of the environment.

## 1. A Specific Environmental Issue in the Development Process

The preceding section has indicated that the environmental problems of developing countries fall broadly into two categories - the problems arising out of poverty (or the inadequacy of development itself), and the problems that arise out of the very process of development. The problems in the first category are reflected in the poor social and economic conditions that prevail in both urban and rural areas of developing countries. For most developing countries these problems are of greatest importance. But as the process of development gets underway, the problems that emerge from it begin to gain significance.

The environmental policies of developing countries must naturally be oriented towards both categories of problems. However, as already noted, the remedial approaches to the first set of problems are closely interwoven with policies for overall development. Problems of poor water supplies, inadequate sewerage, sickness, nutritional deficiency and bad housing need to be considered in the process of planning and policy making.

Goals and objectives in these areas should be incorporated into development plans along with targets for the growth of output. This is because the basic problems to be solved are so much a part of social and economic conditions in developing countries that their treatment is but one aspect of the whole approach to social and economic development. Each country needs to identify, in its own circumstances, the complementari-ties and conflicts that characterise the relationship between its social and economic goals, and to determine its own priorities concerning the allocation of resources.

This section will therefore seek to do no more than draw attention to:

- the urgent environmental problems that arise out of poverty;
- the need for a new awareness of the importance of remedial measures, and above all;
- the need for reinforcing the commitment, both nationally and internationally, to the objective of development itself.

We hope that the emphasis now being given to a more unified approach to development will result in a greater recognition and a more efficient treatment of the environmental problems that arise out of mass poverty.

Therefore, this section attempts in a broad way, to identify some of the negative side effects that can arise out of the process of development in several sectors of the economy. In presenting a selected catalogue of environmental consequences which may be experienced, the aim is to bring together some of the available knowledge on this subject so that the developing countries can draw their own conclusions in the context of their development policies.

In particular, this section will describe the process of development in agriculture, industry, transport and human settlement. The side effects of development in those areas take several forms and may be grouped into a number of categories. These are:

- Resource deterioration: This includes the deterioration of mineral, soil or forest resources.

- Biological pollution: The pollution represented by agents of human disease and by animal and plant pests.

- Chemical pollution: This may arise out of air pollutants, industrial effluents, pesticides, metals and detergent components and similar agents.

- Physical disruptions: This may be represented, for example, by thermal pollution, silting and noise.

- Social disruption: Of which congestion and loss of sense of community are examples.

These side effects manifest themselves in varying degrees depending on the sectors concerned, the particular geographical region involved, and the stage of development attained by different countries. The first two categories are commonly experienced by most developing countries. So are silting and perhaps social disruption. Urban air pollution is becoming a problem of increasing importance in the larger cities of certain developing countries.

Since these side effects are likely to manifest themselves in the process of development, they need to be assessed within a framework which helps to establish their relative importance. Basic consideration should be given to the way in which development activities relates to the carrying capacity of a country's natural and social system. Within an appropriate framework, a country may ascertain the nature of its environmental problems and examine alternative forms of action in dealing with environmental policies.

Environmental side effects which are encountered in the development of various sectors should receive selective treatment

They should first be evaluated in terms of the development priorities which guide the planning considerations of any country. Those side effects which directly frustrate the development objectives should be given the most immediate attention for remedial action:

**Agriculture**
The process of agricultural development often involves the transformation of low productivity systems of agriculture into systems where productivity is relatively high. In the course of this transformation, cultivation practices on existing land are improved, the infrastructure of facilities and services for agricultural production is expanded and new land brought under cultivation through extensive systems of irrigation and river basin development. These changes are crucial to the development process itself. But they may also generate environmental side effects of varying degrees of importance. Some of the most common of these side effects are felt in both traditional and modern agriculture.

## (a) Traditional Agriculture

Environmental side effects may manifest themselves even within the framework of traditional systems of agriculture under the pressure of rapid population growth. These systems have often persisted for centuries, sometimes successfully cultivating the same lands without irreversible damage. But a new situation may be created by the current rapid growth of population. This may impose pressures that were perhaps never experienced before and which could engender environmental problems.

Traditional agriculture, in many tropical regions, is characterised, particularly under stress of expansion, by a range of environmental hazards which include:

- leaching; notably the rapid leaching of nutrients and degradation of planted farmland following the removal of forests;
- rapid soil depletion resulting from permanent cultivation of relatively infertile soils without the addition of nutrients;
- soil erosion through variable and heavy rainfalls and prolonged droughts or flash floods; and
- indiscriminate loss of forest resources through slash and burn techniques of cultivation.

Although much of the environmental deterioration mentioned above can be corrected if unlimited funds are available, some are so costly to correct that they are effectively irreversible. The fragility of tropical ecosystems may cause environmental deterioration to proceed rapidly and to recover slowly.

There are opportunities for preventing some of these environmental hazards through proper planning and anticipatory action. For instance, the under and unemployed labour that frequently abounds in rural areas may be mobilised in terracing and reforestation programmes. Many of Africa's current marginal lands, for example, have all the necessary elements for successful reclamation through new management techniques.

### (b) Modern (mechanised) Agriculture

In the case of modern agriculture, the environmental hazards that arise are mainly due to the chemical control of weeds and pests and from irrigation works.

- fertilisers, on one hand, do not at present or in the near future, appear to pose a serious threat in the developing countries.
- the side effects of insecticides and pesticides need to be watched fairly carefully. Their toxicity to fish and birds, as well as their persistence and mobility, make them a hazard beyond their target area.
- irrigation projects unless matched by drainage facilities, can result in salination and water-logging.
- constant tillage, facilitated by mechanisation, can also damage the soil structure.

It should be reiterated that modern agriculture would be impossible without the use of chemical fertilisers and pesticides, yielding varieties of seeds and irrigation works, and some degree of mechanisation. However, it is important that the side effects of these practices be taken into account while planning and implementing the use of these inputs.

**Industry**

The pollution emanating from industrial development represents more of a potential than of an actual threat at the stage of development existing in many developing countries. However, there are a number of isolated cases of actual industrial pollution already. With regard to pollution, developing countries have an advantage in so far as they can learn from the experience of the developed nations.

By taking sensible decisions on the location of industries and their waste disposal, and by instituting social controls under which the private sector must function, some of the worst environmental problems that have arisen in connection with industrial pollution can be avoided. Developing countries should give careful consideration to the question of local industries and formulate concrete guidelines in the context of their own national situations which would prevent the rise of major environmental problems. Identifying cases where labour intensive technology may produce less environmental disruptions would also be useful.

In the African context, technology gives rise to industrial proliferation whose goals reside in the fulfillment of human purpose. Technology, is therefore strongly influenced by varied social forces; for example, in a country like Kenya, social provision of services and amenities is a priority. On the other hand in most developed countries machines come first. Just as it can be argued that the work of a scientist is very subjective, determined by a variety of personal and professional values, it would be valid to argue that technology with its resultant industrial growth, is even more strongly influenced by the social context in which it develops. In other words, scientific and technological innovations not only cause change but they are also a response to change.

Though technology is meant to improve the living standards of a society, it may and does have a negative impact on the society and environment in which it is implemented. It has been well articulated in various fora that, the technology we use is polluting our environment in many ways; for instance, factories discharge effluents, sometimes obnoxious and always offensive, into rivers, the sea and the atmosphere.

Similarly, in the process of mining (whether coal, iron, or gold), quarries are often left open thereby restricting land use and reducing the aesthetic value of the environment. Quarries should be filled and trees planted to restore the environment to its original beauty. This is evident in countries such as Zambia, Angola and South Africa. In Kenya, as early as in 1985, there were debates and controversies recorded in daily newspapers with regard to the disposal of industrial products in the production of pesticides and fertilisers.

Lack of proper planning for the disposal of industrial waste leads to the problem of bionondegradables, such as plastics, which cannot be easily disposed of. The point here is that the issues of industrialisation are not only technical but are underpinned by social factors. There is fear that if societal needs in developing countries are not considered during industrialisation, one of the consequences will be the bitter experience of acid rain which has become a significant problem in developed countries.

A further point which has particular relevance for Kenya's future industrialisation is the need for a critical analysis of indigenous (traditional) technologies. It can be argued that although the great majority of Kenyans, especially those in the rural areas, are served in some ways by modern technology, their lives are sustained through the skills and techniques of indigenous traditional technology. Such technologies are still widely used on building construction, pottery work, textile weaving, leatherwork, the production of cooking pots and implements, crop storage and preservation , woodwork and iron smeltings.

Although those traditional technologies have over the years remained more or less static, they are still culturally important and should therefore influence Kenyan technology and industrialisation.

A number of desirable characteristics of traditional technology still persists. In general, African technology and industrialisation was identified by the role it played in survival hence it may be referred to as survival technology. Whenever technological activities were undertaken, they were not intended for 'mass production . Instead, they were strictly a response to a need of the time. This characteristic could perhaps be explained in terms of the abundance of resources found in Africa. Thus, there was no urgency for mass production because it was possible to get what one wanted locally when it was required. Today, however, things are quite different. Clearly, the styles and techniques of survival, and hence survival technologies, encouraged certain characteristic skills. It can be seen that since these technologies were need-generated, they encouraged the development of skills and ingenuity in selecting and improvising what could best satisfy people's needs. In contrast with theoretical models of technology, African technology (and specifically Kenyan technology) was craft-based, drawing its materials from the surrounding.

Traditional technology was also characterised by its respect for certain values, specifically those pertaining to specific aspects of the Kenyan culture. However, it lacked a strong knowledge base, which would have been necessary for the improvement of subsequent designs. Designs too were always implicit in the sense of existing solely in the people's minds; they could be handed down to the next generation only through emulation and repetition.

The use of unimproved indigenous technology as a model for modern Kenyan technology cannot suffice because it appears to be incompatible with current aspirations regarding Kenya's development. At the same time, because of its harmony with traditional Kenyan culture, its use raises questions about whether or not there is an inevitable cultural discontinuity between traditional and modern technology.

A similar trend is true of transferred technology and technology in the informal sector. Transferred technology leaves the design characteristics used in the country of origin, 'hidden', thus making it impossible for the recipients to modify or adapt those technologies to suit the new conditions under which they are required to work (this prevents imitation or even adaptation which would result in 'mistransplant). Work has to be done with predetermined blue-prints and workers are simply operators who neither understand the total operations of the plant nor the suitability of the equipment and the materials used. Workers learn how but not why things are done the way they are done. This could be referred to as 'assembly-line' technology.

On the other hand, transferred technology does allow one to develop the ability to operate different kinds of machinery and tools; through this expansion of their skills they are enabled to identify aspects of such machinery and tools which could be replaced by indigenous parts or materials. In car manufacture, for example, operators may learn how different parts fit together and how machines perform such operations.

Similarly, in textile factories, although the design and colour mixture may be pre-determined, the process of producing the design and colouring could still be learnt. Transferred technology therefore leaves some valuable skills and knowledge which could be incorporated into the Kenyan technology particularly if it is carefully investigated; on its own, however, it is inadequate for the developmental needs of Kenya.

Technology in the informal sector (popularly known as *Jua Kali*) exists within dynamic small-scale Industries and is concerned with meeting the needs of the majority of rural and urban low-income Kenyans. The artisans improvise almost everything with waste material obtained mainly from large industries. *Jua Kali* activities depend on-the improvisation and use of simple tools (even obsolete ones), identification of materials and their uses, and modification of techniques. From these activities, certain basic skills are developed.

The knowledge and designs inherited from traditional technologies, however, remains 'tacit' (in the minds of the operators) and are only realised in the artifacts produced. The major problems of this 'improvised' technology include lack of consistency in the methods used, lack of experimental testing on the performance of things made and lack of plans to explore and improve the artifacts for better performance.

Indeed, informal sector technology relies too often on trial and error methods. Besides, operators turn their hands to too many different skills; there is little specialisation if any. In general, technology in the informal sector is characterised by its versatility and its emphasis on repair and improvisation.

The development of a technology should aim much beyond the production of a Kenyan Car or the development of a drug such as KEMRON. Clearly for instance, the development of a Kenyan Car would call for innovations in the design, fuel used, the suspension, engine and the cooling system. Transferring or even adapting existing technologies would not produce such a Kenyan Car. Kenyan technology can and should be understood as need-generated and problem-based. It must focus on identifying and finding solutions to the problems of energy, agriculture, drought, water-supply and health which afflict the lives of the majority of Kenyans. In the process, careful observations and interpretations must be made with regard to the significance of our cultural values while maintaining the goals of 'survival technologies'.

Second, a Kenyan technology must create an awareness of indigenous skills and techniques and aim to use, improve and develop these by incorporating them in the process of designing, making and experimentally testing crucial components.

Third, an important quality of Kenyan technology is its flexibility, especially in the materials, tools and techniques used; it is also characterised by improvisation, re-use and adaptation skills. Both identification and careful use of available materials are vital.

Finally, a necessary component of Kenyan technology would be a determination to pursue the 'unknown' through careful investigation of the local environment, while seeking new or alternative ways of solving any given problem. The invention of new approaches and the discovery of alternatives are of great concern to Kenyan technology.

**Transport Systems**
A basic choice in the field of transportation is between systems that provide mass transportation and the owner-operated vehicle. In the United States, and increasingly in

Western Europe, Japan and some developing countries such as Kenya, the choice of the motor vehicle as the primary means of personal transport is now resulting in critical environmental consequences: air pollution with damage to people, vegetation and landscape, increased accidents, pressure on urban space (as is the case now in Nairobi) and a distorted configuration of human settlements.

There is a clear choice. In the developing countries, some of these environmental problems can be avoided by providing efficient communal means of transportation. The need for owner-operated vehicles is then reduced. This is in any case dictated by a country's own level of development and the need to reduce disparities among various income groups.

## Human Settlements

### (a) Rural Areas

The majority of the population in most developing countries still live in the rural areas. In Kenya, this is estimated at about 80 per cent. Often, these communities suffer from an inadequacy of services of one kind or another. Problems associated with health, nutrition, potable water supplies and drainage are often severely felt in rural areas no less than in towns.

An inadequate infrastructure of agricultural and credit services is also a familiar feature of the rural scene, contributing to the persistence of low levels of production and hence of incomes. The stress of rapid population growth can, in certain situations, aggravate these problems and impose further strains on rural resources.

In such situations, there is a migration of the population to the towns which in turn causes a further worsening of urban conditions. A pre-occupation with growing urban problems could result in a further neglect of rural areas. Modern social, cultural and economic activities capable of attracting educated youth may not exist in the rural areas and this could itself be a contributory factor to growing urban concentration and unemployment. Moreover, the process of rural-urban interaction can result in the disruption of traditional systems of social security (i.e. the extended family) without the provision of suitable substitutes.

It is of utmost importance that the planning process takes these problems into account. Given the rapid population growth, developing countries are likely to face an increasingly urgent problem of employment creation. It is, however, unlikely that the expansion of economic activities in these regions through industrialisation and related developments alone, will suffice to provide employment opportunities for the increased numbers in the workforce.

A substantial part of the increased workforce will need to remain in the countryside, and it is therefore vital that not only employment opportunities be created in rural areas, but also that the whole structure of social and economic services in these areas be developed. This places a new emphasis on rural environment and on planning and policy making in this field. In Kenya, the Government tackles this aspect of planning and policy formulation through the District Development Committees existing throughout the countryside.

### (b) Urban Areas

As has already been mentioned in the previous section, environmental quality is virtually synonymous with social welfare in the urban areas of the developing countries. Urbanisation within a country can, of course, be accompanied by increased economic and social welfare systems while the urban concentration of dynamic enterprises can function usefully as development poles, generating growth throughout wider regions.

However, the carrying capacity of any city submitted to rapid population growth will eventually become over-extended, and when this occurs, economies of size are displaced by diseconomies of inadequate infrastructure. Disease, water supply shortages, lack of sewage treatment, congestion and deteriorating housing are all clear manifestations of environmental stress. More developed urban areas are now confronted with chemical contamination of air and water and the hazards of social disorganisation.

Urban renewal projects such as those in the industrialised countries are one line of attack. Often, however, such projects merely displace the slum population to new slums while more well-to-do people move into the renewed areas.

Another line of attack is urban dispersal, contingent upon planned allocation of new growth poles in conjuction with newly established industries and new urban settlements. Such planning is already underway in many developing countries. Less capital intensive renewal schemes, and especially those which draw upon abundant labour, should be accorded a very high priority.

**River Basin Development**
River basin development projects are instruments of major importance for economic and social development, and are often an essential part of development programmes. However, many environmental problems which are commonly discussed have arisen in connection with the construction of these projects. This fact underlines the need for careful study and

analysis in the design of large dams or the choice of dam sites, so that negative side effects can be minimised through proper planning.

Some of the environmental problems which are generally associated with river basin development projects include: the spawning of waterborne diseases; the filling of reservoirs with sedimentation; the drying up of downstream fisheries; the spread of salinisation and water-logging in areas associated with irrigation projects; the inundation of valuable agricultural and forestry land; the displacement of population; and the loss of mineral resources, wildlife areas or valuable historical sites.

The emergence of most of these adverse effects is generally gradual. Some of them can be readily corrected but others are virtually irreversible because the capital investment is very large and fixed. Some of the consequences can be on a very large scale and may even be such as to frustrate the purpose of the development project itself. However, many of them can be anticipated by preliminary analysis.

## 2. Some Considerations for Environmental Policy Formulation

This section is devoted to discussing a number of considerations which are relevant in formulating environmental policies in developing countries. In describing these, it should be pointed out that no general guidelines or specific formulas can be prescribed at this uncertain stage of our knowledge regarding the interaction of environmental and developmental policies. Each country must find its own solutions in the light of its own problems and within the framework of its own political, social and cultural values. The formulation of environmental goals, and indeed the formulation of economic and social policies in general, falls entirely and exclusively within the sovereign competence of each developing country.

The importance of integrating environmental policies with development planning and regarding them as part of the overall framework of economic and social planning, should be of top priority. As stressed earlier in the chapter, environmental concern is only one dimension of the problem of development in the developing countries. It cannot be viewed separately from development efforts. The objective should be to regard environmental improvement as one of the multiple goals in a development plan.

Developing countries have certain inherent advantages in integrating environmental and developmental policies. Most are already committed to planning so that the imposition or acceptance of social controls is nothing new. They are also making a fresh start in many fields and can anticipate environmental effects and provide for them in their current planning. The overriding constraint in developing countries is, of course, limited resources; this constraint poses fairly sharp restrictions on the choice between various objectives.

Since environmental improvement can be regarded only as one of the multiple objectives of development plans, its priority in relation to other objectives should be determined by each society in the light of its own economic and social problems and in accordance with its stage of development. Essentially, this is a question of deciding on alternative uses of resources within the framework of comprehensive economic and social planning.

The integration of environmental concern in development planning will require national action on a fairly broad front by developing countries. Some of the major policy areas will include: location of industries, land use policy, urban-rural interaction and community development. Greater attention should also be paid to the physical planning of facilities so that individual development projects and programmes can be integrated into the overall physical environment.

In order to formulate environmental policies, the developing countries require considerably more information and knowledge than they currently possess. One of the first priorities should be to broaden the availability of environmental information. It would be useful if developing countries were to undertake a survey of the present state of their environments and the major hazards to which these are exposed.

Studies and research to define the kind of environmental problems that are likely to arise in the process of development over the course of the next two decades and beyond should also be undertaken. It would also be useful to compile all existing legislation regarding environmental control including the regulations dealing with urban zoning, location of industries and protection of natural resources.

This accumulation of information and knowledge should provide developing countries with a clearer perspective of their environmental problems and of the corrective action that may be required at different stages of development. Since public participation in any such programme is vital, efforts should be made to build environmental concerns into education curricula, and to disseminate appropriate information to the general public through the mass media.

Once developing countries have integrated the environmental concern in their framework of development planning and undertaken studies of specific policy action required at the national level, concrete institutional arrangements would be needed to implement policies of environmental control. A few of the institutional arrangements that developing countries can consider include:

• establishing a separate ministry or department to deal with environmental control.

• setting-up environmental standards and indicators and monitoring these by specific institutions.

• establishing environmental, technological and locational assessment boards.

• establishing specific legislation to determine norms for the maintenance of clean air and clean water.

## Conclusion

In summary, it should be re-stated that the aim of this chapter has been to provide an overall framework within which the developing countries can consider their own specific national action for environmental control. As was pointed out at the beginning, no general guidelines or specific prescriptions are possible, or even desirable, at the moment.

As the basis of national action is so much rooted in the varied conditions within each country, the scope of this chapter was limited to highlighting certain overall considerations rather than attempting to prescribe any specific policies.

## Questions

1. The socio-economic development of mankind has created our current environmental problems. Discuss.

2. Critically discuss some of the specific environmental issues relating to the development process.

3. Discuss some considerations for environmental policy formulation particularly for developing countries.

4. What are the main environmental policies for developing countries?

5. Is it feasible for Kenya to evolve her own technology? What should be the main features of such a technology?

## Bibliography

Ahmed, Y.J. *Environmental Decision Making*, (London: Hodder and Stoughton, 1984).

Bolin, B. "The Carbon Cycle" in Boblin, B. and Cook, R.D. (eds) *The Major Biogeachemical Cycles and Their Interactions, Scope Report, No. 21*, (New York: John Wiley and Sons 1983).

Carson, B. Environmental Education: Principles and Practices, (London: Edward Arnold, 1978).

Cavaseno, V. (ed). *Industrial Air Pollution Engineering*, (New York: McGraw-Hill, 1980).

Creekmore, C. "Climate Change" in UNEP *News Africa,* (Nairobi: UNEP, 1988).

Crump, A. "A Lot of Hot Air Over the Ice Continent". *Daily Nation,* Nairobi, Kenya, April, 2 1988 .

Darst, G.B. "Protective Layer of Ozone is Shrinking" *Sunday Nation,* Nairobi Kenya, October 26, 1986 .

Desmann, R.F. *Environmental Conservation,* (New York: John Wiley and Sons, 1959).

Devins, D.W. *Energy: Its Physical Impact on the Environment,* (New York: John Wiley and Sons, 1982).

Dix, H. Environmental Pollution: Atmosphere, Land, Water and Noise, (New York: Wiley, 1981).

C. Enrique, I. "Developing and the Human Environment". A Paper Presented in Switzerland from June 4 - 12,1971.

Evans, L. *Environmental Control of Plant Growth.* Proceedings of a Symposium held at Canberra, Australia in August 1962, (New York: Academic Press, 1963).

Fearnside, P.M. "Deforestation in the Brazilian Amazon: How Far is it Occurring". *Interciencia* (1982) 7 (pp. 82 - 88);

Gadd, P. *The Ecology of Urbanisation and Industrialization,* (Lohaon: Macmillan Education Ltd., 1976).

Gourdie, A. *Environmental Change,* (Massachussets: Oxford University Press, 1977).

Hamilton, A. Environmental History of East Africa: A Study of the Quartenary, (London: Academic Press, 1982).

Hines, L.G. *Environmental: Pollution and Economics,* (New York: W.W. Norton and Co., 1973).

Hodges, L. *Environmental Pollution,* (New York: Hoit Rinehart and Winston, 1977).

Holgate, M.W. *Perspectives of Environmental Pollution*, (London: Cambridge University Press, 1979).

Holum, J.R. *Topics and Terms in Environmental Problems*, (New York: John Wiley and Sons, 1977).

Hugh, W.J., *The Environmental Challenges*, (New York: Holt Rinehart and Winston, 1974).

Hudges, E.D. *Environmental Education : Key Issues of the Future*. Proceedings of Conference held at the College of Technology. (New York: Pergamon Press, 1977).

E. Johnson, K. "Looking Ahead to the Greenhouse After Ozone Agreement Reached", *Nature*, September, 1987, P. 329.

F. Joyce, C. and Mackenzie, D. "Hot Air Threatens Ozone in Montreal" *New Scientist*, (1987).

Kapp-William, G. K. "Implementation of Environmental Policies", A Paper Presented in Switzerland from June 4 - 12, 1971.

Kenyatta University, Environmental Education Workshop on Environmental Training in Africa, Dakar and Paris: UNESCO, (1980).

Korir-Koech, M. "Environment and People: Problems and Consequences, Focusing on the Protection of the Ozone Layer from Chemical Damage", in the Proceedings of the Second Annual General Conference on *The Role of Physics in National Development,* 28th - 30th September, 1988, University of Nairobi, Chiromo Campus, Kenya.

Kuling, J. "Environmental Policies for the Developing Countries and their Development Strategy", A Paper Presented in Switzerland, from 4 - 12 June, 1971.

Lamb, R. (ed.). The Human Environment: Action or Disaster? (Dublin: UNEP, 1983).

Lincoln, A. Environmental Planning: Political Philosophical Analysis, (London: Alien and Unwin, 1975).

Masagate, A. "Is the Depletion of the Ozone Layer a Scare or a Joke," *The Kenya Times*, Nairobi, Kenya, June, 1988.

Morghan, R.F. *Enviornmental Biology*, (Oxford: Pergamon Press, 1963).

Myers, C.B. *The Environmental Crisis: Will We Survive!* (New York: Prentice-Hall, 1976).

Newmann, J.L. Environmental Education and Risk Adjustments in Eastern Africa, (Syracuse: Syracuse University, 1969).

Almeida Ozorio, L. "Economic Development and The Preservation of Environment", A Paper Presented in Switzerland, June 4th - 12th, 1971.

Pittock, B. *Environmental Consequences of Nuclear War*, (New York: John Wiley and Sons,1986).

Postel, S.L. "Atmospheric Warm-Up", Environmental Science and Technology, *America Chemical Society*, (1986) Pp. 12.

Sachs, I.N. "Environmental Quality, Management and Development Planning: Some Suggestions for Action", A Paper Presented in Switzerland, June 4th- 12th, 1971.

Singer, S.F. *Global Effects of Environmental Pollution*, (New York: Springer Verlang, 1970).

Singh, J.J. Environment and Climatic Impact of Coal Utilization, (New York: Academic Press, 1980).

Southwick, C.H. (ed.), "The Study in Belief", in *Global Ecology*, (Massachusetts: Sinaver Associates Inc, 1985) pp. 48 - 49.

Swan, J.A. Environmental Education: Strategies Towards a More Livable Future, (New York: Sage Publications, 1974).

Tolba, M.K. *Sustainable Development*, (London: Butterworths, 1987).

Toufexix, A.P. "Our Filthy Seas", in *Times Magazine*, August 1 1988, p. 44.

United Nations, Environment and Development in Africa: A Study by the Environmental Development Action {ENDA) for the United Environmental Programme, (Oxford: Pergamon Press, 1981).

UNEP, The State of the World Environment, (Nairobi: UNEP, 1987).

_____, Vienna Convention for the Protection of Ozone, (Nairobi: UNEP, 1985).

UNESCO, Regional Training Workshop on Environmental Training in Africa, (Paris: UNESCO, 1978).

UNESCO - UNEP, *Glossary of Environmental Education Terms,* International Environmental Education Programme (1987)

Utton, A.E. Environmental Policy Concepts and International Implications, (New York: Praeger Press, 1973).

Vesilind, P.A. *Environmental Pollution and Control,* (Boston: Butterworth, 1983).

Westmann, W.E. Ecology, Impact, Assessment and Environmental Planning, (New York: John Wiley and Sons, 1985).

World Bank, *Environment and Development*, (Washington, D.C: World Bank, 1975).

Young, A. An Environmental Data for Agroforestry, (Nairobi: KRAF, 1985).

# -9-

# Industrial Pollution and its Effects on the Environment

N.T. Muthiani

## Introduction

*Pollution* may be regarded as the contamination of resources or materials so that they become unsuitable for their intended use. Waste from people and animals pollute water. Air can become polluted from smoke, dust and automobile exhaust gases. Pollution can therefore be viewed as any interference that prevents the beneficial use of air, water, land, plants or animals. In a more comprehensive way, pollution may be regarded as any direct or indirect alteration of the physical, thermal, biological or radioactive properties of the environment that creates an actual or potential hazard to the health, safety or welfare of any living species.

According to this last definition, pollution consists of inserting foreign matter in the wrong place and in quantities that are too large. In the right place and in the right quantity, a given substance may be beneficial: fertilisers are beneficial in a farmer's field but not in a lake where they will promote the growth of water weeds and algae which reduce the commercial, domestic and aesthetic value of the water. The construction of roads, power lines, telephone lines, dams, the establishment of large-scale agricultural development, mining etc, invariably cause disruption of the environment to varying degrees. This may lead to pollution of the environment unless corrective measures are incorporated in the project implementation process.

## 1. The Roots of Environmental Pollution

Early man spent his entire existence surviving. The provision of food and shelter for the family took all of his time. Indeed, until the 16th century, man was still not very proficient in producing food or controlling disease; as a result of this, famines and plagues held the growth of population in check. But with the industrial revolution and the birth of modern medicine, the world population began to climb rapidly as can be seen in fig. 9.1.

The Earth is now crowded with people and all of them consume resources and create waste. The waste must be returned to the Earth in some form, and often this process destroys or alters the ecology. Over-population is not, however, the only danger. In economically and technologically advanced countries, consumption of both manufactured goods and natural resources has increased tremendously within the last few decades.

In fact, the problem in many countries today is that of over-consumption; wasteful use of resources is responsible for 90 per cent of the world's consumption while population growth account for only about one-tenth of the increase in the use of natural resources and the resultant pollution of the environment. The spiral of consumption seems to have no end except when we finally run out of resources. It may be safely stated that the root of environmental pollution problems is a combination of the tremendous resource in human population amplified by an even greater increase in per capita consumption of raw materials, processed goods and services.

In the previous chapters of this book, it has been made clear that the term *environment* refers to the conditions and forces that surround and influence living and non-living things.

**Fig. 9.1 The World's Population Over the Years**

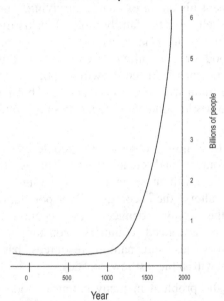

The biotic environment is made up of plants, animals and cultural and social surroundings. The abiotic or non-living environment is composed of: soil, water, air radiation, temperature, living space, built up areas, and man-made structures.

**219**

Industrial pollution of the environment may be sub-divided into:

* air pollution;
* water pollution;
* soil pollution;
* noise pollution.

Though these pollutions have already been discussed in a general way, we will find it useful to look at them once more in their connection with the development of industrialisation.

## 2. Some Effects of Atmospheric Pollution

The atmospheric pollutants emitted by industries into the air are either gaseous or particulates. Particulates consist of fine solids or liquid droplets suspended in the air. The larger size particulates are grit, fly ash, dust and soot; the smaller sizes are smoke, mist and aerosols.

Specific particulate size determines the behaviour of pollutants and the time they are in suspension in the atmosphere.

Larger solid particulates with a diameter of over $50\mu m$ ($\frac{1}{2000}$ m) are collectively visible in the air and fall out or settle fairly fast so that they do not become a long term pollution hazard. They, however, often produce ground pollution because the larger sizes over $10\mu m$ ($\frac{1}{10,000}$ m) diameter are deposited near the point of emission. Consequently, stone and clay quarries, as well as cement and brick works, often cause despoliation of the surrounding land. Particles of the size ranging from $55\mu m$ $0.01\mu m$ are of greater significance in air pollution; these are not easily visible. They

220

can remain in the atmosphere for varying lengths of time and undergo various chemical transformation to produce secondary pollutants.

Particles below a diameter of 10µm are able to act as nuclei for the formation of condensation of water droplets in cloud formation. They may then be washed out of the air by precipitation within a few days of their emission. The smaller particulate solids and gases can remain suspended in the atmosphere for days, weeks, months or even years especially in the upper reaches of the atmosphere, that is, the stratosphere and the mesophere.

The high concentration of particles in the atmosphere over large urban and industrial areas can increase smoke and fumes and consequently atmospheric turbidity. This leads to a reduction of the amount of solar radiation reaching the ground. Solid particles are an element of cloud formation and so urban pollution and increased water vapour emission can produce up to about 10 per cent increased cloud cover, up to 10 per cent more wet days and increased mist, fog and smog. All of these processes combine to increase the deposits of large sized particles on the ground. With the passing of time, these deposits can cause the erosion, corrosion of building materials and metals and destruction of plant life. We will soon discuss these effects more thoroughly.

### 3.  Effects on the Atmosphere and on Built-up Areas

Chemical substances discharged into the atmosphere undergo chemical changes in the presence of water, oxygen and ultraviolet solar energy to form intermediate or secondary products. The overall effect of air pollution upon the biosphere and man-made environment has the greatest impact on buildings and materials, the soil and vegetation including crops, and animal life and people.

### Effects on Buildings

The fabric of buildings exposed for years to heavily polluted air undergoes chemical changes. Gradual corrosion takes place and this becomes evident when the outer surface starts peeling off. There are many examples of the corrosion and erosion of monuments which have become quite unrecognisable over a period of hundreds of years. The process is more rapid on softer stone surfaces exposed to the combined effect of chemical pollution, wind, rain and suspended dust and grit particles.

Gaseous pollutants such as sulphur dioxide ($SO_2$), carbon dioxide ($CO_2$), hydrogen sulphide ($H_2S$) and fluorides, together with rain and solar radiation attack the surfaces of buildings, particularly those made of limestone and sandstone. Sulphur dioxide is converted into dilute sulphuric acid which acts on calcium and magnesium carbonates (limestone) to form sulphates. Eventually, these form a hard surface which blisters and then peels off.

In sandstone, the calcite cement is attacked by sulphuric acid which loosens the sand grains; these are then washed away by the combined action of wind and rain. Stone erosion is also increased by carbon dioxide, which dissolves in rain to form weak carbonic acid; this attacks stone to form soluble calcium and magnesium hydrogen carbonates.

Metal surfaces are also attacked by atmospheric pollutants and may undergo corrosion. The surface of iron and steel in the presence of moisture and oxygen changes into hydrated iron oxide commonly known as rust. The process is aided by sulphur dioxide and carbon dioxide, water and oxygen.

Natural oxidation and corrosion of metallic surfaces occurs in unpolluted air, but the effect is hastened and increased by pollution.

### Effects on Plants

Natural materials such as cotton, wool and linen made into dyed fabrics are also affected by pollutants. Sulphur dioxide dissolved in water droplets forms sulphurous acid which can bleach or reduce the chemical dye used in these materials. The action is accelerated by ozone, and if dilute sulphuric acid is also present, the fabrics will eventually rot and disintegrate.

Plastic materials are more resistant to pollution but some polymers do crack and become brittle. Leather and rubber also absorb sulphurous acid and are affected by ozone, resulting in their deterioration over time. Hydrogen sulphide ($H_2S$) often present in polluted air, affects some paints which contain basic lead carbonate pigment, so that they become discoloured when lead sulphide is formed. Other pollutants also affect paints causing it to crack and peel.

When gases like sulphur dioxide, carbon dioxide, nitrogen dioxide and hydrogen sulphide are in combination with various particles deposited on the soil, they can affect plants. Precipitation containing sulphur dioxide, together with other acidic gases, tends to lower the pH balance of the soil causing it to become acidic.

Similarly, the emission of heavy metallic compounds such as lead and mercury in localised industrial areas, causes toxic concentrations in the soil. Where this toxicity occurs, the range of plant species that can grow is severely restricted. Some species of plants are very sensitive to small amounts of toxicity which inhibit the action of some plant enzymes. Particles such as soot and dust are deposited on the leaves and block the stomata or pores of the plants. This restricts the absorption of carbon dioxide and reduces the rate of photosynthesis; it also restricts the loss of water vapour and the transpiration rate. Both of these physiological effects stunt the growth of plants and reduce the yield of food crops and cash crops.

**Effects on People**

The general and most widespread effects of air pollution on people are caused by smoke and sulphur dioxide gas. These two pollutants are found in high concentrations when smog and temperature inversion conditions exist. For example, in London between December 5th and 9th 1952, heavy continuous smog conditions caused an estimated 4,000 deaths above the normal expectancy rate for December. The chief causes of the deaths were bronchitis, pneumonia and other respiratory complaints.

Smoke and sulphur dioxide are most certainly one cause of bronchitis and the condition is aggravated by polluted moist air conditions. Atmospheric air also contains carcinogenic (cancer causing) organic compounds, similar to those that occur in cigarette smoke, but no clear evidence has been produced to indicate that atmospheric pollution is a direct cause of lung cancer. It may, however, be an additive cause of the disease in heavy smokers. Other chest -conditions that are aggravated by air pollutants are asthma, pneumonia, tuberculosis and heart disease.

Apart from these general effects on human health, there are certain pollutants produced in specific industrial locations which can cause disease. Substances such as asbestos fibres, heavy metallic compounds like lead nitrate, copper compounds from tannery factories (which are known to cause stomach cancer) and numerous organic compounds like pesticides, are all hazardous to our health. Consumption of industrial products and consumer goods is increasing with time as more and more people in the developing world change their tastes in favour of using greater amounts of processed goods and other industrial products. This obviously increases the chance of air pollution and the consequent dangers to health.

## 4. Commercial Use of Nuclear Energy
Occasionally, nuclear explosives have been used in both mining and engineering projects. The Gasbuggy Project was started in December 1967 in New Mexico, U.S.A. After three years it was suggested that nuclear fission should be used in the hope of fracturing rocks and freeing trapped oil or gas. The explosion set free krypton 85 and hydrogen-3 (tritium or heavy hydrogen atom) which became incorporated into the molecules of methane gas and thus made the gas radioactive.

In order to get rid of the radioactivity, it was necessary to burn or flare the gas well for a year and a half. By 1972, 200 million cubic feet of the non-renewable resource had been needlessly wasted and the radioactivity present still prohibited commercial use of the gas. Project Bronco was devised to free oil trapped in oil-shale formations, and Project Sloop to extract copper from low grade copper ores.

The use of nuclear explosives has also been suggested to facilitate preliminary work for highway and rail road construction, through mountain terrain and also for the construction of dam and rockfill structures. The danger of radiation and its deadly effects has so far limited the use of nuclear devices to a prudent minimum.

## 5.  Effects of Radioactive Air Pollution on Man

Exposure to radioactive air pollution produces both somatic effects (which can be seen in people living now) and genetic effects (which are passed on to their offspring). Whole body exposure to radiation (natural radiation) may be experienced when nuclear weapons are tested and when reactor accidents occur. Therapeutical radiation is sometimes administered to parts of the body usually in the form of X-rays.

Acute or short-term effects of radioactive pollution include radiation burns, nausea, changes in blood and disorders of the intestines and the central nervous system. Latent and chronic effects can include a variety of cancers, impairment of growth and development, shortening of one's lifespan and genetic disorders.

Radio nuclides affect man mainly through background radiation, through inhalation and through intake via the food chain. In terms of their effects on man the four nuclides iodine-131 (I-31), strontium-90 (Sr-90), Caecium-137 (Cs-137) and Carbon-14 (C-14) are the most feared.

*Iodine-131* is a β-y emitter with a half-life of 8.1 days; this short-lived nuclide affects the body internally and externally. It is abundantly produced in the process of fission, and via the cattle-milk-man food chain, it is deposited in the thyroid gland. Cancer of the thyroid has been reported to occur in children after fairly low exposures of about 50 rem.

*Strontium-90* (Sr-90) is a B emitter with a half-life of 28 years, and is one of the most dangerous radioactive pollutants. Because of its chemical similarity to calcium (Ca), it is

226

deposited directly in the skeleton. Sr-90 reaches man via the food chain vegetation-milk and meat. Apart from its somatic effects such as leukemia and bone cancer, Sr-90 has been reported to have significant genetic effects on mice.

*Caecium-31* (S-37) is a β-y emitter with a half-life of 30 years and is deposited mainly in the soft tissue but can irradiate the whole body. Fortunately it is eliminated from the body in a biological half-life of a hundred days. Its y-rays are a genetic hazard because they irradiate the gonads.

*Carbon-14* (C-14) is a B-y emitter with a half-life of 5,730 years and is readily absorbed by the body and this may lead to whole body irradiation and to adverse effects both somatic and genetic. Nuclear weapons tests have significantly increased the amount of C-14 present in the world thereby resulting in an 80 per cent increase over natural C-14 levels by the end of 1963.

Long term studies of survivors of atomic bomb explosions in Japan (Hiroshima and Nagasaki) established that certain radiation doses calculated for certain distances from the epicentre correlate significantly with radiation induced disorders and diseases such as abnormalities in cell development, chromosomal damage, leukemia, thyroid, lung and breast cancer, impairment of growth and increase in foetal, infant and general mortality.

Any amount of radiation from man-made pollution adds to the natural background radiation . Clearly, if one considers that man is already the victim of man-made radioactive pollution, any additional exposure to radiation, however small, may affect him through genetic diseases.

As the fossil fuels (i.e. coal, oil and natural gas) reserves become depleted, more and more nuclear power stations will be built, mainly in the industrial countries of the north for the generation of electricity. Increasing industrial development will cause the amount of radiation in the environment to increase thereby aggravating global pollution especially for the next century or until the world's population and the demand for industrial products stabilise.

Nuclear reactor accidents, like the Chernobyl accident (in the Soviet Union on 26th April, 1986), can expose a very large number of people to varying degrees of radiation. This is especially so when radioactive particles such as Radon-222 gas are carried by fast moving air, or even water, to areas of dense human population.

## 6. Impact of Different Types of Development Projects and Industries on the Environment

*Dams*
Certain human activities have considerable impact on the environment by engendering individually small but cumulatively important effects. A good example is the construction of large dams for the generation of hydroelectric power and the storage of water for irrigation. The construction of the Aswan High Dam in Egypt in 1960-1970 cost US$ 1 billion and produced a number of undesirable effects on the environment; these have almost eclipsed the desirable effects of generating electricity, increasing the area of irrigated land and controlling the flooding of the Nile Delta. On the other hand, it had many disastrous effects-120,000 people were displaced from their homes; the fertility of the Nile Valley was decreased because the silt that used to be deposited by the flood waters was now intercepted by the dam.

Downstream river erosion became more pronounced due to the deposition of silt behind the dam. Water-logging in the irrigated fields led to an increase in the incidence of vector borne diseases including malaria and schisostorniasis; and it is also (suspected that the construction of the Aswan High Dam has led to the reduction of fish catches in the Nile Delta-Mediterranean region.

## Timber Industry

Timber production, wood processing and paper manufacturing can deplete vegetation cover and lead to increased rates of soil erosion. This, in turn leads to the pollution of rivers with the eroded soil and chemical effluents from the paper manufacturing industries.

Let us mention once more that industrial developments are necessary in order to satisfy the needs of an increasing population in the developing countries, a population which is diversifying its tastes and uses more and more manufactured consumer goods.

## 7. Solid Wastes and the Environment

Solid waste is any worthless, unwanted or discarded material that is neither liquid nor gas. It includes food scraps, expired drugs and chemicals, raked leaves, crop residues, animal manure, sewage sludge, old newspapers, non-returnable cans bottles, worn out furniture, abandoned cars, food processing wastes, mining wastes and construction wastes. Throwing away resource-rich solid waste often amounts to squandering the Earth's finite resources as well as being a massive waste of energy and a considerable economic loss.

Although some hazardous wastes must be isolated and stored, most of the things we throw away should not be regarded as waste, but as wasted solids that we should either re-use or recycle. In many instances, such as those involving excessive packaging, it is material that was unnecessary in the first place. Most solid waste is produced by agricultural or mining processes, although there is also some industrial solid waste.

### (a) Disposal of Solid Wastes in Urban Areas

In urban centres, the majority of the population is uninterested in whatever happens to the domestic, business and industrial waste as long as it is disposed of in a place where they will neither see it nor smell it. The local authorities use this principle of "out of sight out of mind" to collect the waste and then dump, bury or burn it.

Methods used in land disposal of solid wastes include *open dumps, landfills, sanitary landfills* and *secured landfills*.

An *open dump* is a land disposal site where solid and liquid wastes are deposited and left uncovered often with little or no regard for control of scavengers, aesthetics, disease, air pollution or water pollution problems.

A *landfill* is a waste disposal site that is located with little, if any, regard for possible pollution of ground or surface water due to runoff and leaching. It may also involve covering waste intermittently with a layer of soil to reduce scavenger, disease, aesthetic and air pollution problems. In effect, it is a slightly upgraded version of the open dump.

A *sanitary landfill* is a land waste disposal site that is so located as to minimise water pollution from runoff and leaching. Waste is spread in thin layers, compacted and covered with a fresh layer of soil each day to minimise the problems noted previously.

A *secure landfill* is a land site for the storage of hazardous waste (both solid and liquid). These are normally stored in containers and then buried; the site has restricted access, is continuously monitored and is located above impermeable geological strata in order to prevent any waste entering the ground water.

In the developing countries, urban waste dump sites are generally poorly managed. Local authorities are responsible for emptying septic tanks, cess pools and soakage pits. At regular intervals, a large volume of liquid waste is collected from cess pools. This is then loaded into open drums and transported by truck. This liquid waste is discharged onto the waste dumping site and may enter the surrounding land and find its way to underground water sources.

Uncontrolled dumping of toxic wastes (e.g. outdated or expired medicines) is common. These are sometimes picked up by scavengers and occasionally re-sold on the black market. The wastes often carry infectious diseases which are easily transmitted by humans and animals scavenging on the dump site.

Burning waste heaps and rotting litter often produces noxious odours. The public health situation caused by domestic liquid and solid wastes in urban centres is a major cause of concern to their inhabitants. In the coastal towns of eastern and southern Africa, diseases such as malaria, infectious hepatitis, typhoid, cholera, schistosomiasis and dysentery are almost endemic. Such diseases have a direct relationship to lack of potable water supplies and absence of adequate sanitation facilities. However, governments in many developing countries are making an effort to address this challenge. The Kenya Government, for instance, has taken up the challenge by organising health services to improve facilities and bring them within the effective reach of the rural population.

In small towns and rural areas collection and disposal of solid waste services is unavailable. People dispose of their solid waste by littering, that is, by spreading the waste on the surrounding land. Most of the surface water in dams, streams, rivers and lakes is thus contaminated with human excrement. Water-related diseases often become unavoidable under such circumstances.

### (b) Hazardous Wastes

Some industrial waste consists of hazardous materials that are toxic, flammable or explosive. There is currently no universally accepted definition of the term hazardous waste. The World Health Organisation (WHO) refers to hazardous waste as waste that has physical, chemical or biological characteristics which require special handling and disposal procedures to avoid risk to health or other adverse environmental effects.

Estimates of quantities of hazardours waste produced by industry vary widely depending on the definition used. It is estimated that in 1987, the Organisation for Economic Cooperation and Development (OECD) countries generated about 300 million tons of hazardous waste of which 264 million were from the United States of America. More than 10 per cent of the waste generated by OECD countries is transported across national frontiers for treatment or disposal. In 1983, 2.2 million tons of hazardous waste crossed the national frontiers of the European members states of the OECD countries on the way to treatment, storage or disposal.

The disposal of hazardous waste has become a difficult and controversial issue in waste management. In many cases, existing methods of disposal are not so reliable as to preclude any risk to man and the environment. In many countries, only incomplete data, if any are available at the national level with regard to the amounts of hazardous waste generated or the disposal techniques used by the producers.

Over 75 per cent of the hazardous waste generated by industries in the OECD countries is disposed of on land in the form of land fills, deep well injection and underground disposal. Wastes may be disposed of in bulk or stored in drum barrels or tanks. Hazardous wastes may also be 'exported' to unsuspecting and less developed countries for disposal. Considerable amounts may also be dumped in the sea. This may happen where the alternative disposal method in the country of origin is very costly. Many of the developing countries have no legislation governing the disposal of hazardous wastes. They are even more handicapped by lack of facilities for the detection of hazardous wastes. Some developing countries may also accept attractive payment in return for permission to allow dangerous wastes to be dumped on their territory.

## 8. The 'Greenhouse Effect'

As already made clear in a previous chapter of this book, the atmosphere that surrounds the earth plays an important role in maintaining even temperatures on the Earth's surface. Like the glass in a greenhouse, the atmosphere absorbs some of the long wave radiation emitted by the Earth, and radiates energy back to the Earth. If the atmosphere were not present, temperatures on the Earth would be much lower than they actually are.

233

Industrial activity the world over is slowly changing the atmosphere's structure. As gases, such as carbon dioxide are produced and released into the atmosphere, they absorb more of the Earth's radiation and return more of it back to the Earth. This energy, which would otherwise escape harmlessly into space, is already increasing the Earth's surface temperature, though only by small amounts so far (about 0.5°C over the past 120 years).

Carbon dioxide is the most important of the greenhouse gases and is produced mainly when fossil fuels such as coal, natural gas and petroleum products are burned to provide power. Levels of carbon dioxide in the atmosphere have already increased by some 25 per cent since the industrial revolution; they are expected to increase by a further 30 per cent in the next 50 years due to further industrialisation.

Many other gases have also a greenhouse effect. These include nitrous oxide, methane, neon and chlorofluorocarbons (CFCs) used in refrigeration and other industries. The concentrations of these gases in the atmosphere are much lower than that of carbon dioxide but they are increasing and many of them produce a very strong greenhouse effect. Scientists estimate that over the next half century or so, the temperature rise produced by increasing concentrations of carbon dioxide will be doubled by the effect of other greenhouse gases.

How much is the temperature likely to rise? By making assumptions about how much of each type of gas is likely to be released into the atmosphere, and feeding this information into computers that can model the atmosphere's behaviour, scientists can make rough estimates of what is likely to happen. Current predictions are that the greenhouse effect will amount to between a 1.5 and 4.5°C by the year 2030.

However, because the oceans take a long time to warm up, not all of this increase will actually occur by 2030 - about half of it will occur by then, the other half following in the ensuing decades. Even these apparently low figures will be enough to have a major effect on climate. Temperatures averaged globally over a year disguise what can happen locally in different seasons. Though the Earth's average temperature was only about 5°C colder than now during the last ice age, it was very much colder in some places during some seasons.

Similarly, an average temperature rise of only 3°C could mean increases of more than 10°C at high latitudes in some seasons. In temperate zones, winters would tend to be shorter and warmer, summers hotter and longer. Rainfall would also be affected. Evaporation rates would increase and overall rainfall would rise by an estimated 7-11 per cent a year. Temperate winters might be wetter, and summers drier. The tropics would also become wetter, but the subtropics, already dry, could become drier still.

### 9. Ozone: the Biosphere's Umbrella Against Ultraviolet Rays

*Ozone*, a gas composed of three oxygen atoms, surrounds the Earth like a delicate veil, protecting the planet and all of its inhabitants against the direct glare of the sun. Ozone is our umbrella against ultraviolet radiation. Were it not present in the atmosphere, lethal levels of harmful radiation from the sun would reach the Earth's surface. Ozone is found up to heights of 60 kilometres above the Earth's surface. It is most dense at height of 20 to 25 kilometers up but even there only one molecule in 100,000 is ozone. If all the ozone were collected at the Earth's surface, it would form a layer only 3mm or so thick. But because there is so little of it and because its presence is so important, small changes in ozone concentrations could have dramatic effects on life on Earth.

Ozone is produced naturally, (from oxygen) high up in the atmosphere. Natural forces break it down with the result that the gas is constantly being created and destroyed. The rates at which these reactions occur determine how much ozone there is in the atmosphere at a given time. In addition, these rates can be greatly influenced by chemicals in the atmosphere which act as catalysts in the reactions, speeding up the rates of change without themselves being destroyed. Several chemicals used in or produced by industry greatly influence the rate at which ozone is broken down. These include the chlorofluorocarbons (CFCs) which are used as propellants in aerosols, in refrigeration technology, as foam blowing agents in the plastics industry and as solvents in electronics. Other gases that speed up the breaking down of ozone include nitrous oxide and those substances which [1] contain chlorine, fluorine and bromine.

In trying to predict what will happen to ozone levels in the future, scientists must first make predictions about the rate at which chemicals like CFCs and nitrous oxides will be produced in the future. They must then make models of how these chemicals react with ozone and with one another, and estimate future ozone levels at different heights and at different times in the future. The latest results of this work suggest that ozone levels will fall by a few percentage points during the first half of the 21st century -although any increase of CFC emissions could cause more than a 10 per cent fall in ozone level. Measurements of the total amount of ozone in the atmosphere show that levels have not changed appreciably as yet - though small changes seem to be occurring at particular heights, with low level-ozone concentrations increasing and high-level rates decreasing. Changes of ozone concentrations over the Antarctic have been particularly dramatic as will be shown later.

Changes of a few per cent points in future ozone levels would be sufficient to allow substantially more ultraviolet radiation to reach the Earth's surface. Because ozone affects the Earth's heat balance in a number of ways, climate could also be affected by changes in ozone concentrations. Ultraviolet radiation is responsible for sunburn, snow blindness, eye damage, skin cancer, and the ageing and wrinkling of skin. It affects plant growth by slowing down photosynthesis and delaying germination in many plants, trees and crops. Because algae are particularly sensitive to ultraviolet radiation, fears have been expressed that damage to the ozone layer could upset marine ecology and lower fish populations.

## 10. Some Possible Results on Human Society

The greenhouse effect and ozone depletion are not completely separate problems. Ozone changes will affect climate, and carbon dioxide changes will influence ozone depletion. How are these changes likely to affect human society over the next half century? Three separate effects are involved: climatic change, abnormally fast plant growth caused by high levels of carbon dioxide in the atmosphere and increased levels of ultraviolet radiation.

### (a) Consequences of Climatic Change

The clearest effect of climatic change will be experienced in agriculture. A warmer climate is likely to move the areas suitable for growing specific crops such as wheat, further towards the poles. If soils in these areas are poor, yields will fall. Marginal agriculture - as practised for instance in the drought-prone Sahel will probably suffer most because it will be unable to adapt easily to new conditions. Changes in agriculture will in turn, produce a chain reaction throughout society, altering the economic viability of farming, agricultural employment, commodity prices and patterns of world trade.

There will also be wide-spread changes in natural ecosystems with grassland and desert areas expanding and forested areas shrinking and moving polewards. Problems such as desertification and soil erosion could worsen. A warmer climate might make some cities unbearably hot. A wetter or drier climate would also have major effects on water use and long-term planning, perhaps making large reservoirs or other projects useless long before their normal 50 year life span has elapsed.

As the oceans expand, sea levels would rise causing flooding of low lying areas. While developed countries could afford to protect themselves - as the Dutch have done for centuries, the poorer developing nations, with both capital and technological constraints, might have no choice but to lose large areas of precious coastal land to the sea.

### (b) Effects on Plant Growth

Because carbon dioxide is a natural fertiliser, most plants would grow larger and faster in an environment with a higher carbon dioxide concentration. At first sight, this might be thought beneficial assuming that yields of major crops might increase. While this might be true, there would be many complicating effects: weeds would also get bigger, plants would be less rich in nitrogen and perhaps more susceptible to pests and diseases, and soils might become rapidly impoverished as a result of having to sustain high rates of plant growth.

In addition, natural ecosystems would be disrupted, with unpredictable results, since some species would adapt easily to the new conditions while others would dwindle or become extinct.

(c) **Dangers Posed by Increased Levels of Ultraviolet Radiation Reaching the Biosphere**

Higher levels of ultraviolet radiation would have a number of major effects on society. Skin cancer, already the most common form of cancer in man, would become even more common, possibly in its most deadly form, melanoma. Eye diseases would increase and the ability of the body's immune system to cope with infections might be impaired.

The yields of many crops could fall because ultraviolet radiation slows down many aspects of plant growth. Plastics are also affected by ultraviolet radiation, and the lifetimes of many commonly used synthetic materials could be shortened. Because of this effect, goods might have to be replaced more frequently, than at present, at a great economic cost. In addition, ozone depletion is likely to lead to more smog in cities.

(d) **Social Effects of Damaging the Biosphere,**

The social results of greenhouse effect and ozone depletion are summarised in fig. 9.2.

Fig. 9.2  Social Effects of Damaging the Biosphere

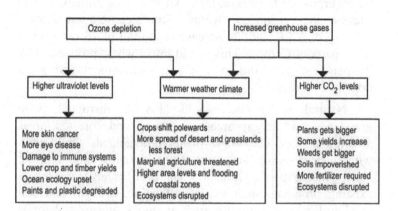

## 11. What Could Happen as the Earth Gets Warmer?

The Earth's climate has not varied by more than 1 or 2°C in the past 10,000 years. The warming expected in the next 50 years will therefore exceed any climatic change experienced in human history. Models of the Earth's climatic system are not sufficiently reliable to predict exactly how a given change in average temperature will affect the different regions of the Earth. However, they do give an indication of what might happen with large temperature changes occurring in the high latitudes, particularly in the world's major grain growing areas. While warmer temperatures speed up crop growth, they do not necessarily lead to higher yields; muggy conditions, for example, provide ideal breeding grounds for pests and diseases.

Because agriculture is fairly well adapted to existing climatic conditions, any major change is likely to prove disruptive rather than beneficial. This is particularly true where crops are farmed on marginal land. One climatic model suggests that greenhouse, warming could cause a temperature increase of 3.4°C and an increase in rainfall of 18 per cent in some parts of Canada. This would lower wheat production by 25 per cent, resulting in a fall in employment and gross domestic product.

Natural ecosystems would also be disrupted, with grasslands and desert areas expanding and forested areas growing smaller. The mix of plants in rangelands would alter, with unclear consequence for the wild fauna and domestic stock grazing them. Climatic change might also exacerbate existing problems such as desertification, drought and soil erosion. Ecological hazards such as floods, storms and forest fires might become more common, and warmer winters could enable more pests to survive cold seasons in which they previously would have perished.

The world water cycle is likely to be profoundly influenced by greenhouse warming, with rainfall increasing in many areas but soils becoming drier as evaporation rates rise. This conjunction of factors would have a major effect on surface water run-off, and many dams, reservoirs and hydro-electric schemes might become useless. Planning would become difficult if the climate began to change rapidly.

### To What Extent Would Sea Levels Rise?

One of the main dangers of a warmer climate is flooding from rising sea levels. However, the greenhouse effect is not expected to melt the Antarctic ice to any great extent; this would require temperature rises of some 20°C and take several centuries. Nor is the greenhouse effect likely to cause the glaciers on the west of Antarctica to slip into the sea (an event that would cause sea levels to rise by some 6 metres). On the contrary, the volume of Antarctic ice could increase as a result of a small global warming because of the increased snowfall that would occur.

However, as the oceans warm up, they will expand. Scientists calculate that this expansion could cause a rise in sea levels of between 20 and 140 centimeters if the average temperature increased between 1.5 and 4.5°C a temperature rise in the middle of this range could increase sea-levels by about 80 centimeters, more than enough to flood huge areas of unprotected coastal land. Nearly one-third of the human race lives within 60 kilometres of a coastline.

A rise in sea level of even half a metre could therefore have profound effects on settlement patterns, causing many people to move and many of the world's most important cities and ports to come under threat of flood.

**Plants May Get Bigger**

As already mentioned in section 10 (b), because carbon dioxide is a natural fertiliser plants will grow faster and larger in carbon dioxide. If carbon dioxide levels double as they may do later in the next century, the yields of many crops (and weeds) could increase by an average of about one third. Plants have widely differing responses to increased carbon dioxide so it is difficult to predict what effect this change would have on agriculture. Yields of some crops might double while others might change very little.

Individual responses depends on how a plant photosynthesises. Plants that produce intermediary chemicals with three carbon atoms, the $C_3$ plants, respond well; those that produce intermediaries with four carbon atoms, the $C_4$

plants, much less so. Of the world's 20 major food crops, 16 are $C_3$ plants. The other four - maize, sorghum, millet and sugarcane, are $C_4$ plants, whose yields would not be expected to increase greatly.

Unfortunately, three of these are the staple foods of most of sub-Saharan Africa, where food is already in short supply. While increased yields would be beneficial in many areas, this would not be true in the United States, the EEC countries or Japan; where overproduction is already agriculture's principal problem. Further yield increase would lower prices and subject farmers to increasing economic pressure.

Bigger plants with higher yields could raise other problems as well. Unless larger amounts of expensive fertiliser were used, the soil might well become impoverished as it struggles to provide the nutrients required by an increased plant cover.

### Consequences of the Reduction of Ozone

If ozone levels are depleted by a small percentage early in the next century, there will be increased levels' of a portion of the spectrum known as UV-B on the Earth's surface. UV-B causes skin cancer and eye disease in man, slows down plant growth, is lethal to marine algae and breaks down the chemical structure of paints and plastics.

Currently, between 10 and 30 per cent of the sun's UV-B reaches the earth's surface. If ozone levels were to fall by 10 per cent, the amount of UV-B reaching the Earth would increase by about 20 per cent. Worldwide , about 100,000 people die from skin cancer every year and UV-B is implicated in most cases.

In the United States, the National Academy of Sciences has estimated that each 1 per cent depletion of the ozone layer would increase the incidence of skin cancer by 2 per cent. On this basis, a 3 per cent reduction in ozone would produce some 20,000 more cases of skin cancer in the United States every year. Other medical effects are harder to quantify. More UV-B will increase eye disease, skin ageing and wrinkling and probably impair the body's ability to cope with infections in general.

Some 200 plants have been tested for sensitivity to UV-B and about two thirds of them respond with slower growth and seed failure to germinate. A 25 per cent ozone depletion, for example, would be expected to lower soyabean yields by 20 - 25 per cent. It is thought that trees and grasses would be particularly badly affected by higher UV-B levels. Fish and the algae, on which they feed, may also fair badly. Recent research shows that a 15 day exposure to UV-B levels (20 per cent higher than normal levels), kill off all anchovy larvae down to a water depth of 10 metres. More UV-B is likely to lower fish catches and upset fish ecology. Worldwide, fish currently provides 18 per cent of all the animal protein consumed.

Even today's levels of sunlight provide enough UV-B to cause substantial economic damage. It is UV-B that causes paints to fade, window glazing to yellow and car roofs to become chalky. These kinds of degradation will accelerate if the ozone layer is depleted.

Finally, more UV-B will mean more smog in cities - an effect that will be accentuated if temperatures rise as a result of greenhouse warming. Urban air pollution caused by UV-B could also worsen the problem of acid rain in cities.

In summary:

- If the emission of chlorofluorocarbons were held constant, some 1.65 million cases of non-melanoma skin cancer might be avoided;

- The cost of adding stabilisers to PVC to counter 27 per cent ozone deplation by the year 2075 would amount to nearly US$ 5 billion;

- Smog levels in certain cities (like Nashville, Philadephia and Los Angeles) could increase by as much as 50 per cent if ozone was seriously depleted and temperatures rose.

**What Can Be Done?**

International action is urgently required to minimise both future greenhouse heating and ozone depletion. Because it takes decades for human actions to produce any discernible effect on the structure of the atmosphere, a start has to be made now. While something has been done to control ozone depletion, little effort has gone into tackling the greenhouse problem which is, in many ways, the more serious issue.

**(a) Sorting out the Greenhouse Problem**

There are four possible solutions to the greenhouse effect:

(i) Reduce the rate at which fossil fuels are burnt and other greenhouse gases produced;

(ii) Dispose of the greenhouse gases as they are produced elsewhere than in the atmosphere;

(iii) Recover the greenhouse gases already in the atmosphere and dispose of them elsewhere; or

(iv) Accept the changing climate and adapt to it.

Only the first and last "solutions appear economically feasible. Carbon dioxide, for example, could be filtered from power station effluents, converted to some other chemical form and dumped in the ocean floor. But the cost would be enormous.

Carbon dioxide, which is already in the atmosphere could, in theory, be 'mopped up' by planting more trees on the Earth which would convert carbon dioxide in the atmosphere into woody tissue. But an area the size of France would have to be planted annually to compensate for the current rate at which carbon dioxide is produced. Even if this were possible, the effects of the other greenhouse gases would still change future climates.

The best solution would be to reduce overall energy consumption (something that is already occurring, thanks to increased oil prices), consume fewer fossil fuels by relying heavily on nuclear and solar energy, for example, and learn to adapt and accept the changing climate. Future actions are likely to include a combination of these three approaches but international mechanisms to formulate an agreed plan have yet to be put into effect.

### (b) Protecting the Ozone Layer

Action has already been taken to protect the ozone layer. Because the major danger comes from the chemicals called chlorofluorocarbons (CFCs), and because these chemicals were widely used as propellants in aerosols, several countries have restricted the use made of CFCs or the amounts produced. The United States banned the use of CFCs in aerosols in 1978. The EEC has introduced its own regulations and some countries, such as Belgium and the Nordic countries, have in effect banned CFC production altogether.

Furthermore, a convention for the protection of the ozone layer was adopted in Vienna in March 1985 by 21 states and the EEC. Though the Convention is not yet in force, it has since been signed by more states. The Convention pledges parties to it to: protect human health and the environment from the effects of ozone depletion; two annexes to the Convention provide for the parties to it to co-operate in research, observation and information exchange on matters connected with ozone depletion.

A protocol to the Convention is currently being framed that will pledge signatories to limit their production or emissions of CFCs. Japan, India, China and Australia, major industrial countries, are not yet signatories. In Africa only Egypt, Morocco and Burkina Faco are signatories.

### (c) The Role of UNEP

Concern with the ozone layer was one of the environmental issues that led to the creation of the United Nations Environmental Programme in the early 1970s. UNEP is working with governments, international organisations and industry to develop a framework within which the international community can make decisions to minimise atmospheric changes and the effects they could have on the Earth. In 1977, UNEP convened a meeting of experts to draft the World Plan of Action on the Ozone Layer. The Plan called for a programme of research on the ozone layer and on what would happen if the layer was damaged. To coordinate this programme UNEP created a special body, the Coordinating Committee on the Ozone Layer (CCOL).

By 1986, the CCOL had met eight times and had assessed the threat to the ozone layer at several of its meetings. Most recently, its group of experts and government representatives framed the Convention for the Protection of the Ozone Layer. This convention also advocates limitation of emissions of CFCs, a question that touches difficult commercial issues because CFCs are important industrial chemicals.

UNEP also took action to tackle the greenhouse problem early in the 1970s when the organisation joined forces with the World Meteorological Organisation (WMO) and the International Council of Scientific Unions (ICSU) to place the study of the greenhouse effect on a firm scientific footing.

The results of that initiative has been a clearer understanding of the nature of the greenhouse effect and its implications for the future. Thanks to the studies made during the late 1970s and early 1980s, much of the guesswork about both ozone depletion and the greenhouse effect has been removed. The reality of both issues is no longer in doubt; the only questions remaining are when to act and how much can be done.

Work in coordinating international legal action with regard to the greenhouse effect has so far not begun except in relation to CFCs - partly because the issues are complex and the solutions less obvious. However, UNEP is working with governments, WHO, ICSU and other international bodies to develop a better understanding of the greenhouse effect. This is planned to lead to a framework within which the community of nations will be able to make informed decisions on how best to minimise greenhouse heating and its social and economic effects.

## Questions

1. Discuss the functions of the ozone layer in protecting life on earth.

2. Give a brief outline of the impact of ozone layer depletion on the economy of East African countries with particular reference to Kenya. (Consider Kenya as an essentially agricultural country).

3. Discuss the impact of the 'greenhouse effect' on the future development of the coastal towns of East Africa.

4. What abatement measures can be incorporated in all industries to avert the depletion of the ozone layer?

5. Why do most discussions on solid waste emphasise the urban solid wastes produced by homes, hotels and other businesses in or near urban areas?

## Bibliography

Adams, D.D. (ed) Acid Deposition: Environment, Economic and Policy Issues, (New York: Plenum Press, 1985).

Anonymous "The Day the Impossible Happened: the Chernobyl Syndrome" *The Sunday Observer,* London, 4th May, 1986.

Goggle I.E. *Biological Effects of Radiation,* (London: Wykeham Publications, 1973).

Devins, W.D. Energy: Its Physical Impact on the environment, (New York: Marcel Dekker 1979).

El-Hinnawi, E.E. *Environmental Impact of Production and Use of Energy,* (Dublin: Tycooly Press Ltd., (for UNEP),1981).

B. Fismock, D. "The Nuclear Reactor that Started an Inferno". *Sunday Nation,* Nairobi, May 4th, 1986.

Fletcher, W.W. *The Pest War,* (Oxford: Basil Blackwell, 1974).

Gadd, P. *The Ecology of Urbanization and Industrialization,* (London: Macmillan Educational Ltd., 1986).

C. Heylin, "The Bhopal Report". *Chemical and Engineering News,* llth February, 1985.

D.Hewitt, B. et. at. "The Poisoning of the Rhine: A Chemical Spill in Europe's Industrial Heartland Raises Questions About the Will to Fight Pollution", *Newsweek,* November 24th, 1986.

Howard, R. and Perley, M. *Acid Rain: The North American Forecast,* (Toronto: House of Anansi Press Ltd., 1980).

E. McCormic, J. "Acid Earth: The Global Threat of Acid Pollution" *Earthscan* Bulletin Vol 8 No 5(December 1985).

Meethan, A.R. Atmospheric Pollution: Its History, Origins and Prevention, (Oxford: Pergamon Press, 1981).

Miller, G.T. *Living in the Environemnt,* (Belmont: Wadsworth, Inc., 1982).

Nanda, M. "Environmental Protection and the Law". *Bulletin of Sciences: A Journal of Science Technology and Society* Vol. (December, 1985) 2 No.l.

Patternson, W.C. *Nuclear Power,* (London: Cox and Wyman Ltd., 1976).

Roggeri, H. *African Dams: Their Impacts on the Environment,* (Nairobi: Environment Liason Centre, 1985).

UNEP, Environment and Health: State of the Environment Report, Nairobi: UNEP 1986.

——, State of the World Environment, (Nairobi: UNEP 1987).

——, Public Health Problems in the Coastal Zone of the East African Region, (Nairobi: UNEP, 1982).

——, *The Public and Environment*, (Nairobi: UNEP, 1988).

——, "The Changing Atmosphere". *Environmental Brief*, (Nairobi: UNEP, 1988).

Vesilind, P.A. *Environmental Pollution and Control*, (London: Butterworth Publishers, 1986).

# -10-

# Perspectives on the African Environment and Development

W. P. Ezaza

## Introduction

Since the Stockholm Conference on the Environment in 1972, the current international concern on development and environment in Africa has hinged on three issues: agriculture, environment and development. For the purpose of the present discussion, *environment*, in the developmental planning context will mean the control or regulation of the interaction between the physical environment and human societies. *Development*, in the environmental management context, will signify the improvement of the quality of human life through rational, efficient and sustainable utilisation of available resources for present and future generations.

Africa is the second largest continent occupying about 22 per cent of the total land surface of the earth. It is richly endowed in terms of resources. For example, the continent contains more land of high carrying capacity and high biological potential than any other continent. *Biological potential* is measured by an adequate degree of precipitation and effective radiation throughout the year. The continent is also rich in culture which has been greatly influenced and modified by alien ideas. Yet, with all this richness, Africa is-perhaps the most fragmented and vulnerable continent in terms of its ecosystems, culture, politics and economy. This diversity and vulnerability has greatly affected the continent's developmental efforts. In the last three decades or so, many changes have taken place in Africa. These changes, particularly in Africa's ecosystems, did not come about as a result of rapid economic development but rather as a result of rapid changes in social organisations.

Although Africa is the second largest and the geologically oldest continent, the processes which brought about radical modification in its entire natural ecosystem have been rather recent. The modification has basically been related to food production and energy requirements. As these are basic needs, they depend heavily on the availability and quality of the natural resources.

The last three decades have also witnessed a rapid growth in population. Africa's population rise of 3.2 per cent a year is the fastest anywhere on this plant. The rapid growth of Africa's population has damaged her soil, water, vegetation, and wildlife in order to meet growing demands particularly in food and energy consumption. The result has been a rapid deterioration of environmental quality; in some parts of Africa, the land can no longer sustain the human population occupying it.

In other words, Africa is facing serious environmental, food, energy, population and poverty crises. The depletion of natural resources and its effect on food, energy supply and human settlement, is a matter of grave concern.

There is widespread poverty, food insecurity, drought and desertification, diseases, and malnutrition, all of which result in massive rural-urban migrations. The concentration in urban centres in turn puts excessive demands on natural resources and pollutes and degrades the surrounding areas.

Urban fuel-energy demands have led to widespread deforestation, soil erosion and changes in micro climate and hydrological systems. In many parts of Africa, arable lands have been expanded into ecologically fragile ecosystems such as steeper slopes, margins of arid and semi-arid areas and wetlands as well, to meet the growing demands. This expansion is an environmental threat. The quest to meet the demands of the rapidly growing population, combined with insufficient attention to the environmental impact of agricultural policies and practices, are, according to the United Nations Environmental Programme (UNEP) 1988, the main causes of environmental damage in Africa.

The United Nations and UNEP have identified various symptoms of the damage and warned that some countries in North Africa could be wiped off the map if the key degrading factors are not reversed (Figure 10.1). The symptoms of the approaching desert include: depletion of top soil and forests, droughts, loss and deterioration of the quality of surface and ground water, reduction in genetic diversity and of fish stocks, damage to the sea floor, water logging, salinisation, and siltation of soil, water and air pollution and entrophication caused by improper use of fertilisers and pesticides and by careless disposal of industrial effluents.

In some African countries, the damage is now so severe that the rural areas are no longer attractive for the able young persons who are expected to engage in agriculture in order to feed both rural and urban populations. It appears then that the current environmental and developmental crises in Africa are merely reflections of the use and misuse of natural resources. Over 10 per cent of Africa's population has been attracted to towns from unattractive rural areas. In Ghana, Guinea, Liberia, Sierra Leone, Tanzania, Togo, Uganda, Zambia and Zaire, nearly half of the total population is found in urban areas.

**Fig. 10.1: Risk of the Desert's Advance in Africa
(after Harold Dregne, 1976 p.15).**

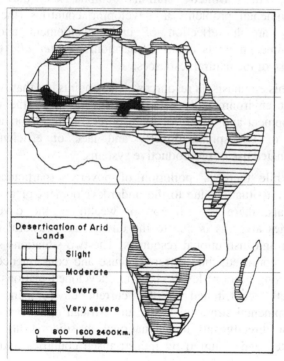

Desertication of Arid Lands

▯ Slight

≡ Moderate

▤ Severe

▓ Very severe

0  800  1600 2400Km.

Nevertheless, the situation in Africa is not entirely bleak. Some African societies have come to realise that there is a limit to the use and misuse of resources. Much has been learnt from past mistakes and experiences. Given the diversity of resources and the rarity of ecological conditions on their continent, Africans have confidently taken the challenge to rethink for themselves how to face their environmental and developmental problems.

## 1. Environmental Perspective

In its International Conference on the Human Environment (1973), the United Nations emphasised that most environmental problems in developing countries (including Africa) are a reflection of underdevelopment and that environmental goals could be harmonised *inter alia* by the wise use of the natural resources.

This emphasis on resources clearly points out that Africa's current environmental concerns are a result of the under-development and misuse of its resources. Both factors arc the cause of widespread poverty and lack of efficient and coordinated use of bioproductive systems.

While there is 'pollution of poverty', (particularly in Africa) a situation due to the underdevelopment of available materials, there is 'pollution of wealth' in the developed countries and this is due to the unwise and wasteful use of human and institutional resources. The two situations should not be confused; they differ in cause and consequence. The high consumption levels of the 'developed nations have indirectly contributed to the current environmental and developmental stress in Africa: the African resources, which do not directly fall under national jurisdiction are being exploited and acquired by industrialised countries under the guise of the Global Common Good. The rationale behind this is that such resources are available and unused locally and should therefore be made available to countries that can use them. This way of thinking is clearly echoed in the International Conference on the Natural Resources and Environment Protection Report where developing countries are advised that they should not duplicate the environmetally unsound policies and practices of the industrialised world. This is interpreted as asking Africa not to develop her industries but allow already industrialised countries to import her resources at arbitrarily dictated low prices. This seems to imply that developing countries should stagnate economically in the interests of environmental protection. The world's richer nations, for their part, would be free to maintain industry-based wealth and to engage in environmental degradation. In other words, developed nations are intent on preserving their own environmental amenities even at the cost of spoiling the African ecosystems. It should be made clear to them that if they want to exploit tropical forests, such as those of the Congo Basin, they should be willing to pay owners reasonable prices and contribute to the conservation of the local natural resources.

For example, Africa's forests contain very important tree species which are valuable in terms of yet unknown food varieties, fats, drugs, fuel, fibre, ornaments, resins and fauna. These forests are being cut down not only for traditional uses, but for commercial, industrial and agricultural purposes. Forests the world over, are vital bioproductive systems because they play both protective and productive roles in development. Their large scale removal represents the most dramatic destruction of habitat for both human and terrestrial biota. It will undoubtedly have dramatic impact on Africa's development.

Similarly, Africa's coastal waters are experiencing over fishing, not by underdeveloped societies but by developed nations with sophisticated technology. The same scenario applies to wildlife reserves. The recent world-wide outcries over the extinction of animal species in the continent are really uncalled for because it is not the wish of the great majority of local inhabitants to destroy their heritage and resources. Throughout the past centuries, African societies have lived side by side with wildlife. It is only recently that, these resources have been wastefully exploited as a result of contract with greedy outside influence.

The diversity and vulnerability of Africa's ecosystems is imposing considerable constraints on food production and energy requirements. Africa's climate, soils, her geology and patterns of disease, all pose severe problems. Rainfall is scant and erratic, its amount and distribution uneven; and it varies too much from place to place to plan for large scale agriculture. Strong radiation, difficult soils and unsettled land tenure, are additional problems that make the situation still more precarious.

Africa is an old continent where the Precambrian rocks (gneisses, granites and sandstones) have been intensively weathered into fine grains under tropical semi-arid and arid conditions. The interaction between Africa's climate and topography has produced, in most countries south of the Sahara, thoroughly leached soils poor in plant nutrients. The removal of the vegetation cover often exposes these soils to the high heat of the tropical sun which breaks down the organic matter rapidly and inhibits the work of bacteria which fix nitrogen from the air. When such interference occurs, the soils usually turn into infertile hard pans (laterites) which do not allow plant roots to penetrate. There are only a few exceptions and these can be found in the East African Highlands, volcanic areas and large river basins. Furthermore, in much of Africa, the arid and tropical climates have also had adverse effects on human populations: they hamper labour productivity and food production and control of these conditions is extremely difficult and expensive. It also requires the adoption of both new technologies and new attitudes.

Again, it must be stressed that the real causes which have accelerated environmental degradation in Africa lie in a chain of events that have forced the majority of Africans into destructive patterns of land use. Population pressure is compelling African societies to deplete natural resources to meet their immediate needs for survival. The relatively low per unit of land and per capita agricultural and fuel wood production should therefore be seen as the real cause of environmental degradation in Africa.

In other words, environmental damage in Africa is associated with lack of development which sometimes arises from an ill conceived use of resources; productive agriculture and profitable utilisation of the forest reserves on which economic development depends, are thus threatened. In the last three decades, governments and aid agencies have tried to break this poverty syndrome but with little success. In several areas, the attempts at improving the solution have resulted in environmental degradation and the destruction of resources since no effect has been made to utilise them in a sustainable fashion.

What has often put the environment and development in Africa at risk is the relationship between the different African societies who have relatively different cultural, economic and political structures, diverse natural resource bases and varying attitudes towards the use of limited resources. The diversity acts as a setback rather than as a stimulant to development. Whatever the approach to solving environmental problems in Africa, it must take these differences into consideration.

As mentioned earlier, the modification of the African environment has been rather recent. It resulted from both external and internal pressures. At no time has Africa's total natural ecosystem been interfered with as much as during the colonial period. One of the most exploitative and destructive policies which brought about widespread poverty and disparity in the distribution, control and access to resources, was the introduction of the policy which vested the very means of Africa's existence in the hands of the State and introduced the capitalist-oriented market economy. Indeed, this policy was intended to phase out the traditional African culture, economy and social organisation.

It should be pointed out here that the traditional African way of utilising resources, was very much in harmony with ecological laws. The method of land cultivation known as swindle or; shifting agriculture depended on *humus economy*, and this represented a form of stable equilibrium between the farmer and the physical environment. Although some people refer to shifting cultivation as essentially a 'no-input' method of agriculture, it was stable and sustainable as long as population pressure was low. It was only when population densities began to rise three decades ago that traditional methods began to degrade the environment. The process has also been accelerated by the pressure put on the rural population by the urban demand for food and fuel.

In an attempt to consolidate and control African population and land patterns, the Europeans upset Africa's traditional ecological harmony. Under colonial rule, traditional economies, which were in harmony with the natural physical environment, encountered increasing difficulties.

For example, in the north-east of Tanzania, the introduction of medical and veterinary services not only changed local dietary habits, but also created income disparities, and increased birth rates and livestock numbers. This was a result of the introduction of wage labour to pay the hut-tax imposed by the colonial government. The decrease in number of cattle-ticks (which resulted in an increase of livestock numbers) also led to extensive overgrazing and soil erosion. Again, the introduction of cash crops was perhaps the most destructive influence on the African environment. Emphasis on cash crops by the colonial powers admittedly made an important contribution to the economic growth of the colonies but produced severe economic and social imbalances as well as ecological damage. It changed the rationality of the African peasants and led to the abandonment of traditional ways of using resources.

For example, cash crop production changed the conditions of access to the means of food production and induced changes in the rationality of individual behaviour with respect to the environment. The colonial policy forced peasants to expand cultivable land into ecologically fragile areas. It restricted African communities from applying their human, material and institutional resources to gradually modify their own environment for a better lifestyle. It is because of these factors that the African environment continued to degenerate under the colonial system of land use. Many societies in settler colonies continued to live on marginal land which was considered unproductive by the colonialists.

Indeed, cash crops were the tool for the development of the European domestic economy rather than the colonial economy. Cash crops were seen as a healthy development tool although such crops as cotton in fact accelerated land degradation. The extension of the cultivated area under cash crops and food crops put pressure on the land, increased population growth, caused soil degeneration and accelerated soil erosion.

The point made here is that the alien standard of money values set before the African by his new master, generated profound changes on the African environment, Yet, the African has come to be blamed for not being able to feed himself under the dilapidated environment left by the Europeans. It is now too late to reverse some of the processes accelerating environmental degradation in Africa.

It is important to consider prevailing external factors which are still exacerbating the environmental and developmental problems in Africa. The world recession, coupled with the high cost of imported energy, sharp rises in Africa's public debts and misguided actions of the international assistance and development organisations, are strangling Africa and forcing African societies towards serious levels of poverty. Under the combined onslaught of the world recession, cuts in government spending and droughts, the average per capita incomes in sub-Saharan Africa fell by almost 2 per cent between 1980 and 1985.

These factors have put considerable pressure on African societies with respect to satisfying their basic food and energy requirements. The world recession has affected Africa to the point where her exports are fetching far less than three decades ago. Primary export crops and mineral ores fetch prices far below their value, while many products and hard goods produced in developed countries are being sold 'at prices which many African states cannot afford. In particular, the freight, brokerage, insurance, banking, factorage, patents and transfers of technology plus other invisible services are taxing Africa's economy heavily and making huge rifts in her balance of payments.

How do all these factors affect Africa's environment? The economic situation is putting more pressure on the rural farmers than on the urban dwellers. Everywhere, national governments are pressurising farmers to produce more and more cash and food crops to pay debts. To produce more cash and still more food, rural farmers in central Tanzania, for example, have been forced to overstretch the carrying capacity of land thereby reducing the resilience of the natural resources. Cash crop production has also absorbed the labour which would otherwise be occupied in food production. This dichotomy has caused a widespread discrepancy between the resource base and economic development. Moreover, farmers are paid far less than what their crops fetch on the world market. For example, farmers in Tanzania, Kenya and Malawi receive only 35 to 50 per cent of the market price for their food grains compared to other farmers in the Far East who receive up to 75 and even 90 per cent of the consumer price.

The expansion of cash crops at the cost of food production (in order to obtain the needed foreign currency) is putting direct pressure on the physical environment. African leaders are to blame when their policies do not aim first at meeting the basic needs of their own people. They must also bear the blame when their ill-conceived policies force the majority into exploiting the natural resources just in order to survive. Much of the damage to the resource base in many African countries may be the consequence of political decisions to cultivate marginal land, strip hillsides of trees for firewood and graze land which is already showing signs of exhaustion. The poor have little choice for they are driven to these extremes by poverty.

The energy crisis has also had a crippling effect on African societies; they have been pushed to depend on energy importation and this heavily constrains their national incomes. The wholesale exploitation of fuel-wood in sub-Saharan Africa for charcoal, wood, twigs and branches, is partly attributed to the high cost of imported energy such as kerosene, diesel and petrol. Because of fuel shortages, crop residues and animal biomass, which were once used to recondition the soil with organic matter, must now be used as fuel for cooking and heating.

The problem of fuel wood in Africa has become widespread. The exploitation of trees has pushed some countries to the point of collapse as energy demands from urban areas continue to rise. In 1987, the United Nations Food and Agriculture Organisation (FAO) estimated that some 7 million square miles of sub-Saharan Africa are seriously threatened by desertification; they warned that if this process continues unchecked, about 16.5 per cent of Africa's rainfed cropland will be lost by the year 2000 (Figure 10.1).

Internally, regional political conflicts, which erupted after independence, have contributed more to environmental damage than ever before. These political conflicts are eroding the quality of resources and of life itself. For the last three decades, the African continent has been besieged by three significant trends: political instability, economic recession and ecological stress. The first two factors have a direct relationship to the third and in fact are different sides of the same coin.

**Fig. 10.2: The Degradation Threat Losses of Rainfed Cropland**

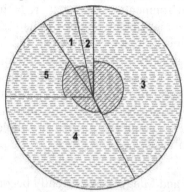

1. Central America [40,95]   2. South-West Asia [13,51]
3. Africa [203,1027]         4. South America [112,1029]
5. South-East Asia [176,319]

Source: U.N. Food and Agriculture Organisation

Political instability in parts of western and eastern Africa has led to widespread social destabilisation, migrations, economic disruption and ecological stress. Similarly, ecological stress in the Sahel Region and in the Horn of Africa has caused widespread social unrest, out migration and political instability. While political unrest erupts suddenly and often with short-lived consequences (unless engineered as in Southern Africa), environmental degradation in Africa has gradually been affecting the environment. The current environmental crisis is in fact a manifestation of a prolonged deterioration of resources.

Nevertheless, the situation in Africa is not all gloomy. Despite the massive environmental problems that Africa is facing, there are some successes which only need to be replicated in other areas. Successes in agricultural production, combating environmental damage, reducing population increase in debt repayments, collecting natural resource data and in developing human resources, have already been recorded in many parts of Africa. For example, Zimbabwe has recently reduced the food problem by mobilising farmers and paying attractively for their produce. Malawi, Botswana, Egypt and Nigeria are on their way to following Zimbabwe's example. In these countries, technical solutions have been fully adapted to local conditions to solve the problem of land degradation.

Zimbabwe and Malawi have recently become exporters of maize to other African countries. Tanzania is trying hard to increase her food production by offering attractive producer prices to farmers for their surplus sorghum production. Ghana is practising a 'no-till[1] method of cultivation which has reduced surface runoff by up to 70 per cent. Kenya's agroforestry practices have increased agricultural production by between 30 and 50 per cent during the past five years.

However, these signs of conservation have yet to be replicated in other parts of Africa. To do this, there is need to provide African countries with information regarding resource potentialities and their environmental consequences. The African farmer is the vital link in incorporating these practices into agricultural planning. Therefore, it is important that such information be made available to him.

## 2.  Environmental Development: Constraints and Prospects

It is not easy to assign every nation or continent of the world to a particular category; e.g. developed or developing or less developed, least developed or even underdeveloped, nor is it possible to distinguish clearly between these classifications. There is no appropriate yard-stick to measure the degree of a nation's development. Development in terms of Gross National Product (GNP) does not really reflect a nation's wealth in human and natural resources nor does it reflect changes in a nation's natural resource assets.

For example, rapid depletion of groundwater, forests, soils and other natural resources, may reduce a nation's potential development. In calculating GNP, the values of depleted natural resource assets are not subtracted from the current economic gains. Even generalisations of income per capita, either in terms of agricultural output or of manufacturing and urbanisation, do not, for example, place Africa anywhere in the previously noted classifications. This ambiguity is clearly seen in the United Nations classification of the African states according to their GNP for 1984 (Table 10.1).

Increasing population growth has subjected natural resources and the African environment to increasing pressure. Although some people argue that Africa is neither overpopulated nor underpopulated, the continent has the fastest population growth rate of 3.2 per cent per year compared to 1.67 per cent per year for the world as a whole. While agricultural production capabilities to provide new materials for agricultural and industrial development have increased and the total food production rose at a rate of over 2.1 per cent a year through the 1970s, self reliance in food has not been achieved (see Figure. 10.3 (a) - (c). According to the UNCTAD's report on Trade and Development 1989, food self-sufficiency has not been achieved due to geographical disadvantages and ecological fragility both of which constitute additional constraints on Africa's development.

Table 10.1: Developing African countries GDP per capita (US$ 19/9), country profiles (C.D.E) criteria, excluding Cape Verde, Saotome & Principe Djibouti.

| | | LDC, UNCTAD (1984) | | | |
|---|---|---|---|---|---|
| US$ 100-199 | US$ 200-299 | US$ 300-399 | US$ 400-499 | US$ 500-999 | US$ 1,000-1,499 |
| Burkina Faso | Chad E | Central Africa Republic | Angola E | Benin E | Algeria D |
| Burundi E | Comoros | Kenya D | Egypt C | Congo D 1978 | Botswana D |
| Equatorial Guinea E | Gambia E | Madagascar D | Kuberia E | Ghana D | Djibouti |
| Ethiopia E | Guinea Bisau E | Mauritania D | Senegal E | Morocco D | Ivory Coast D |
| Lesotho E | Malawi E | Niger E | Togo E | Nigeria D | Mauritius C |
| Mali E | Mazombiqu e E | Sierra Leone D | Uganda E 1978 | Sudan E | Tunisia D |
| Upper Volta E | Rwanda E | | | Swaziland D | |
| | Somalia E | | | Cameroon D | |
| | Tanzana E | | | Zambia D | |
| | Zaire E | | | Zimbabwe | |

Source: GDP per capita: United Nations (1981); Country profile Mchale and McHals (1977)

## Figure 10.3

### (a) Gap Between Population Growth and Food Production in Africa 1970-81 (Indices, 1970=10)

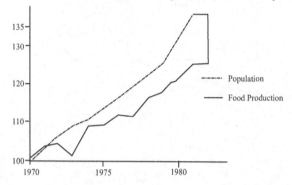

Source: U.N. Food and Agriculture Organisation

Figure (b) and (c):  Index of Per Capita Food Production

B. DEVELOPING REGIONS (1965=100)

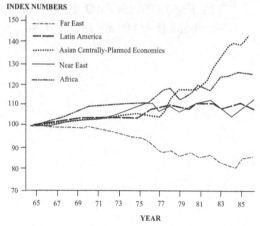

**270**

## C. DEVELOPED REGIONS (1965=100)

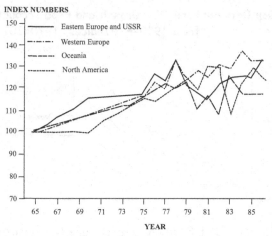

Sources: For 1965,1970: United Nations Food and
Agriculture Organization (FAO), 1987
Country Tables, (FAO Rome 1987), pp. 312-
336. For 1975-86: FAO, 1986 Production
Yearbook (FAO Rome 1987), p. 48.

### Figure 10.4 (c) Agricultural Growth Necessary to Satisfy Needs in 1990

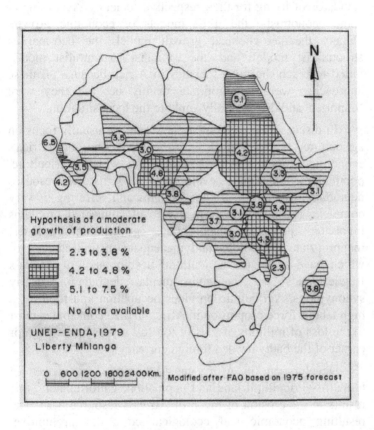

Africans have always blamed the colonial governments for their underdevelopment but if one attempted to reconstruct Africa's development immediately after political independence was achieved in the early 1960s, one 'is able to realise where Independent Africa went off course. Many African countries

272

adopted various capitalist, marxist, socialist and middle economic policies to steer their countries into achieving higher standards of living for their respective societies. According to some economists, the three models of economic growth, namely the neo-classical growth model; the neo-marxist structuralist model; and, the capitalist structuralist model, failed to reach the poor societies in Africa because all these approaches were inappropriate mainly because they were 'imported' and did not really apply to the local situation.

In discussing development in Africa, we usually focus on agriculture because it forms the backbone of Africa's economic growth. But the way in which agriculture, population, economic development and natural resource degradation interact to trigger droughts and suffering, is very complex. These factors form a web of connected problems involving poverty, inappropriate government policies, inappropriate technology and inadequate institutions, all of which have made the agricultural development of Africa's fragile lands and its environmental degradation nearly synonymous. Agriculture provides occupation and food for a high labour force proportion in Africa. It also contributes most to the loss of millions of tons of top soil a year but is a major earner of the badly needed foreign currency.

Development in Africa must, therefore, be viewed in terms of agricultural land and population. Unfortunately, this results in the erosion of much of Africa's resource base. The resulting economic and ecological costs are prohibitive. Wooded areas have been turned into desert; huge investments in irrigation works have caused technical problems and cut the longevity of dams themselves short by sedimentation, floods, and diseases. Africa continues to face crises not only in food production but also general development efforts. Recently, this situation has been exacerbated by natural, economic and political shocks which are far beyond the control of the African farmer.

In 1987, the Food and Agriculture Organisation of the United Nations (FAO) estimated that for the past ten years, the agricultural sector of African countries performed poorly with food averaging only 1.1 per cent and 1.2 per cent per capita. The annual population growth was between 2.5 and 3.1 per cent. By the year 2000, FAO estimates food production increases in Africa to be approximately 1.5 per cent and its population 1 billion.

Even the *Green Revolution* which many African countries saw as a 'short cut' solution to food deficit and rural poverty, (and which did bring about some radical reforms in land, labour and capital in the 1960s), was later found to be a socio-economic disaster. The *Green Revolution*, despite its successes in the Far East Asian countries, aggravated already existing income disparities in Africa and failed to break the back of the rural poverty syndrome.

The present food imports and food relief aid projects frequently do not help Africa in its development but rather offset demands only temporarily. Moreover, the import and export substitutions of food gains given by developed countries have only undermined Africa agricultural products. Exports and import substitutions have in fact aggravated environmental neglect of farmland. Lack of initiative and support from the policy makers has left the majority of African farmers with too little capital to increase their production and the acreage under cultivation.

As a result of insufficient local production, the urban population is offered imported foodstuffs at subsidised prices. Given their already degraded farmlands, farmers complain about low prices paid to them but their demands merely give to heated and fruitless discussions among politicians. The tendency of almost all African governments is to set food prices so as to provide low-cost food to the urban areas rather than adequate incentives to farmers. This remains one of the principal impediments to increasing food production.

Yet, most of Africa's vast natural resources such as forests, rangeland, coastal waters and wildlife could be exploited to boost food supplies. These, however, are largely state-controlled and thus the majority of Africans have no access to such resources. Would privatisation of those resources, or at least part of them, ensure more effective utilisation and improvement of the food situation.

Another aspect of the problem that still complicates it is the gender issue. Although they are responsible for up to 90 per cent of the food production, processing and marketing, African women are rarely given the position they deserve in the household and its development.

In almost all the rural households in Africa, women are the principal source of informal education and values. Yet deeply entrenched cultural values and social patterns inhibit women from access to the educational standards which would allow them to achieve their full potential. This attitude has not only affected decision making in all sectors of development, especially in agricultural development, and planning, but it has also limited the availability of trained manpower for development.

Beset by other chronic problems such as inequalities in the international economy, growing protectionism in the world market, heavy debt servicing and inadequate financial flows, many African governments have found themselves caught up in the difficult situation of having to decide between urgently needed development or conservation of their natural resources. Desperately they dismantle their state-controlled economies by introducing such reforms as devaluation, subsidy-slashing, expenditure cuts and price-decontrols.

These measures are in fact causing much discomfort to ordinary citizens by inexorably reducing their income levels and their standards of living. So far, these new policies have given little sign of productivity improvement despite the widespread structural adjustment programmes. Instead, development has often slowed down entailing negative economic, environmental and social impacts.

### 3. The African Debt Issue and its Impact on its Environment

According to Prof. Adebayo Adedeji, the debt trap adds a heavy burden to the already overloaded African economies. This is because of poor export commodities and the harsh and rigid conditionalities of orthodox structural adjustment programmes (The Standard, Tuesday 16-1-1990). That this burden is particularly heavy can be proved by the fact that in 1984, sub-Saharan African public long-term debt was 53 per cent of the region's GNP. Sub-Saharan debt service consumption was 21 per cent of the region's export income.

How did Africa come to incur debts? There are several reasons for this. First, the price in constant dollars for some 18 to 20 major commodities exported by Africa between 1973-1983, fell by an average of 5 per cent. The rising indebtedness coincided with an erosion of Africa's ability to service debts, as export revenues further declined in 1986 and 1987. In both years, most of sub-Saharan Africa suffered severe terms-of trade losses, as the dollar prices of their primary commodity exports fell or remained depressed, while the dollar prices of their manufactured imports from Europe and Japan rose sharply.

In 1988, the debt service obligations (Tables 2 and 3) amounted to 47 per cent of the regions total export revenues while the actual debt service ratio amounted to 20.5 per cent. This is according to the World Bank as per 1988/1989.

The rise in protectionism in the European Economic Community and the subsidies provided to their farmers has encouraged European farmers to over-produce. So local over-production and protectionism against agricultural products from developing countries has led to surpluses which are dumped on the world market. For example, between 1973 and 1983, sugar and vegetable oil prices fell three times faster than coffee, tea and cocoa the latter being crops which are grown in developing countries only.

Oil prices and the price of manufactured items abroad caused a rise in the prices of Africa's imports. Moreover, the brief commodity booms of the mid - 1970s were neither ploughed back into further promotion of agricultural export crops nor used to pay back debts. African governments spent the boom proceeds rapidly and thereafter shied away from cutting back on expenditure.

Since the 1970s, external debt servicing has continued to rise, followed by rapid inflation, large budget deficits, excessive money creation, rapid accumulation of internal debt, high real interest rates, transfer of wealth abroad and repeated currency depreciation. The debt-crisis has therefore posed an immense problem as it has contributed to the decline of living standards in African countries since the 1970s.

The World Bank singles out the low level of investment in Africa as the main cause of decline in health and education services; this decline is associated with the widespread resurgence of poverty and malnutrition. The crisis has forced national governments in Africa to put pressure on rural farmers to increase the acreage of cash and food crops in order to earn badly needed foreign currency with which to pay external debts.

**Table 10.2: Debt Indicators, 1985-1988**

| Country Group | Debt Service Ratio (a) | | | | Debt Export Ratio (a) | | | |
|---|---|---|---|---|---|---|---|---|
| | 1985 | 1986 | 1987 | 1988 | 1985 | 1986 | 1987 | 1988 |
| Developing countries | 23.1 | 24.6 | 22.6 | 21.5 | 163.6 | 189.0 | 180.7 | 170.0 |
| Low income | 12.7 | 14.8 | 14.0 | 14.5 | 156.7 | 177.1 | 182.1 | 180.0 |
| Middle income | 24.8 | 26.3 | 24.5 | 23.0 | 164.5 | 190.8 | 182.2 | 175.0 |
| Memorandum items | | | | | | | | |
| Sub-Saharan Africa | 24.2 | 21.7 | 18.4 | 20.5 | 191.8 | 273.4 | 307.6 | 315.0 |
| High income countries | 33.3 | 36.7 | 30.6 | 35.5 | 246.3 | 308.8 | 309.9 | 295.0 |

(a)     Debt are based on long-term debt and associated service payments (on a cash basis) and do not include short-term debt or arrears.

In turn, peasant farmers are being forced to encroach on ecologically fragile ecosystems thereby causing serious deforestation, soil erosion, sedimentation and loss of biological diversity. Environmental degradation has been compounded by periods of drought, famine and floods which have caused ecological stress and political conflicts over resources. Under such circumstances, African societies have become vulnerable.

In turn, peasant farmers are being forced to encroach on ecologically fragile ecosystems thereby causing serious deforestation, soil erosion, sedimentation and loss of biological diversity. Environmental degradation has been compounded by periods of drought, famine and floods which have caused ecological stress and political conflicts over resources. Under such circumstances, African societies have become vulnerable.

An Introduction to Environmental Education

Table 10.3  Africa Debt Crisis

| GNP per capita ($/year) | | Agric prod (1979-81 = 100) | | | Food production (1979-81 = 100) | | | Food prod per cap (1979-81 = 100) | | | Export fob ($ mn) | | | Imports fob ($ mn) | | | Total external debt | | | Debt/exports ratio | | |
|---|---|---|---|---|---|---|---|---|---|---|---|---|---|---|---|---|---|---|---|---|---|---|---|
| | 1986 | 1985 | 1986 | 1987 | 1985 | 1986 | 1987 | 1985 | 1986 | 1987 | 1985 | 1986 | 1987 | 1985 | 1986 | 1987 | 1985 | 1986 | 1987 | 1985 | 1986 | 1987 |
| Algeria | 2,590 | 121.4 | 123.3 | 129.2 | 120.6 | 122.6 | 128.4 | 103.7 | 102.0 | 103.5 | 14,108 | 9,179 | 10,511 | 12,990 | 11,736 | 11,471 | 15.33 | 19.30 | 22.88 | 108.7 | 210.3 | 217.7 |
| Angola | | 99.3 | 100.6 | 102.7 | 119.9 | 103.0 | 104.5 | 89.8 | 88.3 | 87.3 | 1,976 | 1,278 | | 1,384 | 1,062 | | 2.70 | 3.07 | 3.8 | | | |
| Benin | 270 | 134.9 | 143.1 | 143.6 | 131.6 | 138.4 | 137.9 | 113.5 | 115.7 | 111.8 | 384 | 386 | 211 | 384 | 386 | 471 | 0.82 | 0.94 | 1.13 | 310.3 | 400.8 | 536.9 |
| Botswana | 840 | 89.5 | 95.0 | 99.9 | 89.5 | 94.9 | 99.9 | 73.9 | 75.5 | 76.6 | 875.2 | 1038.1 | 1066.2 | 875.2 | 1038.1 | 1406.2 | 0.34 | 0.39 | 0.52 | 38.6 | 36.6 | 27.7 |
| Burkina Faso | 150 | 129.7 | 146.1 | 137.6 | 128.6 | 144.0 | 135.2 | 114.3 | 124.6 | 113.9 | 439 | 650 | 382 | 439 | 650 | | 0.54 | 0.67 | 0.86 | 340.4 | 175.0 | |
| Burundi | 240 | 111.4 | 116.6 | 118.5 | 114.6 | 118.4 | 119.2 | 100.0 | 100.3 | 98.2 | 238 | 268 | 151 | 238 | 268 | 299 | 0.45 | 0.55 | 0.76 | 362.9 | 365.8 | 686.5 |
| Cameroon | 910 | 107.5 | 111.4 | 113.3 | 109.1 | 111.0 | 110.9 | 95.4 | 94.3 | 91.6 | 28.20 | 25147 | 2120 | 2458 | 3074 | 3124 | 2.92 | 3.67 | 4.03 | 103.4 | 143.9 | 190.0 |
| Cape Verde | 460 | | | | | | | | | | | | | | | | 0.10 | 0.11 | 0.13 | | | |
| Cent Afr Rep. | 290 | 106.2 | 108.6 | 109.8 | 106.1 | 108.7 | 109.6 | 94.7 | 94.7 | 93.2 | 181.0 | 180.0 | 184.0 | 295 | 339 | 379 | 0.34 | 0.46 | 0.59 | 190.4 | 253.4 | 317.8 |
| Chad | | 119.5 | 121.2 | 118.6 | 119.2 | 121.5 | 117.9 | 106.3 | 105.7 | 100.1 | 99.5 | 147.4 | 170.0 | 327.5 | 389.1 | 480.1 | 0.18 | 0.24 | 0.32 | 184.2 | 159.5 | 187.0 |
| Comoros | 320 | | | | | | | | | | 24.7 | 33.3 | 30.0 | 66.1 | 73.7 | 85.4 | 0.13 | 0.17 | 0.20 | 539.9 | 499.3 | 676.2 |
| Congo | 990 | 106.4 | 108.0 | 109.8 | 106.3 | 108.1 | 109.9 | 93.4 | 92.5 | 91.5 | 1,229 | 782 | 1045 | 1393 | 1400 | 1296 | 3.08 | 3.72 | 4.63 | 250.4 | 476.0 | 443.6 |
| Cote d'Ivoire | 730 | 125.6 | 123.4 | 127.4 | 130.8 | 129.6 | 131.7 | 109.0 | 104.3 | 102.4 | 3,200 | 3705 | 3624 | 2879 | 3482 | 3881 | 9.84 | 11.14 | 13.56 | 307.4 | 300.7 | 374.0 |
| Djibouti | 760 | | | | | | | | | | | | | | | | 0.14 | 0.14 | 0.18 | | | |
| Egypt | | 114.5 | 117.4 | 121.7 | 118.6 | 122.9 | 128.1 | 104.8 | 106.2 | 108.3 | 11727 | 10906 | 11735 | 17074 | 14684 | 15308 | 34.60 | 37.86 | 40.26 | 296.7 | 347.2 | 343.1 |
| Eq Guinea | | 100.0 | 104.3 | 101.8 | 105.5 | 103.1 | 103.1 | 89.5 | 88.5 | 88.2 | 337 | 347 | 384 | 333 | 383 | 763 | 1.13 | 1.16 | 1.16 | 592.3 | 461.1 | 498.1 |
| Ethiopia | 120 | 100.0 | 104.3 | 101.8 | 105.5 | 107.2 | 103.1 | 87.0 | 67.3 | 66.2 | 553 | 885 | 1013 | 1176 | 1089 | | 1.80 | 2.19 | 2.59 | 340 | 319.2 | 140.3 |
| Gabon | 3080 | 104.8 | 107.3 | 108.2 | 104.7 | 107.2 | 108.1 | 97.0 | 87.9 | 79.7 | 2119 | 1209 | 1398 | 2188 | 2921 | 1481 | 1.13 | 1.61 | 2.07 | 53.5 | 132.6 | 148.3 |
| Gambia, The | 230 | 154.8 | 151.8 | 135.8 | 135.2 | 152.6 | 136.2 | 122.9 | 135.7 | 118.6 | 87.9 | 104.0 | 115.0 | 80.0 | 99.5 | 113.0 | 0.25 | 0.27 | 0.32 | 279.5 | 260.3 | 277.3 |
| Ghana | 390 | 121.2 | 129.6 | 131.5 | 122.2 | 130.8 | 132.7 | 103.9 | 107.5 | 105.5 | 676.0 | 819.0 | | 952.0 | 105.6 | | 2.18 | 2.66 | 2.12 | 321.5 | 324.2 | |
| Guinea | | 103.0 | 108.0 | 110.9 | 102.9 | 108.8 | 109.8 | 91.7 | 94.0 | 92.5 | | | | 3.20 | 4634 | | 1.47 | 1.57 | 1.78 | | | |
| G-Bissau | 170 | 105.7 | 148.0 | 151.6 | 105.9 | 148.5 | 151.7 | 123.4 | 132.0 | 132.1 | 13.1 | 16.5 | 23.8 | 83.8 | 89.8 | 89.0 | 0.30 | 0.32 | 0.42 | 2267.3 | 1929.5 | 378.3 |
| Kenya | 300 | 109.2 | 111.9 | 110.9 | 108.3 | 110.3 | 107.7 | 92.7 | 97.0 | 89.2 | 553 | 1907 | 1740 | 1893 | 2158 | 2451 | 1.02 | 1.13 | 1.36 | 362.5 | 413.1 | 448.5 |
| Lesotho | 370 | 101.6 | 94.2 | 98.8 | 98.9 | 92.5 | 97.1 | 87.9 | 96.7 | 92.8 | 469.0 | 312.7 | 335.0 | 358.3 | 286.5 | 427.0 | 0.77 | 0.19 | 0.24 | 592.2 | 59.9 | 72.0 |
| Liberia | 460 | 113.1 | 115.7 | 115.5 | 114.5 | 117.0 | 116.0 | 97.8 | 107.5 | 105.5 | 469.0 | 433.0 | 415.0 | 476.0 | 412.0 | | 1.23 | 1.41 | 1.62 | 262.2 | 324.4 | |
| Libya | | 171.1 | 141.3 | 150.4 | 171.8 | 141.7 | 150.8 | 143.9 | 112.4 | 115.4 | 10353 | 5682 | 415.0 | 3.20 | 5326 | 745.0 | 2.46 | 3.01 | 3.38 | 732.4 | 734.6 | 8131 |
| Madagascar | 230 | 113.2 | 113.4 | 118.1 | 113.6 | 113.5 | 113.2 | 98.8 | 95.9 | 97.1 | 336.0 | 410.0 | 304.0 | 622.0 | 677.0 | 389.0 | 1.48 | 1.74 | 2.02 | 581.2 | 576.9 | 620.4 |
| Malawi | 180 | 109.2 | 111.9 | 110.9 | 104.5 | 106.3 | 105.1 | 96.8 | 88.2 | 84.4 | 282.0 | 274.0 | 304.0 | 389.0 | 363.0 | 655.0 | 1.53 | 1.82 | 2.04 | 378.5 | 404.1 | 430.2 |
| Mali | 420 | 116.1 | 122.8 | 122.4 | 111.8 | 122.0 | 120.7 | 100.5 | 93.2 | 90.8 | 255.0 | 451.0 | 325.0 | 578.0 | 581.0 | 619.0 | 0.62 | 0.66 | 0.78 | 107.1 | 74.4 | 64.2 |
| Mauritania | 1200 | 98.6 | 111.2 | 111.8 | 111.2 | 117.0 | 118.4 | 101.0 | 104.6 | 104.1 | 403.0 | 891.0 | 120.8 | 644.0 | 848.0 | 1202 | 16.27 | 18.85 | 20.71 | 396.1 | 379.9 | 381.8 |
| Mauritius | 590 | 119.0 | 144.9 | 118.9 | 112.2 | 145.0 | 116.3 | 104.8 | 125.1 | 98.6 | 578.0 | 4961 | 5424 | 5126 | | 5821 | | | 3.59 | | | |
| Morocco | 600 | 97.5 | 99.8 | 100.0 | 98.4 | 101.0 | 101.7 | 85.0 | 84.9 | 83.2 | 4128 | | | | | | | | | | | |
| Mozambique | 210 | 123.4 | 129.2 | 130.5 | 123.7 | 129.6 | 130.6 | 104.7 | 106.0 | 103.1 | 1299 | 6931 | 7782 | 11507 | 6427 | 7884 | 19.52 | 24.47 | 26.71 | 150.2 | 363.1 | 369.0 |
| Nigeria | 640 | 103.9 | 106.7 | 109.1 | 101.9 | 105.2 | 107.4 | 86.4 | 86.2 | 85.2 | 171.5 | 237.9 | 176.4 | 350.7 | 428.9 | 432.6 | 0.35 | 0.44 | 0.58 | 206.9 | 185.2 | 330.7 |
| Rwanda | 290 | | | | | | | | | | 91.5 | 12.7 | | 30.3 | 36.6 | 36.1 | 0.44 | 0.08 | 0.09 | 677.7 | 592.4 | 949.7 |
| S.T & Principe | 420 | 123.5 | 122.7 | 122.9 | 123.1 | 121.9 | 121.9 | 108.2 | 104.3 | 101.5 | 843.0 | 1050 | 1290 | 2280 | 1690 | 1970 | 2.44 | 3.01 | 3.69 | 267.9 | 287.9 | 266.4 |
| Senegal | 3088 | | | | | | | | | | | 1303 | | 150.0 | 173.0 | | 0.04 | 0.11 | 0.12 | 658.6 | 620.0 | |
| Seychelles | 310 | 100.7 | 113.2 | 114.2 | 101.2 | 112.2 | 112.9 | 92.7 | 100.6 | 99.4 | 160.0 | 153.0 | | 200.0 | 164.0 | | 0.54 | 0.60 | 0.66 | 336.7 | 389.7 | |
| Sierra Leone | 280 | 115.0 | 122.4 | 125.1 | 115.0 | 122.4 | 125.1 | 098.9 | 103.6 | 103.2 | 128.0 | 116.0 | 712.0 | 448.0 | 487.0 | 1664 | 2.07 | 2.31 | 2.53 | 16.3 | 198.8 | 1562 |
| Somalia | 320 | 118.7 | 122.6 | 119.5 | 116.1 | 122.5 | 117.0 | 100.8 | 103.4 | 95.9 | 1245 | 837.0 | 506.9 | 1887 | 1914 | 513.5 | 8.93 | 9.57 | 11.13 | 717.2 | 1143.6 | 57.8 |
| Sudan | 690 | 112.5 | 133.4 | 123.4 | 112.7 | 135.8 | 124.5 | 97.0 | 113.2 | 100.6 | 2657.8 | 363.5 | | 365.1 | 421.3 | 1173 | 0.21 | 0.24 | 0.29 | 78.5 | 66.8 | 966.4 |
| Swaziland | 250 | 104.7 | 108.7 | 112.5 | 108.0 | 113.3 | 115.1 | 90.6 | 90.0 | 89.8 | 395.0 | 445.0 | 449 | 1099 | 1173 | 1284 | 3.88 | 4.07 | 4.34 | 983.4 | 914.6 | 269.7 |
| Tanzania | 250 | 106.4 | 109.6 | 112.6 | 103.6 | 106.5 | 109.7 | 89.7 | 89.2 | 89.1 | 363.0 | 403.0 | 453 | 427.0 | 576 | 590 | 0.94 | 1.07 | 1.22 | 265.2 | 283.9 | 269.7 |
| Togo | 1140 | 133.7 | 119.7 | 135.1 | 134.6 | 119.7 | 133.6 | 120.9 | 105.6 | 116.9 | 3018 | 3111 | 3794 | 3607 | 3814 | 3939 | 4.92 | 5.88 | 6.90 | 162.8 | 189.0 | 182.1 |
| Tunisia | 230 | 147.4 | 152.6 | 151.0 | 146.3 | 152.2 | 150.3 | 124.1 | 124.7 | 118.9 | 372.0 | 410.0 | 372 | 389 | 479 | 702.0 | 1.16 | 1.26 | 1.41 | 310.6 | 307.7 | 377.9 |
| Uganda | 160 | 116.5 | 117.6 | 120.6 | 116.0 | 117.1 | 120.1 | 100.2 | 98.1 | 97.6 | 2007 | 2028 | 1930 | 2369 | 2546 | 2720 | 5.89 | 6.93 | 8.63 | 293.3 | 341.9 | 447.1 |
| Zaire | 300 | 114.8 | 122.2 | 122.5 | 114.3 | 121.9 | 119.3 | 96.9 | 99.8 | 94.4 | 667.0 | 732 | 955 | 1043 | 1170 | 979 | 4.64 | 5.63 | 6.40 | 535.3 | 768.4 | 670.2 |
| Zambia | 620 | 126.4 | 128.1 | 108.0 | 121.5 | 124.2 | 89.2 | 102.4 | 101.0 | 70.0 | 1301 | 1531 | 1650 | 1403 | 1556 | 1640 | 2.20 | 2.34 | 2.51 | 168.7 | 152.8 | 152.2 |

707

In general, African leaders are either incapable of solving or unwilling to take a firm stand in, political conflicts arising from the lack of control of access to the ever scarcer resources. Many African governments have been forced to cut imports and development projects. For example, between 1982 and 1983 Niger and Ghana cut their health expenditure by 3 and 10 per cent respectively. Sudan spends 6nly 1.4 per cent of its budget on medical services. Ethiopia, Burkina Faso, Chad, Rwanda, Mozambique and Zaire spend the equivalent of $1 per year per person for health services. Compare this to Sweden's $550, Canada's $457, France's $370 and Japan's $171 health expenditure per person.

## Conclusion

Development problems in Africa are closely interwoven with 'the continent's environmental degradation. While environmental destruction has partly contributed to underdevelopment, the latter has driven the majority of African societies into desperate exploitation of the remaining resources in order to meet their basic food and energy requirements. This situation clearly differs from that experienced in developed nations, Africans have overstretched the carrying capacity of their ecosystems through rapid increases in population. They have drastically reduced the resilience of their environment, thus, causing widespread disparity in the distribution of resources and creating a wide gap between population growth and food production.

On the brighter side, some countries are beginning to realise that there is a limit to the use and misuse of resources. Unhappily, those countries are few and their efforts to conserve environmental resources and share information find few imitators. Again, the current world recession coupled with heavy debts and wide gaps in the balance of payments, is diluting Africa's efforts to develop economically and to fight environmental problems. Much rethinking, policy orientation, mobilisation and participation obviously has to come from within Africa; yet there is need for the wealthier nations to assist Africa in her efforts to save her ecosystems. Africa is part of this planet and global efforts are necessary for the good of all.

## Questions

1. Discuss the main factors which have brought about rapid modifications of Africa's environment.

2. Differentiate between 'pollution of poverty' and 'pollution of wealth'.

3. Why is it said that Africa's ecosystems are both diverse and vulnerable?

4. Despite many external and internal efforts to break Africa's poverty syndrome, the continent has achieved little in terms of economic development. Discuss.

5. Discuss the implications for cash crop economy during and after the colonial era.

6. Why are energy and food crises the most serious causes of the present environmental degradation in Africa?

7. Discuss the probable effects of the advance of desertification in Africa south of the Sahara

8. Suggest possible solutions to the population crisis in Africa south of the Sahara.

9. Discuss the relationship between political instability and ecological stress.

10. How does environmental degradation lead to social unrest and food insecurity?

## Bibliography

Acharya, S., "Perspectives and Problems of Development in sub-Saharan Africa" *World Bank Reprint Series*, 77, 9 (London: Pergamon Press Ltd., 1981). pp 109-147.

Allan, W. *The African Husbandman*, (London: Green Press, 1965).

Bartelmus, P. *Environmental and Development*, (London: Pergamon Press Ltd 1985).

Biswas, A. "Facts and Trends - World Bank and Environment", 6 (Bonn: German Foundation for International Development 1989).

Dregrie, H.E. "Desertification: Symptoms of a Crisis. Desertification: Process, Problems, Perspectives. Arid/Semi-Arid Natural Resource Programme",. (Tuscon: University of Arizona (TUSCON), 1976).

Dumont, R. and Mollin, M.F. *Stranglehold on Africa,* (London: Andrea Dentich, 1983).

Ecoafrica, "An Environment and Development Magazine for Africa NGO's " (Nairobi: UNEP, 1987).

Ecoafrica, "In Partnership with the People to Promote Sustainable Development, "(Nairobi: UNEP 1988).

Egger, K. "Methoden and Moqlichkerten des Ecofarming in Berglandern Ostafrikas" Giessen: Tropisches Institute Reihe 1 Symposium Band 8 1982.

El Ashry, M. "Projects in Conservation" in *Splash*, 3 (1987) 2; 2-6.

Ezaza,W. and Othman, H. "Political Instability and Ecological Stress in Eastern Africa," (Uppsala: Scandanavian Institute of African Studies, 1989).

B. Forge, J. "The Pornography of Poverty and the Need for Alternative Internal Development Strategy (IDS) in Africa", *Journal of Eastern African Research and Development, (1989).*

Goddard, C. "Environment and Development Planning: Some Methodological and Institutional Consideration Environment and Development in Asia and the Pacific. Experience and Prospects" (Nairobi: UNEP, 1982), 332.

Grigg, D. Food Problems in Geography. The Harsh Lands. A Study in Agricultural Development, (London: Macmillan Press Ltd, 1970).

Grosjean M. and Messerle, B. "African Mountains and Highlands: Potential and Constraints Mountain Research and Development (MS) 111-121.

Harrison, P., *The Greening of Africa: Breaking Through the Battle for Land and Food*, (London: Collins Publishing Group Earthscan Study, 1987).

Holman, M. Africa Editor Financial Times. Development Network", London: Aga Khan Development Institutions, 1989.

International Union for Conservation of Nature "World Conservation Strategy" UNEP and WWF (1980).

International Institute of Environment and Development, "An Assessment of the Resource Base that Supports the Global Economy[1]" (Nairobi: UNEP 1988/89).

Mascarehnas, A. *et. al.,* "Land Use and Farming Systems: Kenya, Tanzania, Zambia, Mozambique,". Younde, 1986 17-21.

C. Mumm, R.E. "Towards Sustainable Development. An Environmental Perspective'. *Journal of the Society for International Development (SID)* 1989.

Richard, P (ed.), "African Environment. Special Report 1. Problems and Perspectives,". (London: Internal Africa Institute (I.A.I), 1975).

Shivji, I., "The Roots of Agrarian Crisis in Tanzania - A Theoretical Perspective III, OSSREA Publishing, Volume III Number 1 1987 1, 111-134.

Strong, M. "Ending Hunger through Sustainable Development," Society for International Development (SID) (1989) 4 3-5 1.

United Nations Commission on Environment, *Our Common Future,* (London: UNEP, 1987).

UNEP, "General Assembly Regulations of the llth December 1987 on Environment - Perspective for the year 2000 and Beyond ",.42/186, (1988)

UNEP, "Environment and Development in Africa. A study for the UNEP Action in Third World". (ENDA) (London: Pergamon Press Ltd., 1981)4.

United Nations Conference on the Human Environment, "Report and Working Paper of a Panel of Experts", (1972)

United Nations Conference on Trade and Development (UNCTAD), "Trade and Development Report," (1989) 2

United States Agency for International Development (SAID),"American Research and Development Abstract, (ARDA)" 14 (1989) 4,11-15.

Westing, A. "The Environmental Component of Comprehensive Security. Ecology and Politics - Environmental Stress and Securing in Africa". (Uppsala: Scandanavian Institute of African Studies, 1989).

World Bank, *World Debt Tables. External Debt of Developing Countries*, 1, Analysis and Summary Tables 1988/1989, (Washington D.C.: World Bank, 1989).

# -11-

# Policies and Laws Affecting the Environment

J. W. Kabeberi-Macharia

## Introduction

Development of environmental law gained momentum after the Second World War. During the period of reconstruction, the war-devastated countries of Europe embarked on a rapid programme of industrialisation which had extremely damaging effects on the environment. Some of these effects have taken a long time to be remedied. The need for legal protection of the environment was motivated by two interests: first, the need to protect scenic resources for both present and future generations; and second, concern towards the protection of public health. The latter took into consideration the ever increasing population in the cities and the few facilities available to such a population. Other consequences of environmental degradation began to be felt; these included water, air and noise pollution, pollution from hazardous and conventional wastes, radiation, and of late the threat of global warming and depletion of the ozone layer.

The present state of the world's environment calls for immediate action if we are to ensure that the future generations will be able to sustain themselves. Rapid economic development has been achieved at the cost of the environment, resulting in untold sufferings to mankind and unprecedented ecological problems.

Annually, according to the 1987 report by the World Commission on the Environment and Development (WCED) - Brundtland Report, the state of the world's environment is worsening, making immediate action necessary to arrest the situation. Six million hectares of arable land are turned into worthless dry land, whilst more than 11 million hectares of forests are destroyed annually. This has led to increased changes in rainfall patterns, loss of animal and plant species and disappearance of the rain forests.

### 1. International Management of the Environment

International awareness of the need to properly manage our environment gained momentum around the middle of this century. In 1947, the United Nations Economic and Social Council adopted resolution 32 (v) which asserted that the world's natural resources were important for the reconstruction of economies ruined by the Second World War. In the 1950s and 1960s, it became more and more evident to various countries that increasing environmental degradation could not be prevented by individual states but rather required the intervention of regional groupings or organisations of interested states.

In 1972, the United Nations Conference on the Human Environment held in Stockholm (Sweden) affirmed the urgency for a properly managed environment if sustainable development was to be achieved. The conference adopted the

Declaration on the Human Environment (Stockholm Declaration) which asserted that human beings are entitled to a healthy environment which it is their duty to protect and improve for future generations. The United Nations Environmental Programme (UNEP) was created on the basis of the recommendations of this conference.

The UNEP has undertaken to develop guidelines and principles on various aspects of the environment and a number of reports have been prepared which focus on the environment and sustainable development. Other than these guidelines, there are currently some 114 conventions and protocols which touch on the environment. These conventions indicate various global concerns for the natural environment ranging from regulations on the use of water, plant protection, pollution, global warming, hazardous wastes and the protection of the ozone layer.

The most up-to-date report on the world environment is the WCED report which emphasises the need for harmonising environmental issues with developmental issues if we are to ensure sustainable growth on a global scale. In recognising that there is an accelerated ecological interdependence amongst nations, the report calls for more global co-operation in ensuring that the global ecology is not overstretched. Sustainable development can only be achieved if present needs are met without compromising the well being of future generations.

Finally, the report calls for effective management through legislative and other means by international or regional bodies especially in the areas of shared resources. The United Nations General Assembly has called upon regional organisations to undertake measures in accordance with the findings of the report.

## 2. Role of Law in Environmental Management

In the scope of environmental protection, law has a facilitative function in both national decision making and in the implementation of policy. However, it is argued that law should not be seen only in the rather passive role of a facilitator of policy implementation: it must actively work towards establishing policy where the game is wanting (Okoth Owiro, 1988). Law also assumes the role of articulating environmental policies and regulating existing programmes.

In environmental management, law assumes a three dimensional role (Ogolla Bondi, 1987).

(i) Providing for the allocation of natural resources.

Firstly law provides for the allocation of natural resources and states the rules and regulations governing their use and development. Where there is misuse of such resources, the law provides sanctions for any violations.

A good example is seen in the legislation protecting the forests in Kenya, that is the Forest Act (Chapter 385) which "makes it an offence for anyone to remove any produce from the forest or to carry out any activity within the forest which is harmful to the environment

(ii) Providing set standards for effecting resource management.

In regulating the uses of available natural resources; the primary concern of the law is to ensure appropriate resource management and guard against possible environmental deterioration. In ensuring further effective resource management, law may undertake to establish institutions which are given the responsibility of carrying out legal provisions to ensure effective management; for instance, the establishment of agricultural boards, conservation

**290**

commissions, water boards or pesticide control boards. We shall discuss these boards in greater detail later in this chapter.

In carrying out its second role, the law undertakes to provide set standards which have to be complied with in order to ensure effective resource management. This is carried out effectively through a licence or permit system, which requires the permit or licence holder to ensure compliance with set standards; failure to do so would result in the withdrawing of the permit or licence. This system is effectively used in the regulation of the uses of air, water, insecticides or pesticides. The legal issuing authority issues a permit or licence to a person, group of persons or to a company, and indicates the requisite standards which have to be met and constantly maintained. Such a permit or licence should also indicate the sanctions or penalties that one may face in the event of a violation of the stated standards arising out of environmental degradation.

Besides providing standards for using a resource, law may also prescribe the standards which have to be complied with in the event of by-products or waste being discharged into the environment. Thus, those responsible for such activities have to ensure that such discharges will be treated in such a way as to ensure that only minimum damage is caused and no harm will be done to human beings, plants and domestic or wild animals. Such requirements are often imposed upon industrial plants or local authorities.

(iii) Establishing the institutional mechanisms for controlling the impact of development projects and human activities on the environment.

These two activities are the major causes of environmental degradation and as such, they have to be checked. Development activities include the building of dams,

291

industrial plants and the introduction of new farming technology. Human activities include the clearing of land for cultivation or for settlement, agricultural practices and building of houses.

In order to protect the environment from degradation caused by such activities, the law seeks to create institutions which are competent to assess the possible impact on the environment arising from such activities. These institutions may, as in the case of development projects, require that the initiators of such projects prepare a full environmental impact assessment statement. This statement should show the possible impact of such a project and any present and future measures that will be undertaken to ensure environmental protection. Institutions demanding such a statement may also appoint independent experts to determine the provisions of an Environmental Impact Assessement Statement (BIAS).

Today, in both developing and developed countries, existing environmental legal regimes are falling or have fallen behind development activities. This makes it necessary to constantly reformulate existing laws or enact new laws in order to keep pace with such activities. Whereas the need for an effective environmental law cannot be overemphasised, one should bear in mind that by itself, law is ineffective and it requires the close cooperation of every member of the society if it is to be successful. In cases of shared natural resources such as rivers, lakes and seas, there is also a need for close co-operation among the affected countries, to ensure the protection of the shared resource.

## 3. Basic Environmental Management Laws and Policies of Developed Countries

The notion of environmental protection in order to achieve a sustainable development initially developed amongst the industrialised nations but later spread to the Third World. It was in the developed countries that environmental degradation, caused by rapid industrialisation, was most evident. As a result, the last twenty years or so have been characterised by campaigns to ensure the proper use and protection of the environment. One also finds that most international agreements on the environment have resulted from problems which have reached a crisis point within the developed countries. In discussing developed countries, we shall look at the United States of America, and how it has managed to make provisions for environmental protection.

### United States of America

Concern for environmental protection in the United States was first expressed in the last century with the enactment of the River and Harbours Act of 1889 which prohibited the dumping of waste material into navigable waterways. However, until the middle of this century, environmental concern was mostly limited to pollution control expressed through legislation or ordered by the court (Grad, 1985).

The rapid growth of industry during the two world wars, had devastating effects on the environment especially on air and water. To regulate water pollution, the Federal Water Pollution Control Act was enacted in 1948, and its primary objective was to ensure that states undertook the regulation of water pollution. This Act, however, needed to be strengthened, in order to ensure effective control. In 1965, the Water Quality Control Act was enacted to provide for the establishment of

293

water quality standards for inter-state waters, which the federal agency would use for combating pollution.

Water control was later comprehensively provided for by the 1977 Clean Water Act which amended the previous Water Acts. In seeking to achieve a no pollution water level, the Act set uniform effluent standards to be met by dischargers. The Act requires that, first, all states establish treatment management agencies; second federal effluent standards be met and enforced; and, third, states are to set ambient quality standards and provide for their enforcement. The last requirement indicates that before effluents are discharged, a permit must be granted. This ensures that any effluent discharged, meets the already set national effluent standards.

*Air*

Concern for air quality , was given legal recognition in 1965 by the Clean Air Act. This Act required that all states were to set air quality standards and make their own plans for implementing and enforcing them. The Attorney General was also given powers to ensure that any air pollution substantially dangerous to health should cease.

The Clean Air Act underwent various amendments culminating in the 1977 Clean Air Act. This amended Act provides for the establishment of national primary or secondary ambient air quality standards. These national standards are to be achieved in each air quality control region (Grad, 1985).

In addition, individual states are required to set their own standards and also indicate how they intend to attain the objectives set by the national standards. Where there is a contravention of the standards set, and pollution results, the Environment Protection Agency is empowered by the Act to undertake to prosecute the polluters and bring an abatement to the pollution.

Pollution from solid waste (either conventional or hazardous) is an ever increasing problem arising out of industrialisation. The growing concern over this problem culminated in the 1965 Solid Waste Disposal Act. Despite this enactment, solid waste was considered a lesser problem than air and water pollution. But in 1976, the enactment of the Resource Conservation and Recovery Act indicated that this problem should no longer be marginalised. The 1976 Act requires the safe disposal of hazardous waste materials and bars open dumping. Disposal of this waste should be carried out in permitted disposal facilities, and contractors doing the dumping must keep a record of the type, quantity and locations where hazardous waste is disposed of. Although states must operate their own programmes, they have to meet the stated national requirements on waste management.

In addition to the threat of pollution, the threat of radiation (which is harmful to health and to the environment) is also taken seriously in the U.S.A. The Atomic Energy Act of 1946 established an Atomic Energy Commission to set standards for radiation protection with regard to nuclear installations. The Commission has also prescribed standards for protecting the general environment from radioactive materials. It may grant, modify or revoke licences where it deems necessary.

*Noise*

The need for a noise free environment, led to the Noise Control Act of 1972, which gives the Environmental Protection Agency (E.P.A.) administrator power to develope and publish criteria on noise, identify those products which are major sources of noise and formulate noise emission standards for them.

### The N.E.P.A

Perhaps the most important environmental statute to enhance evironmental awareness in the U.S.A. is the National Environmental Policy Act (NEPA) of 1969. This Act established the Environmental Protection Agency to oversee the protection and conservation of the environment. The EPA is empowered to set standards which are to be met by states with respect to various aspects of the environment, for example, air or water quality standards.

In situations where development practices affect the environment, the N.E.P.A. requires that development agencies must provide an environmental impact assessment statement outlining how the agency intends to deal with environmental damage arising from the activity, both presently and in the future.

However, these statements are only necessary where it is a federal activity which is major in scope and will significantly affect the quality of the environment. Unhappily, this leaves out private developers who cause a great deal of damage and who may claim that their activity is not "major" (Grad, 1985).

It is evident, from the facts and legislations mentioned in this section that the U.S.A, among other developed countries is very much concerned with the environment. Where industrialisation has led to environmental degradation, the U.S.A. is fortunate enough to have advanced technological means of addressing and managing existing and future environmental problems.

## 4. Environmental Management Policies and Laws in Third World Countries

The need for efficient environmental management in order to ensure a sustainable economic growth, has not escaped the governments of most Third World countries. The policy makers in these countries are faced with the difficult task of making decisions which will promote economic development and yet have minimum impact on the environment. Development and the environment are complementary to each other and this is why there is a need to harmonise environmental conservation objectives and natural developmental aspirations and goals (Okoth Owiro, 1988; WCED, 1987).

However, environmental considerations have often been viewed by various developing countries as hampering economic development. As a result of such shortsighted policies, economic and social development has been achieved at the cost of the deterioration of the environment. The need for rapid economic growth in order to improve the standards of living, was voiced by African countries at a regional seminar on the Human Evironment in 1971. In their declaration, they stated that economic and social development is essential for ensuring a favourable living and working environment for man and for the improvement of the quality of life. This lays a heavy burden upon the environment in the name of development.

Today, most African countries are faced with the threat of continuous desertification, which, coupled with the 1984 - 1985 severe drought has resulted in untold sufferings. These deserts could have been avoided by effective management to ensure that the environment is not overstrained.

Most developing countries (including those in Africa) are also faced with the problems of deforestation and pollution which result in immense environmental degradation, and may eventually lead to the loss of animal and plant species, changes in rain patterns and the disappearance of rain forests (WCED,1987).Therefore, where the environment is overstressed because of the urgency for immediate development, future economic progress is threatened. This can produce negative results as the quality of life and that of the entire environment continue to deteriorate. In discussing the position of Third World countries, we will concentrate on the Kenyan situation.

## 5. Environmental Management Policies and the Law in Kenya

Kenya has to balance environmental protection against socioeconomic development in planning the future. We are clearly aware of the harsh consequences of environmental deterioration already too common in other African countries.

### (a) Policy

Since her Independence, Kenya has formulated her own environmental policies and has established an effective institutional framework to implement these. The initial concern was voiced in the 1965 Sessional Paper No. 10 on African Socialism and its Application to Planning in Kenya. It stated that:

> While many of our domestic resources are not fully utilised, still others are being dissipated, wasted and in some cases destroyed. The use of outmoded farming techniques may result in erosion; the cutting of wind - breaks, and the burning of vegetation may turn fertile acres into desert; and

the destruction of forests may eliminate important water supplies. Practices tending to harm rather than conserve our physical environment must be curbed through education and legislation.

Therefore... concern to the quality of the environment must be put on equal footing with the need for its exploitation.

The sessional paper further recognised that the well-being of future generations would depend on the adoption and implementation of policies which were expected to ensure the conservation of natural resources and create an enjoyable physical environment.

Besides showing an early concern for environmental protection, Kenya's initial awareness was enhanced by the Stockholm Declaration of 1972, and the creation of the United Nations Environmental Programme whose headquarters are in Nairobi. This made Kenya the first developing country to be chosen as the headquarters of a United Nations Organisation. In 1976, the United Nations Human Settlement Secretariat (UNHSS - Habitat) was also established in Kenya. Hosting such major bodies renewed Kenya's concern for the need to protect the environment. Today, Kenya has emerged as possibly the leading African nation in environmental protection.

Kenya's environmental policy cannot however be found in one specific document; it is laid down in ministerial statements, development plans, sessional papers and various legislations.

The 1974-78 Development Plan recognised the competing interests in land use as the population increased. The 1979-83 Development Plan further stated that environmental considerations must motivate and influence development decisions taken at every level from family to government. The

1983-88 Development Plan recognised that there is a need to control human behaviour in order to maintain a proper balance between the nation's development and the protection of the environment.

The current 1989-93 Development Plan formulates Kenyan's best policy (so far) on environmental protection. The Plan, which devotes a chapter to resources and environment, recognises that there are developmental activities which, white conferring benefits to the individual and the nation, have the tendency of generating diseconomies in the form of soil erosion , gaseous emissions, liquid effluent and toxic accumulations from industrial activities, all of which pollute the environment.

It is clear that certain projects which may temporarily benefit the nation as a whole often do not in the long run result in positive economic development. To obviate unwise and wasteful use of resourses, there is a need for sound environmental management. In our country, the government wants to ensure that development does not take place at the expense of the natural environment (Development Plan, 1989-1993). Within the plan period, the government will insistute measures to attain a balance between the development needs of the nation and environment protection. Such measures include:

(i) Assessment of the impact of individual projects and the setting of standards by the Government for sustainable use of resources and disposal of wastes, in situations where human health and safety may be at stake.

(ii) The imposition of surcharges by the Government on those concerns and activities which pollute the environment. Such surcharges will be used to compensate those affected by such actions and to pay for the cost of rehabilitation.

(iii) In the exploitation of non-renewable resources, the exploiters will be required to develop new technologies that use less of such resources or seek alternative resources in order to maintain a careful balance between the needs of the present and those of future generations.

(iv) The Government will, during the Plan period make provision for the enactment of a National Environment Enhancement and Management Act (NEEMA).

This Plan provides a more comprehensive policy and reflects the government's concern for sound environmental management in order to achieve sustainable development. Whereas such a concern was present in the past development plans, it was not so explicitly expressed.

### (b) Law

In discussing evironmental law in Kenya, we shall look at both common law and statutory law.

### Common Law

"Common Law" refers to English common law which is applicable in Kenya by virtue of Section 3 of the Judicature Act This Act states that Kenya accepts common law principles in existence in England as of 12th August 1987; doctrines of equity, statutes of general application, and English judicial decisions. This applies so far as the circumstances of Kenya and its inhabitants permit and is subject to such qualification as those circumstances may make necessary.

Such rules are applicable unless varied by Kenyan statutes or judicial decisions. The phrase "Common Law", however, usually refers to that law which is created by the customs of people and the decisions of judges.

Under common law, the owner or in some cases the mere possessor of property has an almost unrestricted right to the use of his property. However, such owner or occupier has a duty, first to avoid causing injuries to individuals within or near that property and second, to safeguard the interests of other parties on that property.

### (i) Torts

Environmental protection under common law is carried out through the law of tons which provides remedies for nuisance, trespass, negligence or abnormally dangerous activities which are harmful to others.

Damages are payable by the defendant if he has committed an act or omitted to perform his duty without any just cause or excuse.

However, tort law is concerned mostly with injury to the human being rather than damage to the physical environment: therefore if damage to the physical environment does not cause any form of injury to human beings, it is not actionable per se.

### (ii) Nuisance

Nuisance arises from unreasonable, unwarranted or unlawful use, by a person, of his own property, causing obstruction or injury to the rights of another or to the public. Such activity becomes actionable if it results in material annoyance, inconvenience and discomfort which harms or injures others, and prevents their reasonable enjoyment of the property they occupy.

There are, however, three forms of nuisance, that is public, private and mixed. A *public nuisance* is that which affects an indefinite number of persons although the extent of injuries suffered need not be equal. A *private nuisance* is that which "affects either an individual or a few persons by causing damage or deterioration of property and hinders the useful enjoyment thereof". The injury suffered should be a special injury which is different from injuries suffered by the general public. Lastly, a mixed nuisance is a mixture of both private and public nuisance in that it affects and injures the general public and also produces special injuries to certain persons.

*Common nuisances* are those of air and noise pollution and their control or prevention is provided for by way of injunctions. Injunctions may be either temporary or permanent and their effect is to require the perpetrator to remove the nuisance and prevent its continuation.

### (iii) Trespass

The term *trespass* refers to an unlawful entry and stay upon another's premises without lawful permission. In the course of , trespassing, the trespasser may also commit an act which is harmful to the interests of the owner or occupier of the premises. Trespassing may occur when certain gases, fumes or noxious matter are emitted or discharged into the premises of another.

The tort exists when such emission is caused either intentionally or negligently; its occurrence must be direct. Examples include releasing sewage water or oil into the land of another, or allowing the emission of noxious fumes which directly enter another person's premises. In bringing an action for trespass, unlike in nuisance actions the affected person need not prove that any damage has occurred and therefore trespass is actionable *per se*.

### (iv) Negligence

The Law prescribes certain standards of conduct which a person has to conform with in specific circumstances, and where one fails to do so and others are injured as a result, this amounts to actionable negligence. Negligence is, therefore, no more than heedless or careless conduct which results, in damage suffered by a person "who is owed a duty by another, the breach of which results in the damage".

Thus, a person is required to take such reasonable care as to avoid acts of omissions which can be reasonably foreseen to be likely to injure a neighbour. In the scope of environmental law, thus, a person is required to take such reasonable care as to avoid acts of omissions which can be reasonably foreseen to be likely to injure a neighbour. In the scope of environmental law, this duty has been treated, damage has been caused, to the property or the person of another.

However, the injured party must establish that a duty of care was owed to him and that the damage suffered is a consequence of the breach by the polluter. The damage suffered should not be too remote a consequence of the breach, which a reasonable man could not have foreseen. Examples of negligent acts include releasing sewage water into a river used by both human beings and domestic animals; discharging oil into the ocean resulting in marine pollution, the negligent handling of chemicals which results in a major industrial accident; or the dumping of noxious matter without taking reasonable care to protect the environment.

(v)   Strict Liability

There are situations where persons are not negligent in their actions, but are nevertheless found liable for any damages which arise from their action. In the case of Rylands Vs Fletcher I (1968 L.R. 3.H.L.330) the defendants employed independent contractors to build a reservoir on their land. Beneath the reservoir was a mine whose shafts were not blocked during the construction of the reservoir.

When the reservoir was\filled, water escaped down the shafts and flooded the mine of the plaintiffs. The court found that the defendants should be held liable for the damages suffered by the plaintiff. A ruling was made in this case: in the non-natural use of his land, a person is responsible for the accumulation on it of anything likely to do harm if it escapes and interferes with the use of the land of another.

The category of 'things' is, however, restrictive and it must be established that they are things which are likely to escape and cause harm. This includes, waste accumulated in dumps, noxious gases and fumes from an industrial plant, fire and things likely to cause fire, explosives, water, and harmful plants. However, the accumulation of these things must be proved to have been carried out in the non-natural use of one's land, that is artificially if the accumulator is to be held liable in the event of escape.

In protecting the environment, common law has limited application in that the relief awarded is either in the form of damages or in the issue of an injunction to prevent the occurrence of the activity complained of. The protection of the environment against future recurrence of the same action was never guaranteed although in essence an injunction should guard against recurrence.

In the above case, the perpetrator of the damage was not required by common law to clean up his mess and the extent of his liability depended on the extent of damage caused. The only enforcement agency for common law is the court which plays a minimum role in ensuring environmental protection. As society develops, statutory laws are formulated to regulate competing interests in the use of natural resources.

**Statutory Law**

Kenya's environmental law is sectored and administrative in nature and is mainly concerned with the regulation of the use of water, land, minerals, forests and the protection of both wild and marine life. Today there are some 66 statutes in force which touch and affect the environment.

(i)   **Use of Land**

The protection of the environment, the conservation of natural resources and pollution control are basically tied up with the question of the permitted uses of land. Land is the - most important resource, available in that it provides the means of livelihood for more than 80 per cent of Kenya's population. About 18 per cent (104,844 sq.km) of the total land in Kenya is arable land which is used for agriculture, whilst 36,300 square kilometres are set aside for wildlife conservation and only 2,008 square kilometres are under forest cover. The remaining land is either arid or semi arid.

The rising population has also placed heavy demands on the available arable land in order to sustain itself. Competing and conflicting interests in the use of land have increased. Such uses include agriculture, forestry, wildlife protection, mining and urban settlement. These interests have also placed heavy demands upon the environment and this situation has inevitably resulted in environmental degradation. In the last twenty years or so legislation has been enacted to regulate these interests, although it must be, admitted that environmental concerns are not adequately covered by law.

Kenya's land use policy is not clearly defined and is mainly found in scattered legislation, sessional papers, ministerial statements and development plans. The most important individual interests and legislative regulations are discussed here below.

**Agriculture**

Kenya's emphasis on agricultural development cannot be overstated as Kenya is largely an agricultural country. The overall agricultural policy of the government is to achieve internal self-sufficiency, maintain adequate levels of strategic reserves and generate additional supplies of food for export. Because there is limited arable land, there is a need for the intensification of agricultural practices and techniques if we are to achieve internal self sufficiency in food and meet the demands of the ever increasing population.

In the past two decades, Kenya has relied more and more heavily on the use of pesticides, fertilisers, and modern methods of animal husbandry in order to boost her agricultural production and achieve higher levels of agricultural development. This has been at the cost of the environment as soil depletion, soil erosion, water and air pollution occur due to poor farming

Land preservation and soil conservation is ensured through Land Preservation Rules made by the Minister under Section 48 of the Act. Such rules regulate, control, and prohibit the clearing of land for cultivation, grazing, and watering of livestock where the Minister considers it either necessary or expedient for purposes of conservation of the soil, or prevention of erosion. These Rules further protect land against flooding, landslides, formation of gullies and storms; they also endeavour to ensure the preservation of the soil and its fertility. These rules may also provide for the maintenance of water level in a body of water.

Besides making rules regulating the clearing of land, the Minister is further empowered to make rules which regulate and control afforestation and reafforestation, protection of slopes and catchment areas, drainage of land, construction and maintenance of artificial or natural drains, terraces, contour banks, and diversion ditches. Where a person who has been served with a land preservation order fails to comply, the Minister is empowered by Section 56 of the Act to authorise another person to enter the land and carry out such works as are necessary to comply with the order. Where this is done, all expenses incurred shall be paid by the owner or occupier of the affected land.

Under Section 184 of the Act, the Minister may make general rules for the preservation, utilisation and development of agricultural land. These include requiring owners or occupiers of land to abide by rules of good husbandry, and estate management, and regulate the kinds of crops grown, methods of cultivation used and the keeping of livestock practices such as over cultivation, overgrazing and misuse of agricultural chemicals.

In empowering the Minister for Agriculture to make land preservation rules and management orders, the Act attempts to prevent practices which lead to the degradation of land. The Act recognises that total mismanagement of land can lead to disastrous results such as desertification, a process which is difficult and very costly to arrest. Desertification is an ever present threat in Kenya considering that four-fifths (473,000 $Km^2$ of the land is either semi arid or arid.

Keeping livestock for domestic purposes may be devastating to the environment due to overgrazing and overstocking both of which result in soil erosion. The Crop Production and Livestock Act Chapter 321, seeks to regulate and control overgrazing and overstocking. Section 4A of the Act empowers local authorities to make by-laws for purposes of prohibiting the keeping or grazing of cattle on any agricultural land; regulating the number of livestock kept and providing for the compulsory reduction of livestock. The Crop Production and Livestock (cattle) Rules (1959) also empower a District Commissioner to order a person grazing livestock in a problem area to cease doing so.

The Act also makes provision for the improvement of crop production and, under Section 4, the Minister is empowered to make rules regulating the improvement of a crop's cultural condition and prevent its destruction or waste.

The use of pesticides, herbicides and fertilisers is widespread all over the world. Fertilisers used in agriculture have been known to persist for long periods on the land and may be washed off by rain water into the rivers. This eventually results in water pollution which can be injurious to both humans and animals. Legislative control of the use of such chemicals is discussed separately in this chapter.

The present land tenure system and certain cultural practices have often been accused of assisting the uneconomic subdivision of agricultural land. The Land Control Act, Chapter 302, provides against the uneconomic parcelling of agricultural land by requiring that before such subdivision is carried out, consent is sought and given. There is special provision by the Trust Lands Act, Chapter 288, which regulates the use and occupation of such land. The overall control over the trust lands is vested upon county councils which are empowered by the Act to grant licences for purposes of livestock grazing, removal of forest produce extraction of common minerals, opening of roads and establishment of "temporary accommodation.

Section 65 further empowers the Minister in charge to make rules which provide for the control of grazing and pasturing of livestock reconditioning of land and prohibiting or regulating its occupation, regulating the use and conservation of any productive area, (including forest), and lastly regulating the ways in which county councils grant licences.

Plant protection is provided for by both the Plant Protection Act, Chapter 324 and the Seed and Plant Varieties Act, Chapter 326. The Plant Protection Act seeks to prevent the introduction and spread of diseases which are destructive to plants. Plants include any member of the vegetable kingdom ...(including) any part of a plant whether severed from the plant or not.

Plant protection is provided for by the Plant Protection Act, Chapter 324 and the Seed and Plant Varieties Act, Chapter 326. The Plant Protection Act seeks to prevent the introduction and spread of diseases which are destructive to plants. Plants include any member of the vegetable kingdom ... (including) any part of a plant whether severed from the plant or not.

The Minister for Agriculture is empowered by Section 3 to make rules to prevent and control the spread of pests and diseases. Under Section 4, owners or occupiers of land are under a duty to remove pests or diseases when they are requested to do so by an authorised officer. The Act thus plays a dual role of providing protection both to the specific plant species and to the habitat. This ensures a healthy environment for plants.

The Seed and Plant Varieties Act also regulates the production and marketing of seeds, approves varieties of plants and restricts the introduction of new plant varieties Section 3 of the Act empowers the Minister for Agriculture to make regulations which deal with the, control of production, processing, testing, certification and marketing of seeds.

Regulation of seed production is also done through the control of plant breeding which is a licenced system under Part V of the Act. It is only plants or seeds which are adaptable to the environment and thus not destructive to it that are regulated by the Act.

In order to protect the plant environment from noxious weeds which are destructive, the Suppression of Noxious Weeds Act Chapter 325, empowers the Minister in charge by notice in the Kenya Gazette to declare a plant to be a noxious weed. An owner or occupier of land where such a weed is found is required to remove it: failing this, the relevant authorities may enter the land and eradicate the weed.

**Forestry**

From time immemorial, forests have provided the Kenyan people with wood fuel and raw materials. Today, forests cover some 2,008 square kilometers and this includes indigenous forests, exotic plantations forests and the mangrove forests of the coastal areas. In recognising the need to protect, manage and conserve her forests, Kenya's forests policy (declared in the present and past development plans) provides for inter alia reservation of land for forestry; protection of forest resources; increased tree planting; conservation of forest resources and promotion of forests for public amenities and wildlife protection.

Kenya's forest law is mainly found in the Forest Act Chapter 385. This Act provides the structural framework within which national forest policies are set, it also reflects Kenyans objectives and priorities in this regard. The Act mainly deals with the conservation and management of forest resources and provides for the establishment, control and regulation of forests and forest areas on government land.

The Minister in charge of forests is authorised by Section 4 of the Act to declare any unalienated government land to be a forest area or cease to be a forest area. Under Section 6, the Minister may declare a forest area to be a natural reserve in order to conserve its natural flora and fauna. Where such a declaration has been made, no person (unless licenced by the Chief Conservator of Forests) may undertake any activity in the area. Such activities include tree felling, burning of grass or vegetation, removal of any forest produce; erection of buildings, grazing of livestock, clearing or cultivation, road construction, or even poaching.

Sections 10 and 11 of the Act further empower a magistrate, forest officer, police officer or chief game warden to demand the production of licence by a person found in a forest area. They may also arrest or search any person suspected of committing an offence under the Act. These officers may also seize any forest produce found in the illegal possession of someone and also seize and detain cattle found in a forest area. Any activity within the natural reserve, which will involve the disturbance of the flora or fauna is prohibited unless licenced by the Chief Conservator of Forests.

The administration of forests is done through a licencing system backed by a criminal law framework, whereby penal sanctions are provided for those who commit an offence under the Act. However, the Forest Act is silent on the question of wood fuel for purposes of providing energy. Currently, the demand for wood fuel energy for usual households has been on the increase, necessitating proper management strategies for the preservation of existing forests.

The other legislations offering protection to forests are the Agriculture Act Chapter 318 and the Timber Act Chapter 386. The Agriculture Act empowers the minister for Agriculture to issue land preservation rules which regulate, prohibit or control afforestation or reafforestation. These rules further regulate or prohibit the clearing of land and the uprooting of vegetation for purposes of agriculture. The Timber Act is not however a forest conservation legislation in that it is primarily concerned with regulating the export the, sale, grading, inspection and marketing of timber.

### Human Settlement and Urbanisation

As growing population puts increasing demands on the available natural resources, due to this increase, problems of planning urban systems and of improving existing human settlements, are on the rise. In Kenya, these problems are further aggravated by rural-urban migration which has been attributed to the growth of urban centres to unmanageable proportions. Hence, the growth of slum settlements in some of the major towns such as Nairobi, Mombasa or Kisumu. These settlements, which offer shelter to the lower income groups, lack basic services such as water, proper sanitation or waste disposal services all of which pose a grave danger to the people living in the settlements.

313

These problems call for systematic land planning to ensure that these developments do not destroy the environment. Where land planning fails, the result is deterioration in the quality of land and other natural resources. Due to the rapid growth of Kenya's population, there is an increasing demand for both housing and other basic facilities, making it a major concern of the government to provide for these. Thus, in planning and managing human settlements, effects on the environment have to be carefully considered in the provision of basic shelter, infrastructure and services.

Land planning law in Kenya is found in the Planning Act Chapter 134; the Town Planning Act Chapter 303; building by-laws, and the Local Government Act. The main purpose of land planning legislation is to control the physical planning of human settlements, which is of great importance since it affects the environment. Under the Land Planning Act, a local authority may, with the minister's authority, prepare a "town plan" for a municipality and an "area plan". These plans must contain descriptive materials such as maps, and materials indicating existing developments, roads or density zones.

Where an owner seeks to develop a plot of land which is within the jurisdiction of a local authority, consent from the area's interim planning authority is required. Where consent is sought in order to change the use of agricultural land and such land exceeds 20 acres, consent of the land control board is a requisite, and it may or may not be granted. This Act further defines development to mean any material change in the use or density of any buildings or land. Use, for purposes of the Act, includes such activities as settlements, effects on the environment have to be carefully considered in the provision of basic shelter, infrastructure and services. Land planning law in Kenya is found in the Planning Act Chapter 134; the Town

Planning Act Chapter 303; building bylaws, and the Local Government Act. The main purpose of land planning legislation is to control the physical planning of human settlements, which is of great importance since it affects the environment. Under the Land Planning Act, a local authority may, with the Minister's authority, prepare a "town plan" for a municipality and an "area plan". These plans must contain descriptive materials such as maps, and materials indicating existing developments, roads or density zones, as well as deposit of refuse, scrap or waste materials on the land.

The Local Government Act, (Chapter 265), which establishes local authorities, defines their functions by providing that each municipal council has the powers to establish and maintain inter alia sanitary services or any other services used for disposal of refuse and effluent, public lavatories, control of slaughter houses, destruction and suppression of rats and vermin and the planting of trees in public places. In vesting the duty on the local authorities to establish and maintain these services, the Act ensures the protection of the environment through administrative control and regulations.

The Public Health Act, Chapter 242, further imposes a duty upon local authorities to ensure that the areas of their jurisdiction are kept clean and in sanitary conditions. The Act further provides that no owner or occupier shall cause a nuisance or cause to exist on his land or premises any condition injurious to health. Under conditions that are considered nuisances, Section 118 of the Act lists roads, vehicles or buildings which are in bad state and can be injurious to health.

Also included in the list are polluted water, noxious matter, deposit of refuse, accumulation of stones or timber which are likely to harbour rats or vermin, and dirty factories or work-houses. In order to control the nuisance or its recurrence, the Medical Officer of Health within the local authority, is required to issue a notice to the author of such nuisance requiring its removal within a prescribed time. Failure to comply with such a notice shall cause one to be brought before a court; an order to effect the same is then issued. Failure to comply with the court order amounts to an offence under the Act.

The Minister for Local Government may make by-laws under Section 126A regarding unsanitary housing and providing for proper sanitation. Any building declared to be unfit for human habitation is required by the law to be demolished.

The Public Health Act further imposes a duty upon local authorities to ensure that public water supplies are protected from pollution. The Local authority is thus under an obligation to ensure that purification of polluted water is carried out. In order to ensure prevention of water pollution, the Minister for Health is empowered by Section 130 to make rules for the protection of these supplies.

**Wildlife Protection**

Animal resources, together with plant resources and abiotic natural resources, form the basis of economic development. It is therefore very important that vital habitats be protected in order to prevent extinction. As a result of the rapid growth of population, the land put aside for wildlife conservation is currently threatened by increasing demands for agricultural land. This has led to the numbers of wildlife decreasing as their habitat is cleared or reclaimed for farming or other uses. This is coupled with an increase in poaching activities which threaten animals such as elephants, rhinos, leopards and crocodiles.

In recognising that wildlife conservation is an important factor in preserving the ecological balance and our natural heritage, the Government, in the Sixth Development Plan, points out the need to establish the optimal balance between devoting such lands to wildlife and demand for human settlement

Conservation strategies that will be undertaken include: suppression of poaching, carrying out research for enhancing conservation, translocation of threatened species to parks or reserves to enhance their conservation, special protection of endangered species; training of wildlife personnel, educating the public on the need to protect the environment, and protecting the public and domestic animals from damage by wildlife.

Legislation related to wildlife conservation and management is provided for in the Wildlife Conservation and Management Act, Chapter 376. The Act, which provides for the establishment of a department of wildlife conservation and management, empowers the minister in charge of wildlife to establish certain areas as national parks or reserves for purposes of wildlife conservation.

In order to protect animals within the game parks or reserves, the Act makes provision for the control of hunting, whereby hunting licences are issued to persons who want to hunt within such areas. Failure to obtain a licence for hunting amounts to an offence under the Act. However, one may kill an animal without a licence where this is in defence of human life. In situations where game animals have caused considerable damage to crops or killed or wounded domestic animals, an occupier of land or his servant may kill such an animal. One should bear in mind that this killing is only permitted in defence of property.

However, where one causes unnecessary or undue suffering to any protected or game animal, or keeps a wounded animal in his possession without permission from the game warden, such a person is guilty of an offence and is liable to pay a fine of Ksh 5,000.00 or face a term of not more than eighteen months in prison or both. In seeking to regulate the trade in trophies and live animals, the Act provides that any trophy found without an owner and any game or protected animal or bird, whether live or dead, is the property of the government. Where a person is in possession of any of these without a licence, such a person is guilty of an offence and is liable to pay a fine not exceeding Ksh 10,000.00 or face imprisonment for 1 year or both.

Although the law seeks to protect wildlife against poaching activities, there is also a need for other controls to be undertaken to curb these activities. The antipoaching units should consist of well trained and equipped personnel. Because of the ivory and rhino horn trade, some countries have taken stronger measures, such as refusing to buy ivory or rhino horn from countries where poaching is rampant. By ending the market for such goods, it is hoped that the poachers will either cease or reduce their activities.

### Mining

*Mining* is the excavation of mineral substances from open earth workings or from underground. It is one activity which has great and often disastrous impact on the environment. In Kenya, over 400 mineral resources have been identified, the main ones being soda-ash, fluorspar and salt. In the past, some deposits of gold, silver and base metals were also exploited but not on a large scale. Recently, some potential oil deposits were identified in Northern Kenya, at the coast and in several offshore locations within Kenya's exclusive economic zone. There is also some mining of precious and semi-precious stones in the Taita Hills, soapstone is also found in a number of areas. It is the Kenya government's policy today that careful and systematic mineral exploitation should be encouraged in order to provide mineral development. In the current development plan period, the government will undertake various strategies to ensure and promote mineral development.

Legislation to govern mining activities is provided for by the Mining Act, Chapter 306, which is largely concerned with the issuing of mining licences to authorised persons in locations where such activities are permitted. It is not directly concerned, therefore with environmental protection or conservation, but it does provide that where damage or nuisance to land, crops or livestock results from such activities, the owner or occupier of the affected land is entitled to compensation from the prospector(s).

On the other hand, where a prospector abandons or forfeits a location, he is under a duty to fill up or secure all shafts, pits, holes and excavations, to the full satisfaction of the Commissioner. This does not make it obligatory for the prospector(s) to undertake the restoration of the land to its original state although some companies such as the Bamburi Cement factory have undertaken measures to rehabilitate the area from which materials have been mined. This should be but is not yet made mandatory by law.

### (ii) Use of Water Resources

The Kenya government's water policy seeks to provide for the proper management and development of water resources in order to achieve development especially in areas of hydro-power development, irrigation or drainage, while minimising grave environmental consequences.

In any country and possibly more in Kenya, development is to a great extent dependent on effective use of water resources. Our inland waters have already suffered greatly due to such increasing and uncontrolled activities as cultivation, human settlement, livestock rearing and industrialisation. Development has resulted in a number of problems such as siltation, pollution or flooding.

Today, pollution is identified as a major threat to water resources and policies or laws have been formulated, to govern water uses. Water pollution arises in various ways including untreated effluent from industries or factories and runoff of toxic chemicals from agricultural lands or mining activities.

Management and use of water resources in Kenya is regulated by the Water Act, Chapter 372, which makes provisions for the conservation, control, apportionment and use of water resources and for purposes incidental thereto. Under the Act, water is defined as either surface water (i.e. rivers, lakes, ponds, swamps and marshes), or ground water in the form of springs, streams, aquifers and swamps often situated underground but also appearing at the surface to give rise to water courses.

Sections 4 and 5 of the Act provide for the control and use of every body of water. The Minister for Water Development is authorised to make regulations to control and use water, taking into consideration the need for its conservation. Water control is also carried out through a permit system, whereby certain uses of water have to be authorised before hand. These include provision of water for municipalities, steam raising on railways, irrigation, industrial uses and development of power.

Application for licences is made to the Water Apportionment Board which is established by the Act. The granted licence contains terms and conditions on the quantity of water to be used and the quality of effluent which is permitted. Where a licence holder fails to comply with the set conditions, the licence may be cancelled.

As indicated earlier, water pollution is a major environmental hazard, which causes great concern today. The most dangerous pollution is from industrial concerns and agricultural chemicals. Yet both industries and agriculture require great quantities of unpolluted water.

Water pollution control is carried out through making provisions for the standard of effluent discharged into a body of water not to be harmful to the aquatic environment. The standards set for effluent emission are incorporated into the permits; the water must be of such purity that it satisfies the Water Apportionment Board.

There are however, no set national effluent standards and it is the board's responsibility to formulate such standards for each industrial undertaking.

A water user may, under Section 145, take necessary steps to protect himself and his property against the pollution of either surface or ground water. He may do so with the approval of the Minister for Water Development.

On the other hand, Section 158 of the Act makes it an offence for a person to cause the pollution of water for human consumption, domestic use, food or drink through his own negligence. However, this does not prohibit lawful methods of cultivation or watering of livestock. It also allows reasonable use of oil, tar or other substances on any highway or road so long as reasonable steps are taken to prevent any water pollution. Lastly, it permits the disposal of water or effluents in areas approved by the Minister.

The Water (general) Rules make it an offence for any person to deposit, or cause to be deposited in any body of water, any vegetable or mineral refuse, sawdust, effluent from a sheep or cattle dip, factory or sewage which is harmful to fish and fish life. A fish warden is authorised by the Rules to order any person or factories depositing such refuse to stop doing so. Under Rule 80, a person undertaking construction work, where effluent may be deposited in water, is required to present the Water Apportionment Board with plans showing the methods he intends to employ to render such effluent innocuous.

Under Section 74 of the Water Act, the Minister may declare an area to be a conservation area if and where he feels that it is in the public interest. In that case, users of water in a conservation area are required to obtain permits if they wish to continue using that water or if they intend to construct wells. This Section however, applies exclusively to the management of resource water.

There are other Acts which are concerned with the protection of water resources against pollution. The Public Health Act places a duty upon a local authority to ensure that all reasonably practicable measures are undertaken to protect any supply of water for public use, against pollution. Where there is pollution, the local authority is required to undertake the purification of that supply. The Penal Code, Chapter 63, also makes it an offence for anyone to foul water intended for human consumption or other specific uses.

Agricultural practices or activities which may affect a body of water and its maintenance may be prohibited by the Minister for Agriculture under Section 48 of the Agriculture Act. This may also be done for the protection of catchment areas and the drainage of land. Under the basic (land usage) rules, agricultural activities within two metres of a water course, which is more than two metres wide, are prohibited.

Regional management of water is also provided for by the Lake Basin Development Authority Act, Chapter 442 and the Tana and Athi Rivers Development Authority Act, Chapter 443. The former provides for the establishment of an Authority whose functions include examining the hydrological effects and subsequent ecological changes of development programmes and how they affect the economic activities of those persons dependent on the river and lake water environments; to coordinate the administration and use of national resources (especially water) and to cause the construction of any works which are deemed necessary for the protection and utilisation of water and soils in the area.

Similar provisions are found in a later Act, Under the Lakes and Rivers Act, Chapter 409, one is prevented from dredging a lake or river without a licence from the Minister concerned.

### Marine Environment

The importance of protection of the marine environment cannot be overstressed considering the important role it plays in the chemical, biological and physical cycles on which life depends. This environment (which consists of both living and non-living resources) has recently been threatened by pollution which results from man's activities. The critical marine habitats threatened include the coral reefs which are important breeding areas for fish, the mangrove forests and the estuaries.

There is a clear policy covering the conservation as well as the utilisation of marine and coastal resources outside the gazetted marine parks and reserves. The current Development Plan (1989-1993) does recognise the need to enforce regulations on fishing methods, and to monitor the threat of pollution. Currently, fishing in the Indian Ocean is carried out by foreign trawlers which are exploiting this resource. Local fishing is hampered by poor fishing technologies and marketing problems as well as a lack of effective management of this sector. Clearly the fishing industry is being threatened by pollution.

Marine pollution is both a national and international environmental concern. It is often caused by the exploitation of land based resources, oil leakages and man's activities, such as the disposal of untreated waste or the sludge from bilge water and petroleum tankers. There are a few statutory laws which seek to regulate and control marine pollution as well as promote conservation of the marine environment. The Merchant Shipping Act, Chapter 389, makes it an offence for a ship to discharge any oil or oily mixture into either a harbour or into the sea within 160 kilometres from the Kenyan coast. It is also an offence for a Kenyan ship to do likewise within 100 kilometres from the coast of any land.

Perhaps the Maritime Zones Act of 1989, can be considered the only statute that is specifically concerned with the conservation of the marine environment. The Act's objectives include the conservation and management of the resources of the maritime zones. These zones include both the living and non-living resources of the seabed and the subsoil thereof and the waters above the seabed. Section 5 provides that Kenya in the exercise of its sovereign rights, shall undertake the regulation, control and preservation of the marine environment. The Act goes on further to empower the Minister in charge to make regulations to enforce the same.

On the question of overexploitation of the fishing industry, the Fisheries Act of 1989 provides the regulations for development, management, exploitation, utilisation and conservation of fisheries. For commercial fishing, a licence must be applied for first. This includes both local and foreign fishermen. Failure to apply for a licence amounts to an offence under the Act.

### (iii) Use of Air

The importance of our air supply and the need to ensure its conservation, cannot be overstated as it is a matter of survival. Air quality control is, however, relevant to the entire world, and not to the industrialised countries alone. The problem of air pollution is largely a characteristic of urban living where the capacity of the air to dilute the pollutants is overburdened (Grad, 1985).

Air pollutants come from a number of sources, including transportation, industrial processes, smoke, and solid waste disposal. The effect of air pollution can be felt in many ways: for example, the growth of plants can be stunted, man's health endangered and visibility reduced where there is smog. A number of deaths have occurred as a result of respiratory diseases or cardiac conditions caused by air pollution. For example, in 1952, more than 1,600 people died from a 'killer smog', when the weather conditions prevented the disposal of air pollutants, (Grad, 1985). Smog is a combination of smoke and sulphurdioxide ($SO_2$) gas which is produced when fuels are burnt.

Common air pollution emissions include carbon-monoxide, hydrocarbons, nitrogen oxides, sulphur oxides and particles (Grad, 1985). Air pollution also leads to changes in weather patterns and the corrosion of materials as well as damage to plant life. The World Health Organisation (WHO) has prepared guidelines related to air quality standards and, if the concentration of pollutants is higher than these standards, then the air is considered to be polluted.

Recently, there has been a lot of concern over the depletion of the ozone layer, due to the use of halogenated chlorofluorocarbons (CFCs) and other chlorine containing substances. In 1987, the United Nations Environment Programme (UNEP) adopted the Vienna Convention for the Protection of the Ozone Layer which called upon parties to the Convention to undertake all appropriate measures to protect human health and the environment from the likely effects resulting from the human activities which modify the ozone layer.

The Convention also calls for alternative substances or technologies to be used in eliminating CFC and protecting the ozone layer. It also calls for further research and exchange of information in order to assess the effects of human activities on the ozone layer.

The Montreal Protocol, on substances that deplete the ozone layer, was also adopted in 1987. It recognised that worldwide emissions of certain substances can significantly deplete or otherwise modify the ozone layer. The Protocol calls upon states to undertake control measures regarding the level of consumption of those substances which deplete the ozone layer.

Other than the depletion of the ozone layer, there is yet another global problem arising from burning fossil-fuels and the cutting and burning forests; both activities release carbondioxide ($CO_2$) into the air. This has Ied to the so called 'greenhouse' effect (i.e when $CO_2$ and other gases accumulate in the atmosphere and trap solar radiation near the earth's surface (WCED, 1987). Unless urgent measures are undertaken, the greenhouse effect will result in increased global temperatures, raised sea levels and will upset agricultural production systems.

It is clear that air pollution like water pollution, has reached threatening levels and this calls for urgent control measures. However Kenyan law regarding control of air says little about air pollution compared to water quality control. This may be because water pollution is more easily observed and can thus be dealt with immediately. Air pollution must become quite serious before it is observable. There is also the problem of lack of appropriate technology to assess the quality of air.

However, there are a few statutes in Kenya which deal with air pollution. The Public Health Act provides, under Section 119, that smoke emission from any machinery in such quantities as to be injurious or dangerous to health amounts to a nuisance and its author can be ordered to suppress it. An all purpose clause further states that: any act or emission which is, or may be dangerous to life or injurious to health, amounts to a nuisance. Any emission of pollutants into the air may fall under this clause. There is, however, no requirement for the author of the emission to undertake emission control measures to ensure that whatever is emitted into the air will not adversely affect the quality of the air.

The rules under the Traffic Act do provide some measures on emissions by motor vehicles. The rules prohibit the emission of smoke or visible vapour from motor vehicles.

However, there is no legal provision made for any standards or conditions which have to be met by car manufacturers to ensure that fumes and gases emitted into the air by their motor vehicles will not adversely affect air quality.

The Factories Act, Chapter 514, provides for better regulation of gases and fumes than the above two legislations, but it is mostly aimed at ensuring the health of workers. The Act requires that all workers be supplied with suitable clothing and equipment, in order to protect themselves from dust, fumes, smoke or other hazardous gases in their workplace.

The Merchant Shipping Act, provides regulatory control over emissions from ships. Thus, where a ship or vessel emits black smoke, or soot or ash or grit or gritty particles for more than 5 minutes in any one hour this amounts to an offence under Section 310 of the Act. The Act empowers the Minister in charge, to prescribe methods of determining what is *'black smoke'*.

What is evidently lacking in the above legislations, is a set of national standards of air quality to be achieved and maintained. Due to the inadequacy of the laws, pollution of air continues, since polluters do not have to control the standard of pollutants emitted into the air. It is hoped that the proposed Clean Air Act will provide set standards of air quality and a legal enforcement machinery to ensure that they are met. It should also provide heavy penalties for those who fail to comply.

### (iv) Chemical Management

The misuse of chemicals for industrial, agricultural or domestic use has been cited as a major cause of environmental degradation. For example, the misuse of agricultural chemicals such as herbicides, pesticides or fertilisers has already resulted in harmful depletion of the soils nutrients. Where the chemicals are washed into water bodies, water supplies become polluted.

The present ad hoc laws are mainly geared towards regulating the manufacture and sale of chemicals rather than their safe use so as to ensure a minimal effect on the environment.

The Food, Drugs and Chemical Substances Act, Chapter 254 prevents the adulteration of food, drugs and chemical substances. The Act defines chemical substance as those which may contain germicides, pesticides and insecticides. The Act ensures that the manufacture and sale of pesticides and insecticides satisfy the prescribed standards regarding their quality, safety and composition. The Act also provides for the prevention of water contamination through the use of chemical substances that could make the water injurious to health.

A person licenced to sell chemical substances is required by the Act to follow prescribed standards set by the Public Health Standards Board with respect to packaging, labelling or sale of chemical substances. When a person sells adulterated, decomposed, rotten or filthy chemical substances, such a person is guilty of an offence. Contravening the provisions of the Act is an offence and the penalty prescribed is a fine not exceeding Kshs 2,000.00 or a three months' term of imprisonment. A subsequent offence attracts either a fine not exceeding Kshs 4,000.00 or a six months' term of imprisonment or both.

The Pharmacy and Poisons Act Chapter 244, seeks to regulate and control the pharmaceutical profession and the trade in drugs and poisons. Under Section 25, the Pharmacy and Poisons Board is required to prepare a list of approved poisons, including those which can be sold by authorised dealers as mining, agricultural and horticultural accessories. Persons who deal in these poisons must be licenced. This indirectly controls the misuse of chemicals which may prove harmful both to one's own health and to the environment as a whole.

The Cattle Cleansing Act Chapter 358, prescribes standards for regulating the type and composition of chemical substances used in cattle cleansing. It is an offence to a sell a chemical substance which does not conform to the prescribed standards. The chemical substances used in cattle cleaning are mainly composed of organic chlorides which may contaminate water when they come into contact with it.

The Fertilisers and Animal Foodstuffs Act, Chapter 345, seeks to regulate the importation, manufacture and sale of agricultural fertilisers and animal foodstuffs. Under Section 19, the Minister may make rules to prescribe standards of composition, efficiency and purity, prohibit certain substances, and limit the percentages of other substances used in fertilisers and animal foodstuffs.

The Pests Control Products Act No.20 of 1982 asserts that the Pest-Control Board may refuse to register a product if the Board has reasonable grounds to believe that such product poses a risk to public health, animals, plants or the environment in general. This is the only Act which expressly shows concern over damage caused by chemicals to the environment.

One problem that plagues the effective management of chemicals is the creation of various boards under different Acts; the powers of those boards either overlap, or conflict with each other. Clearly, there is a need for the establishment of one single chemical management board with powers over the control of all chemicals.

### (v) Protection Against Radiation

The dumping of radioactive waste in West African countries has caused worldwide concern. In such areas, the environment and the health of people living in these countries are both at stake and for a very long time. One also has to consider the trans-boundary effects of depositing such wastes. Radiation does not only result from nuclear fission; but it is also a side effect of the use of some forms of modern technology such as x-rays, electronic devices as well as radioactive materials. It has been proved that high levels of radiation may lead to various forms of cancer whilst genetic damage may result from low levels of radiation.

Legal protection against radiation in Kenya is provided for by the Radiation Protection Act Chapter 243, whose principle objective is to protect the public and workers who are using radioactive devices or materials which have an ionising effect. In case a person seeks to manufacture, export, import , possess or dispose of radioactive material, he must have a licence before doing so. The Act can also be used to prevent the dumping of radioactive waste within Kenya and its territorial waters by either locals or foreigners.

Under Sector 18, the Minister in charge may make rules prescribing precautions to prevent injury caused by radiation, especially to persons working with radioactive materials. Such persons are required to wear appropriate clothing and undergo a medical examination every six months. This Act aims at protecting all humans, plants or animals in the environment.

## 6. Defects of Present Environmental Laws

There is no comprehensive law on the environment in Kenya; what we have is scattered legislation which deals with what may affect the environment. These various Acts were passed as a response to competing interests in the use of our natural resources: forestry, agriculture, land and water. Another characteristic of this legislation is that the majority of it was passed during the colonial period, when the administration was primarily concerned with exploiting the environment; at that time, conservation was obviously not a primary concern. As a result, most of these laws just happen to have some connection with the environment but do not effectively protect it.

The more recent laws do provide rules and conditions to be met; they further provide various institutional frameworks to enforce those rules and conditions. Unfortunately, the functions of the administrative bodies sometimes overlap and in some cases the bodies do not agree on certain issues such as the use of a particular resource, for example, water or land. This may lead to conflicting interests when one board encroaches on another board's powers. The management of chemicals seems to be the most difficult to achieve to the satisfaction of the various existing boards.

Another problem is that the exact powers of ministers or boards in enforcing the objectives of legislations are not defined. Because of this, discretionary powers cannot be challenged since they are not indicated and there is no provision for their being challenged. For example, if a board is charged with the duty of ensuring that water quality in the urban areas is of a particular standard, and it fails to do so, there should be a legal provision for a person or group of persons to challenge the board's acts, omission or failures.

Yet another problem in our present laws on the environment is that the emphasis is on prohibitions and penalties for breaking the law; this is a major setback in the management of the natural resources. Using criminal penalties but not requiring the offender to repair the damage he causes, serves little purpose in environmental protection. In fact the offender may well repeat the offence since he knows that the sentence is light and he will not be asked to pay damages.

Whereas there is a major need for sound environmental management, the current policy is geared towards the conservation of land and the preservation of forests. It therefore fails to address itself as it should to the major environmental problems such as air, water, marine pollution, disposal of solid and conventional wastes, energy use and misuse, or mismanagement of both renewable and non-renewable resources. It becomes more and more clear that both laws and policies on the environment in Kenya have to address themselves to these emerging issues.

What then would be the best form of environmental legislation for Kenya? When enacting laws on the environment, it has to be understood that the law must be based on local circumstances and that the legislation so enacted must be enforceable through established control and enforcement mechanisms which are able to work. Moreover, the law should be management-oriented and provide practical incentives for using the environment wisely, Legislation can, for example, provide for alternative ways of exploiting renewable resources such as using biogas from cow dung, or using solar energy for energy sources.

In addition, legislation might enhance preservation of forests through the 'cut one tree plant two more' rule; a practice which is preferable to the use of criminal law in enforcing forest preservation. Legislation might also set quality standards for air or water and require that all appropriate measures be taken to ensure that all individuals and industries meet these standards. Offenders should be required to undertake measures to restore the quality standards of effluents or emissions and this may turn out to be expensive. An effective enforcement agency should be set up to ensure that such standards are observed.

Environmental law should make environmental impact assesments (E.I.A) mandatory before a development project is undertaken. The E.I.A. basically provides information regarding an intended project; it evaluates its possible significant environmental effects and specifies whatever mitigatory measures will be undertaken. This information helps and guides policy makers to decide on the acceptability of the projects. For example previous to the construction of a dam, an E.I.A. would indicate the possibility of the spread of certain water-borne diseases, and point out what measures are foreseen in order to deal with the problem. In general, an E.I.A. statement should provide a description of practical alternatives, an assessment of the potential environmental impacts (both short and long-term) and a set of alternatives. However, the law requiring the submission of an E.I.A. should indicate which activities are exempted from this requirement. Currently, the National Environment Secretariat (NES) of the Ministry of Environment and Natural Resources, carries out E.I.As, but lacks the legal powers to ensure that their recommendations are adopted.

If any legislation is to be enforced successfully, it is important to create awareness regarding the need for sound environment management. For instance, different incentives can be given to those persons or companies which undertake to conserve the environment and environmental education must be offered at all levels of education within the society if we are to have a conservation-minded population.

Finally, it is important that an effective environmental agency be established which will act as a 'watch-dog' for the environment and will undertake to enforce environmental laws. This agency should be established by law and be given the legal powers to enforce environmental conservation measures.

## Questions

1. What do you understand by sustainable development? Do you think it can be enhanced by the law?

2. If you were a legislator, what recommendations would you make towards the reform of environmental law in Kenya?

3. Is there a need for a comprehensive law on the environment in Kenya? Discuss what such a law might involve.

4. It has been suggested that pollution of air and water is an urban problem, and that since most of Kenya is rural, there is no need for comprehensive laws on pollution. Do you agree?

5. Other than the law, what other mechanisms can be used to encourage sound environmental management?

## Bibiliography

Grad, F. *Environmental Law* (New York: Mathew Bender, 1985).

Ferries R.N.T.W. *Ecology and Earth History* (London: Helm, 1976).

World Commission on Environment and Development (WCED) *Our Common Future*, (Oxford-New York: Oxford University Press, 1987).

Ogolla - Bondi "Role of Environmental Law in Development" *Journal of the Indian Law Institute*, 29, (1987), p. 188.

Okoth-Owiro "The Limitations of Kenya's Environmental Legislation" (Unpublished).

Mumma, A., "The Law on Westlands in Kenya"; (Unpublished).

N.E.S. "1988 Report on the state of Kenya's Environment," (Unpublished). Montreal Protocol on Substances that Deplete the Ozone Layer, UNEP, 1987. Vienna Convention for the protection of the Ozone Layer, UNEP, 1987.

Documents, Plans and Sessional Papers 'African Socialism and Its Application to Planning in Kenya' Sessional Paper No. 10 of 1965 (Nairobi: Government Printer, 1965).

Development plans of Kenya for, 1974-1978; 1978-1983; 1984-1988; and 1989-1993.

# Index

**338**